Richard Wollheim was born in and educated at Westminster School and Oxford. He served in the army during the Second World War, seeing action in France and Germany. From 1949, Wollheim taught philosophy at University College London, becoming, in 1963, Grote Professor of Mind and Logic. He retired from UCL in 1982, and from then until 1985 was Professor of Philosophy at Columbia University. Between 1985 and 2003 he was Professor of Philosophy at the University of California, Berkeley, and, from 1989 until 1986, he was also Professor of Philosophy and Humanities at the University of California, Davis.

Wollheim was married twice, to Anne Powell in 1950 (dissolved 1967) and to Mary Day Lanier in 1969. He had two sons by his first wife, and a daughter by his second. He died in November 2003.

Acclaim for *Germs*:

'This is a moving and funny book, an extraordinary book, richly exposed to the Home Counties, in touch with the world created by Proust, and yet not in the least old-fashioned or archaic. He was the son of an impresario and dandy, and a maddening comic masterpiece of a mother. For some, the memoir may seem to conform to a pattern of compulsive behaviour which gets a lot of attention these days: the boy makes lists, which include one of royal mistresses, drawn up in ignorance of what royal mistresses did'
Karl Miller

'A great book, strange and beautifully written, candid yet ornate, as if Rousseau were being rewritten by Proust, with interpolations by another author familiar with Beckett. Wollheim's spoilt childhood – eccentric parents, important visitors (Diaghilev, Kurt Weill, Serge Lifar), grand houses and grand hotels – was lonely and sad and strange enough, but immensely more interesting than most. The child became an intelligent and sensitive observer, and what he recalls of those early days is here treated mostly with delicate irony. This is not a book to be admired for a season or a year, but to be counted among those masterpieces of which the fading memory continually demands return and refreshment'   Frank Kermode

'The 1935 cover photograph of Richard Wollheim's masterpiece of early biography, *Germs: A Memoir of Childhood*, gives a hint of what to expect: a serious twelve-year-old in school uniform, flanked by his elegant mother and Kurt Weill. Wollheim's childhood was spent observing the glamorous company kept by his impresario father, trying to understand his distant and dissatisfied mother, and balancing the demands of love and fear; he explores it by methods which owe an equal debt to Proust and Freud, and it does much to explain the remarkable philosopher and aesthetic analyst that he became. The voice is inimitable: subtle, seductive, moving from deadpan hilarity to aching sadness'   Roy Foster

'Wollheim's powers of description astound. Topographically or architecturally, no one has ever depicted London's more prosperous suburbs with such exactitude. His prose is the verbal equivalent to Pre-Raphaelite painting, crowded with lovingly observed and richly coloured detail … [An] elaborately subtle and disturbing book … Because of the intensity with which a remarkable man has offered us a view of his inner self. I doubt whether anyone who has read it will forget it'   Diana Athill, *Literary Review*

'*Germs* is not only elegantly written, it is a human document of considerable power and importance. In *Wilhelm Meister*, the first great *Bildungsroman*, Goethe sets his hero's formal transition to adult maturity in a library which contains the secrets and confessions of men who enjoy worldly success. Only in the light of such admissions can the hero sanely assess himself. Wollheim avoids the two vices to which self-revelation is inclined: exhibitionism and apology. *Germs* is simply the sober, tactful admission by a highly cultivated and competent man of the reality of his inner world'   John Armstrong, *Independent*

'*Germs* [is a book] in which childhood experience, described with Proustian subtlety and thoroughness, remains invested with lasting power and singularity . . . In Wollheim's hands the sentence – often half a page long, full of sinuous purpose and subtle qualification – takes on extraordinary interest as he searches for the precise colour and purport of a childhood memory. The effect is of intellectual exactness given expression as a work of art. For all the book's rigour it is its poetry – the play of charged imagery, the sense of something impalpable that outlasts analysis – that one most remembers' Alan Hollinghurst, *Guardian*

'[A] precise, intensely reflective and above all literary sensibility . . . lies at the heart of *Germs* . . . At first sight [it] might seem a variant on the Holroyd/Cobb/Lewis brand of English autobiography, which achieves its effects by way of the meek self-effacement and the bumbling near-anonymity of the subject. In fact it is a very different kind of animal. Wollheim knows, or doesn't mind admitting, his intelligence and his intellectual precocity, is confident, above all, that these things are worth writing about. Richard Wollheim died in 2003, before the manuscript was submitted for publication. One hopes that an early reader or two had assured him of its abiding quality'
D.J. Taylor, *The Times Literary Supplement*

'*Germs* evokes a prelapsarian world of infantile ecstasy and nightmare with uncomfortable honesty and almost hallucinogenic power'
Hilary Spurling, *Daily Telegraph*

'Wollheim regarded *Germs* as "the best piece of work" he had "ever done". The book . . . portrays the Thames Valley life of his affluent parents – the distant, dandified father he revered; the beautiful, mindless "Gaiety Girl" mother he came to regret loathing – in dazzling detail. However, the dark heart of the book is the merciless, microscopic examination of the development of Wollheim's psyche, not least of his realization that the price of love is fear. So long as Richard was alive, I found the sheer density of this book painful. Since his death, I am able to read it with delight. It must not be allowed to become a *chef d'oeuvre inconnu*' John Richardson, *Independent*

'[A] frighteningly good memoir'
Andrew O'Hagan, *London Review of Books*

'A small masterpiece . . . The intensity, delicacy and precision of the act of memory in *Germs* have provoked comparisons with Proust. Just comparisons perhaps, but this is a Proust who can also make you laugh out loud . . . In this fine memoir, Richard Wollheim has transmuted his childhood hurt and loneliness into an artful, precise, self-deprecating detachment. It is a very English sublimation' Edna O'Doherty, *Irish Times*

'Posthumous publication reveals [this memoir] to be a masterpiece – an unclassifiable work of startling originality in which the acutely sensual and confusedly cerebral experience of infancy, boyhood and adolescence is brilliantly recreated. Although it carries self-scrutiny to an extreme of scrupulous candour which I believe to be unique, the term 'confessional' – with its suggestion of apology and therapeutic exhibitionism – does not apply. There is little here of personal secrets being exposed to public view, but rather of the reader being intimately drawn into the heart of a deeply private life . . . [A]s a writer, Wollheim is entirely and gloriously his own man. Everything he tells us is totally unpredictable and, however surprising, always convincing . . . *Germs* is destined to be a classic' Francis Wyndham, *Spectator*

'Wollheim's writing is indescribable – except possibly by him. It is as though he were both the analyst and the patient on the couch, both of them with a remarkable and idiosyncratic prose'
New York Review of Books

'[A] densely evocative book, achiev[ing] a degree of self-examination rarely found in the words people write about themselves . . . [The] exquisitely written investigation of an inner landscape . . . [T]here is a Proustian feel to the memoir, although W.G. Sebald is probably the nearest in style and unremitting excavation of every detail in this testament of an alienated youth' Emma Tennant, *Observer*

Also by Richard Wollheim

AUTHOR
On the Emotions (1999)
The Mind and Its Depths (1993)
Painting as an Art (1987)
The Thread of Life (1984)
Art and Its Objects: With Six Supplementary Essays (1980)
On Art and the Mind: Essays and Lectures (1973)
Freud (1971)
A Family Romance (1969)
Art and Its Objects: An Introduction to Aesthetics (1968)
On Drawing an Object (1965)
Socialism and Culture (1961)
F.H. Bradley (1959)

EDITOR
Philosophical Essays on Freud (1982)
(with James Hopkins)
Freud: A Collection of Critical Essays (1974)
The Image in Form: Selected Writings of Adrian Stokes (1972)

Germs

a memoir of childhood

Richard Wollheim

BLACK SWAN

GERMS

A BLACK SWAN BOOK : 0 552 77314 X

Originally published in Great Britain by The Waywiser Press

PRINTING HISTORY
The Waywiser Press edition published 2004
Black Swan edition published 2005

1 3 5 7 9 10 8 6 4 2

Set in 12/14pt Garamond by
Falcon Oast Graphic Art Ltd.

Black Swan Books are published by Transworld Publishers,
61–63 Uxbridge Road, London W5 5SA,
a division of The Random House Group Ltd,
in Australia by Random House Australia (Pty) Ltd,
20 Alfred Street, Milsons Point, Sydney, NSW 2061, Australia,
in New Zealand by Random House New Zealand Ltd,
18 Poland Road, Glenfield, Auckland 10, New Zealand
and in South Africa by Random House (Pty) Ltd,
Endulini, 5a Jubilee Road, Parktown 2193, South Africa.

Printed and bound in Great Britain by
Bookmarque Ltd, Croydon, Surrey

Papers used by Transworld Publishers are natural, recyclable
products made from wood grown in sustainable forests. The
manufacturing processes conform to the environmental
regulations of the country of origin

CONTENTS

Wollheim and Angela
(1980)
by
R.B. Kitaj

CHAPTER ONE

My Land

It is early. The hall is dark. Light rims the front door. The panes of violet glass sparkle. The front door has been left open. Now I am standing outside in the sun. I can smell the flowers and the warmed air. I hear the bees as they sway above the lavender. The morning advances, a startled bird runs fast across the dew. Its breast quivers, in, out, and its song scratches on my ear. Lifting my eyes, I see that the garden, and everything in it, moves. The flowers move, and the lavender moves, and the tree above me is moving. I am standing in the sun, my body is tipped forward, and I am walking. Walking I shall trip, and, if I trip, trip without a helping hand, I shall fall. I look above me, and I feel behind me, searching for the hand that is always there. There is no hand, and therefore, if I trip, or when I trip, and now at long last, the waiting is over, and I have tripped, and I am, am I not? I am falling, falling – and was it then, in that very moment when magically I was suspended in the early light, when the soft smells and sounds seeping out of the flowers and the insects and the birds appeared to be doing for me for a moment what the hand that was not there could not do, or was it, not then, but in the next moment, by which time the magic had failed, and the path was racing towards me, that I did what I was to do on many later occasions, on the occasion of many many later falls, and I stretched out my hands rigid in front of me so that my fingers formed a fan, not so much to break my fall, or to make things better for me when I hit the ground, but rather to pretend, to pretend also to myself, that things were not so bad as they seemed, or disaster so imminent, and that this was not a fall but a facile descent through the air, which would leave me in the same physical state, clean, ungrazed, uninjured, that I was in before I tripped, and that the urine would not, out of sheer nervousness, pour out of me?

When I landed, a large rose-thorn, which had been lying in wait on the gravel path, most probably since the early hours of the morning when it had fallen from its stalk, confronted me, and met no resistance as it slid itself under my thumb-nail, and then, like a cold chisel, worked its way up into me, making its own channel as it went, until it came to rest on the pad of pink, quivering flesh that forms a cushion underneath the nail.

Cries of surprise, cries of pain, cries of outrage, resounded through the garden, and tore apart the morning serenity.

Within seconds, someone, alerted to my absence, has run out of the house, and brusquely collected me up into her arms. Held with what was to be memorable pressure against the surface of a starched apron, I was hurried back, breast-height, along those few yards of path which my feet had just traversed in an outward direction. But now the sounds and smells that had lured me onwards were blotted out by the protective breast. And it was only when I was safely returned to the house from which it was made clear to me that I should never have escaped, and I was set down in the darkness, and the dank smell of the hallway rose up and blended with the sharp, chastising smell of the apron, that my senses slowly came back to me. And then it was the turn of oblivion.

Oblivion came down. It came down with a swish, with the great, heavy swish of velvet curtains suddenly released from the high gilded arch of an opera house, or an old music hall, stirring up as they fell the smell of sawdust aerated with the cold dusty draught that blew in from the wings and dried the nostrils. At school I knew that I differed from other boys in that I could recognize this smell, and they could not. It was familiar to me from early visits backstage with my father, which sometimes brought with them moments of excitement as well as the more usual embarrassment, as when, of a sudden, a troupe of eighteen-, nineteen-year-old girls, rushing off the stage, shouting to one another, "Darling", "Dearest", "Did you see him?" as they headed for their dressing-rooms, accidentally surrounded me, and I dared to hope that, as they drew themselves up on their toes, I might, by some mischance or some misunderstanding, brush against their strong, horse-like bodies. But never so. It never happened. Forced to look down through artificial eyelashes, past cascades of ringlets stuck to their cheeks with sweat, and so eventually to take stock of my little boy's body, they reacted with a quick intake of breath, a "Tut" or a "Tss", and, then resuming their speed, swerved past me and on to their dressing-rooms.

Into that brief gasp of theirs I read much. On the surface, there was surprise, surprise at my mere presence; below that, there was some desire, in a sisterly way, to protect me; then below that, there was shame at whatever it was about them from which I needed protection; and then, deepest of all, there was, I knew, their withering contempt for whatever weakness there was in me that made me need, or made them feel I needed, protection from them. Why, they wondered, was what was good enough for them not good enough for me? Whenever I recalled such moments, I noticed how a look of apprehension passed over my father's face as he turned from them to me, and then a look of relief as he turned back from me to them.

It was, as my reader will have guessed, a long, a very long, time before I succeeded in brushing against a woman's body.

For many years, and all of them long before I set out, with Dr S as my pilot, to sail back up the stream of my life – an image I clung to for those strained, pipe-filled sessions, in which the unity that I longed to find in my life seemed to slip further and further away into incoherent anxieties – I loved to trace back to this isolated event, of which I know no more than I have set down, a number of the emotions that have patterned themselves over the subsequent years of my life. In doing so, I gave way to the most persistent of all these patterns: that the earliest identifiable self, with its primitive desires and its exorbitant demands and its own special kind of inconsolability, was the real thing, tap it and it rang true, so that any change I contemplated in myself would be a betrayal of myself by myself.

First of all the things I have connected to this early misadventure is a long-standing resentment, very readily aroused, against places of repose, places where calm and quiet are customarily offered to the senses, places where long afternoon shadows, and gentle breezes, and the low hum of conversation, are natural accompaniments to the day. Loved by most people, by, for instance, my father, and, in his later years, seemingly to the exclusion of all else, such places, of which I give as examples lawns by the side of swimming pools, with tables under striped umbrellas, and the splash of water, and the cries of the bathers, and the gentle, rising smell of chlorine; or bowling greens in municipal parks, where men in the autumn of their lives hone new skills; or the parapeted terraces of large, ornate hotels, which at that time I knew exclusively from the labels pasted over my father's luggage, where waiters move aimlessly amongst the tables, here adjusting a napkin, there pausing to look out over the view of lake, and shoreline, to the distant mountains; or my bedroom where, as a child, I would be set down to rest after lunch, with the curtains drawn against the day, so that only the gentle sounds of the house, like water running, or a stair creaking, or the purring of a vacuum cleaner used late into the afternoon, could percolate through to me – all such places arouse in me, however well things start, the same anxiety: that the pleasures that I am about to receive are not rightfully mine to enjoy. There is someone from whom they have been filched, and, if I even try to enjoy them, I shall have to pay, and the price will be high, and the currency in which it is reckoned will be cruel. As a small child I lived under a rule of my father's making, which he insisted upon and with such strictness that he must have once suffered under it himself, and it forbad me, no matter the circumstances, ever to use the word "boredom", and boredom would be the currency in which I would pay for the pleasures of calm and quiet. As the first pleasurable sensations start to quieten my body, they congeal somewhere behind the eyes, somewhere at the back of the nose, and, the next moment, they are driving their way into me with the insistence of a drill spinning on its screw, blasting away what little there is left of the serenity for which I am being asked to pay before I have tasted it. When Dr S pointed out to me that we should never overlook the literal understanding of the idea of boredom, I recognized that this was how I had always understood it.

To this day there are certain moments, moments at which I am alone, moments at which I seem to myself most pleasurably engaged, when I am perhaps closest to happiness, when I am certainly unprepared for a change of fortune, and I hear a voice inside myself, which seems to have something to tell me, though for a moment the words it uses bleach themselves of all meaning, only to regain it the next. "I cannot tell you," the voice says, in slow, abstracted, somewhat delicious tones, "I cannot begin to tell you," and the individual words are always the same, and they come in the same order, with the same phrasing, echoing the same dying fall, "I cannot even begin to tell you of the horror, the terror, the awfulness, of my life." That is what the words say, and, when I do not simply take all this as a fact of nature, which I do readily, the only explanation that I can give is that, in uttering these words, I am declaring – "declaring" in the sense in which one declares something to a customs officer – that there is nothing in my life on which I owe anything to anyone else, nothing for which I need write out a cheque, made out to the miserable of the earth, drawn upon myself, and calculated in such and such units of boredom. I am declaring that there is nothing I have taken from someone else, nothing I enjoy, and so the drill need not spin. – Perhaps I am not saying or doing this, but then I do not know what I am doing or saying.

Another association that I have to this early memory is the lure, the persisting lure, of danger. The lure, I say, not the love, of danger, for I have never loved danger, though the presence of danger certainly makes the frightening less frightening. But the lure of danger is a familiar of my solitary hours, so that, even now, as I write these words, knowing well that they are not the words that you, the reader, will read because, before you can, I shall write and rewrite them over and over again, even now, as I sit here, in a large, shambling apartment in St. Louis, the "perk" of a visiting professor, with a third-floor view over the moonless park, and it is eleven o'clock, I might – and vary the circumstances only the smallest amount, and I certainly would – get out of this chair, go to the door, open it, turn right, turn left, go down the corridor with its threadbare carpet, pull open the door marked "Exit", go down the concrete stairs to the parking-lot, where a murder might easily take place, frog-march myself into my blue, rented car, insert the key, start the engine, and drive across this city, past what are always referred to as "the great old buildings", past brick warehouses, past office blocks with pediments and quoins, past superannuated department stores with the original owner's name still carved in the stone, until, clattering over the rusty iron bridge, I arrive deliriously in East St. Louis, which locally they call "the battlefield". In the becalmed, southern night, women stand on the curbside, arms akimbo, and the drabbest of pleasures beckon to me. As the lights turn red, and men, men in berets or leather hats pulled down to their eyebrows, look me over, one of their number, a young man of fierce appearance, strolls over to the car. The terror I have come for grips me. Then, as the lights change, I make my getaway, I accelerate, safety looms up ahead, and I have to ask myself, But is it not here, where danger lurks, that I belong? – And all these, I must remind myself, are the thoughts of someone who has never been able to go on a switchback, who has never walked through the Haunted House, who has never watched a horror film, who has neither done nor wanted to do any of these things: they are the thoughts of someone who as a schoolboy would feel sick for up to three days in advance when he knew that he would have to hang upside down for half a minute on the trapeze. Such things, though also frightening, carried with them no compensating lure of danger.

Or, to continue the associations, I could cite the shame that was to persist through the years of childhood and adolescence and also later at the unreliability of my body, of that constant companion which was to let me down so often and so regularly. When I most needed its support, or its cooperation, it proved ungainly, weak, awkward, faint-hearted, incontinent. As a child, I loved lists of all sorts, and found that all sorts of things could be listed. I listed the sails on a windjammer, not knowing how they worked, and the names of philosophers, not knowing what they were, and, a particular source of pleasure, the names of royal mistresses and of royal favourites, not knowing how they earned their keep. I listed the flags of the different nations, and their capital cities, and the rivers on which these cities stood. I listed butterflies, and the names of Napoleonic marshals, and shirtmakers in London, in Paris, in Venice, of which more later. When on a journey I had, as a matter of singular urgency, to list in what became a succession of small red notebooks the names of the places we went through, often with a pencil that went blunt when I needed it most, I learnt out of necessity countless ways in which place-names could be discovered by a small boy sitting in the backseat of a car, and craning his neck so as to see out of a passing window. There were the wasp-coloured AA signs, black and yellow, there was the writing over the local post office, there were ancient milestones, and, in many counties, signposts had a finial, cone-shaped or circular, giving the name of the nearest town or village. To grown-ups, or those I met, these clues were unknown, or were so until the war came and they were ostentatiously swept away so as not to give assistance to enemy parachutists, but to a small boy, always in doubt that he had been anywhere unless he could write the name down with a pencil in a notebook, these signs had a value born of desperation. And, of all these lists, the most necessitated – though, even if I could have, I never would have entrusted it to paper – was a catalogue of the various ways in which the unreliability, the incontinence, of the body forced itself on my attention. I memorized the different shapes, and colours, and outlines, sharp or

17

blurred, with which scabs, and bruises, and grazes, can mark the skin, nor was I content until I also had a mental list of the yet more formless stains that shame a child's underclothing as the secretions of the body spread outwards, and I would try to commit them to memory even as, in the sanctuary of the lavatory, I endeavoured to remove their physical traces.

Or I could associate to this scene – and here I am on the most dangerous of territories – the conviction that punishment, administered in circumstances over which I needed to have the most rigid control, could bring me closest to what, from little more than infancy, or so it seemed to me, I esteemed most in life: innermost knowledge of my self. From punishment to confession: from confession to a knowledge of those things which I had done, and ought not to have done: and then, buried in the awareness of what I ought not to have done but so much wanted to do, was, I felt, the core of myself. The word "forbidden" was, for many years, the most heart-rending word in my vocabulary. Forbidden pleasures, forbidden thoughts, forbidden books, forbidden foods, forbidden pictures, and, the loveliest metaphor to embrace them all, "forbidden fruit".

I could – I must emphasize this word – I could make all these associations to this first memory. But I have always realized that they would be mere associations after the fact, telling me nothing about the past, or why it has the power to repeat itself in the present.

꙳

I was born on the 5th of May, 1923, in a London

nursing home, which occupied a house in what was then part of an early nineteenth-century square. The square, Torrington Square, was destroyed in the war. One side of the square still stands as a terrace, but I do not know whether this includes the house where I was born, even though I know the number of the house, and, if the house still stood, it would not be more than two or three hundred yards from the department in which I taught for over thirty years. And, if I add that, for the last twenty of those years, my department was in the very square, and more or less directly across from the very house, where my mother was born, and where she lived for the first five or six years of her life, and that I never went to look at the house, it might look as though my life has had a unity to which I have been indifferent. I can only say that coincidences are not unity.

My mother was much impressed by coincidences: these and others. She treated coincidence as a fact of life, and she tended to think of it as the most powerful link that could unite two lives. She asked me if I didn't think it a coincidence that someone had been to the same school as my brother, or that I shared my initials with a friend of hers. She would say to me sometimes, "Do you believe in coincidence?" meaning, Did I accept the importance of coincidence? If, in later years, I asked her something about the Russian ballet, or about my father's life, she was likely to say, "That's a coincidence, for last week I overheard someone talking about the Russian ballet," and she might add, "Has the Russian ballet come back into fashion, because I have a lot of things I could tell people?" or "That's a coincidence, I was thinking about Daddy only today, and you couldn't have known about that," and she might add,

19

"Or could you?" and these coincidences she then took, and expected me to take, as more interesting than what I had asked her. Certainly she never gave me the information I asked for. But she never answered any question that I put to her. She did not like it if one person talked to another.

From time to time my mother would say how much she would like it if one day I would arrange for her to visit the house where she was born, which by now belonged to my university. If her next question was not, Why wouldn't I do this for her? she talked of the visit, which she now assumed would take place, as though it would be of as great an interest to those who presently worked there as it would be for her. Not that this was a distinction she often made: for she seldom found a reason for any course of action that was as strong as the interest that others took in what she might do. She did not want to disappoint the world.

My parents, once married, always lived outside London. This was a decision of my father's. Before he married in 1920, he had, from the time he arrived in England from Paris in 1900 – with just one exception, when, during the Great War, as we called it in my childhood, he had evacuated himself to Aylesbury – always lived in London.

Marriage, he thought, required a change. A family needed fresh air. I paid dearly for this decision, but it was what he would have thought, had he worked in Paris or in Berlin, and, once I recognized the unEnglishness of the thought, I was willing, at least intermittently, to forgive him for it. I colluded by trying to think of the roads, and the

houses, and the woods where I grew up as part of some leafy
French or German suburb, Neuilly-sur-Seine, or Wannsee,
or Schwabing, where the air is perennially fresh. Where I
actually lived was the first issue over which I asked myself
whether reality mattered, or how much.

As to what the decision meant for my father, I do not
know. It certainly gave him freedom from the family for
whose sake he had made it. The weekends apart, he dined
at home at most eight or nine times a year. Generally he
returned from London well after midnight. He rose after a
breakfast in bed of stewed apple, toast melba, tea, a glass of
hot water, and some pills, and he left the house briskly at
8.20. His face was delicately shaved, he selected his overcoat
with great care, put one arm in the sleeve, shook the coat up
on to his shoulders, inserted the other arm, picked up his
letters and a newspaper, and ran the short distance from the
front-door to the waiting car. The only friends he had were
friends who came down from London.

That I was born in London came about because my
father thought that, at least for a matter as serious as birth,
there was no reliable doctor outside London. Indeed it was
only for us, us English as he must have thought of us, my
mother, my brother, and me, that an English doctor would
do. For himself, until history put a stop to it, he always
went to Berlin to see his doctor, and, when his doctor came
to London for a few days, my father would take him out to
an expensive restaurant, and there order for both of them all
the rich food which he had travelled several hundreds of
miles to hear himself forbidden. In two other respects, he
tried somewhat harder to follow his doctor's orders. Every
summer he started a cure at Marienbad, or Carlsbad, or

Pau, though he invariably broke it off after a week, and spent the rest of his holiday on the Lido or the Riviera, or at Biarritz. And every morning, he stood on a pair of scales, and, taking out a gold pencil from his dressing gown pocket, he wrote down his weight in fine German numerals, on a pad which was attached to a metal ashtray.

Three years earlier my brother had been born in the same nursing home. He had been breast-fed for a little while. In my case my mother decided not to make the attempt.

My birth was in itself uneventful, but I am sure that it caused my father to pine. It was a small death for him, one of a series of which his life came to be constituted. Thus far he had survived, in some measure, the departure of strange women from his life; the Great War; marriage; abandoning London; the frequent company of my mother's mother; the birth of my brother, which also gave him pleasure; and now

there was my birth. Other small deaths were to come, from which the big death, with all its terrors, was ultimately to bring relief. Not that my father was austere. I do not think that he willingly denied himself anything, nor would he have thought that there was virtue to doing so. He took a crueller revenge upon himself. He converted the luxuries of life into necessities, so that, when they were absent, he missed them, but he took their presence for granted.

Shortly after I was born, I was circumcised. It was done by a rabbi, and with, I was led to believe, a cigar cutter. I was circumcised for health reasons, though there might have been other vestigial reasons. I imagine that my father was circumcised, but I never knew. I do not believe that I ever saw my father naked, even though I often watched him dress in the morning. These levées, to which I was certain to be invited within a day or so of my father's return from one of his frequent trips abroad, when he would lay out at the end of the bed the dozen or so ties he had brought back, were, with one exception about which I shall have more to say, the total of the moral education that I received from him. However, from them I learnt many things, which I value highly. I learnt how to choose a shirt in the morning, I learnt how to hold up my socks with garters, I learnt how to use the forefinger of the right hand to make a dimple in the knot of my tie, I learnt how to fold a handkerchief, and to dab it with eau de cologne before putting it into my breast pocket, and, above all, I learnt that it was only through the meticulous attention to such rituals that a man could hope to make his body tolerable to the world. But, as to the body itself, what I learnt was strictly limited by the fact that, at a certain moment, my father invariably turned his back to me, and, manipulating the long tails that shirts had in those days, passed the back of his shirt between his legs, and so deftly pulled it up towards his waist, that, by the time he turned round to face me, the lower part of his body was completely swaddled in linen shirt and silk underwear.

It was another thirty years or so before I came to realize the loss that I, and perhaps both of us, had suffered through my father's reticence. We were on holiday in North Wales, where we had taken for the summer the upper part of a rambling nineteenth-century castle, and, one late afternoon, various members of a large and famous Bloomsbury family, children and grandchildren of the old lady to whom the house belonged, had settled down in deck-chairs under the window where I was trying to write. Some of them had been swimming in the sea, some reading, one had been writing in pencil in a large notebook, and now they had gathered, with bottles of white wine standing on the grass between them, and they were settling down to discuss a member of the family whose arrival had been delayed. Was he a contented person, or a discontented person? Did he really belong to the town, or to the country? Would he have been more at home in Tolstoy or in Turgenev? What painter could have done justice to his appearance? How did he look at his best? On all these matters conflicting views were expressed, and, when it came to the last question, a dry, shrill voice, coming from a young man, rose to a peak, "I think Dad looks best stark naked." There were restrained cries of "Oh, yes, yes," and generous applause.

As these words reached me, sitting at my desk and writing a partly confessional work, which I recognized at the time would never, on one pretext or another, be allowed to see the light of day, I was made to feel how different my life would have been, what a happier fate at least my manuscript would have had, had I only been in a position to make that remark, or had my father, just once, turned to confront me as he was arranging himself within his trousers. I am not suggesting that my father was emotionally reserved with me. Indeed I never felt him to be more himself than when, leaning forwards and taking off his spectacles, he tickled my cheeks with his eyelashes, and gave me what he called "butterfly kisses". With me, he was, I suspect, more bored than reserved. It was the thought of having, within the dullness of his own house, exposed to a young boy the vagaries of life, the excitements that awaited him in later years or in foreign cities, that he found so daunting.

To remarks overheard, and to things unexpectedly seen, particularly in hot weather, of which I have had more than my fill, I have given a finality, going well beyond what their content, however dramatic, might warrant.

At a period when, having finished one undergraduate degree, and unable to decide what to do next, I was briefly working at an editorial job in London, I suffered greatly from the fact that I was separated from a girl who was still in Oxford, and whom I loved, and who, I eventually allowed myself to believe, loved me. A young friend had found me rooms in a shabbily respectable boarding house in Cliveden Place, and I used to talk to M regularly on the payphone in the hall, but, on this particular weekend, though she had asked me to telephone, I couldn't get through to her. It was a sunny day, and I decided on impulse to go to Oxford. I walked from the bus station in seedy Gloucester Green, memorable for late-night drunkenness, to the convent where she boarded, but, after many inquiries, all met with a resolute display of tact, I gave myself up to walking round and round the city that I knew so well. The lilac was in heavy bloom, and the laburnum cascaded over it, and every corner was associated with some small agonizing sentiment. Early summer in Oxford I had always found heavy and ominous, with a sense of life wasted though not yet begun. On this Saturday, there was a normal blue sky, with, high in it, a normal bright sun. It shone all day, and all the foreboding, all the cloud cover, was inside me. Eventually the day drew to a close, and I took the last bus back to London. Night had fallen, and we were climbing a steep hill near Marlow. Large trees, with trunks white in the glare of the headlamps, grew immediately by the side of the road, and at the very moment at which I looked out from the right-hand side of the bus, I could see down into a large chauffeur-driven car coming in the opposite direction, with its inside lights full on, and there I saw the girl I had gone to see. She was wearing a blue satin dress, and she was lying across the lap of a very white-faced young man in a dinner jacket, with skin like toothpaste.

Within seconds the car had disappeared, and for several days I put off talking to M. When I finally went down to Oxford, she told me, in the soft tones of truth, that she had been taken to a night-club, had drunk too much, and had no particular interest in the young man, despite the eligibility he would have for her mother as a member of an old Catholic family. I believed her completely in so far as belief in such matters is ever complete. But I think I knew that I would never have seen into the lit car, the car would never have had its lights on when we passed, I would never have believed what I saw, alternatively my mind would never have invented the whole story, if things between us had not got to some pass that the words we so gently exchanged were not already useless. When the rupture came, it was not the less painful for this premonition.

A few months before, while I was still at Oxford, I was working on my weekly essay, and both my windows and the windows of the set of rooms above me, which belonged to MBC, who was then my closest friend, were wide open on to the summer night. The noise of conversation drifted down to me, but the words were mostly inaudible. Then I heard my own name, and there was a silence lasting for a few seconds, broken by my close friend who was saying with that authority to which he always aspired, "Richard is a total masochist." There was a rumble of quickened speech, and I had no way of knowing whether the topic was developed or abandoned. What I had heard was a new thought to me, but I allowed it over many years, at moments of choice, to alter my conception of myself and my desires. Part of its power over me was the way I had not expected anyone to have such a well-defined thought about me.

Earliest of all such incidents that I can recall took place when I was about eight or nine, and I had said goodnight to a group of my parents' friends, who had come down to the house for Sunday. The group included a woman whom I thought of as much on my side in childhood, Lea S, a mezzo-soprano from Vienna, Lehár's favourite singer, and, having gone upstairs, I was planning upon making a surprise return to the company, which I thought would be taken as a sign of total worldliness. I had crept some way down the stairs when, already luxuriating in the laughter, the applause, that I expected to greet my arrival, I was halted by the melodious voice of my friend, my ally, in which I seemed to hear the warm golden tones that she carefully inserted into her hair. She was saying, "Such a nice-looking boy, but, Eric, those ears, such a pity. Believe me, I know a surgeon in Vienna, he could do it, he would do it for me. No more than a small cut, snip, snip, and they'll lie down. Close to the head, very neat." I think she added, "Like a cap," but by this time I was creeping back up to my bed. The velvet curtains at the foot of the stairs,

which a moment before I was planning to burst through, gave cover to my retreat, but, as I climbed the stairs, I suddenly found myself thinking of another pair of curtains, which I had seen just a few weeks before on a visit to Madame Tussaud's. The purpose of these curtains was to conceal an exhibit that children under the age of sixteen were strictly forbidden to see, but, being about six inches too short, they revealed stark, twisting shadows cast on the ground, from which a child who could not stop himself from imagining the worst could readily reconstruct the scene in full detail. What was public knowledge was that what was replicated the far side of the curtains was a torture practised in Algiers under foreign dominion, and the brightness of the lighting, which accounted for the way the shadows revealed all was intended to simulate the Mediterranean sun at midday, which was taken to be the hour of punishment. The instrument of torture was a large wheel, set up horizontally to the ground, but with the rim of the wheel removed, and instead, at the end of each spoke, a long, curving blade had been stuck into the raw wood. Around the wheel, forming an outer circle, was a wooden bench or scaffolding, and, at the appointed hour, when the fat, indolent jailers woke from their long sleep, the condemned prisoners would be brought out of their cells and strapped to the bench, and then the great wheel with its knives would be set in slow motion. The prisoners, as the shadows on the floor made clear, had not been strapped down in any standard position, but they had been made to assume postures, some grotesque, some humorous, according to the whims of the jailers. The different ways in which the bodies were lacerated, and the time it took for death to arrive, depended directly upon the postures in which the prisoners had been set. In some cases the prisoner was bent backwards over a pole so that the passing blade ripped open his stomach, and then the next time round, most probably despatched him: in other cases the body of the prisoner was placed so far back that a mere hand or knee cap was sliced off, and the prisoner, now out of reach of the knives, would be left to bleed to death: and sometimes the prisoner had been forced to his knees, and then tied into this position, so that, more mercifully, the knife decapitated him on the first turn. – I have to recount that, of all the discreditable things I felt obliged to reveal to Dr S, nothing caused me more shame than recalling the words of the Viennese singer, for which I, of course, bore not the slightest responsibility. She spoke, I merely overheard.

As the years progressed, the notion of what it is to over-hear greatly enlarged, as did the class of things overheard. At one end were the diagnoses of disease pronounced by doctors, but which I felt to be vacuous unless they were listened to, or overheard, but, when listened to, inevitably brought about the very diseases of which some thought they merely informed us. At the other end were folk songs, traditional music, the lyrics of popular songs, which were addressed to no one, and did not ask to be listened to, but in which I believed the great truths of life were embedded, half audible in the rhythm even when the words were buried in the obscurity of an unknown language. Over many decades, in poor hotels in Portugal, in Italy, in Malawi, in grand hotels in the Sudan and in Iran and in India, I have paused to overhear a maid, making the beds of those who have risen early to visit the archaeological site, or a young laundress at the well or the water-tank, singing lyrics of love and misfortune, or an epic of hope and fidelity after death, and I have envied the singer her secret wisdom. There have been many moments when I have been convinced that, if only I could bottle the hot morning air, and then decant it at my leisure, I would, with time enough and the aid of a good dictionary, know how to hold together in my life the demands of the head and the arbitrary needs of the heart. Of such things important people in high places must always be deprived.

After my birth, I was brought back to the house that my father had rented while he and my mother were looking for something more suitable, and it was there that the incident I have recounted, the fall, was to take place. I was somewhat less than two at the time.

Very shortly afterwards we moved to another house, and this house my father also rented. The truth was that there were only certain things that my father liked owning. He liked owning paintings, and, to a somewhat lesser degree, he liked owning books, of which more later. He liked owning the things that he turned out of his pockets at night and laid out on the dressing table. These were a gold pencil, and a gold case for a toothpick, a very thin Swiss pocket watch in a shagreen case, which, when pulled open, became a small bedside clock, a special key for opening first-class compartments on the Southern Railway, a silver cigarette-lighter, a few carefully folded five-pound notes, printed, as they were in those days, on the finest transparent paper and held in place by a gold clip, some spare coins, and a small pearl tie-pin, which smelt permanently of eau-de-cologne. My father liked owning suits, and he liked owning ties, in both cases in profusion, and the latter passion he communicated to me, though, in loving ties, I possibly loved the shirtmakers they came from, or at least the names of the shirtmakers, even more. In time I came to believe that, through associating my father's ties with the labels sewn inside them, I would, when expensive foreigners came down to lunch on a Sunday, be able, through observing how the silk was ribbed, or how the dots were formed, or the precise shape of the knot, to know one of the most important things about them, or the shirtmaker they went to. Another thing my father liked was paying for everyone when he ate out: he liked owning, for a brief while, his own airy portion of a restaurant or a grillroom.

The "we" who took part in this move were my parents, my brother, our nanny, a cook, my mother's two dogs, one from her days on the stage, a Pomeranian, and another, a Pekingese, and myself. We also had a parlour-maid who was black, which was a rarity in those days, and she was called – to her face, I believe – "Black Mary". It was not till some two or three years after we moved that my father found it necessary to have a chauffeur, and then there was a succession of chauffeurs. One, named Keith, had a spidery handwriting in which he wrote out the weekly accounts of petrol and the hours he had worked, and my father, mis-reading his name, called him "Heath". It was a sign of the times, either of the prevalence of respect, or of the scarcity of jobs, that the mistake was never pointed out to my father until Keith came to leave us and asked for a reference. He was a pale, sickly young man, with a moustache that was like hair sprouting out of a mole.

The one I knew best was the last, who also stayed the longest: a thick-set, sandy-faced man with heavy tortoise-shell spectacles, called Allen, who had a strong temper, which was known to erupt in the early hours of the morn-ing after my father had kept him waiting at the wheel outside an hotel, or on holidays abroad, when crossing some high Alpine pass between one Central European spa and another. A particularly terrible quarrel broke out between Allen and my father on the descent into Innsbruck, while my mother and my brother, sitting in the back of the car, white with tension, clung on to the silk tassels that hung down from the pale wood panels. The year was 1928, and, at that very moment, while they were on

their way to Venice, where, as a photograph shows, they would sit on the Lido with the Russian dancers, I was on a holiday at Felpham with my nanny, playing on the stony beach with my bucket and spade. I passed that summer playing a game that I had invented, which I called Butchers. To set up the game, I collected into a big pile the largest stones I could find in the immediate vicinity, and the game itself began with my picking up the first stone, holding it up to my eyes, and turning it over and over until I detected, or pretended to detect, which was a difference the game obscured, a hairline crack running across it. Holding the crack firm in my sights, and keeping my head completely rigid, I reached down with my empty hand, felt for my spade, tipped it on to its side so that it was now, not a spade, but a cleaver, and, raising it a few inches, brought it down on the stone with a quick sharp tap. If all went well, the stone, colluding with my thoughts about it, fell apart along

the line I had imposed upon it, and revealed a blood-red interior, veined with grey and white. A second blow followed fast upon the first, then a third, perhaps a fourth, until the stone was now in many fragments. I repeated this with stone after stone until the original stock was disposed of, and instead there was a pile mostly of red meat, but also of fragments to be rejected. These fragments I had already classified as gristle, as bone, or as fat, and, with deliberate roughness, I grabbed them and hurled them far away on to some imaginary sawdust floor. I was now ready for the last part of the game, in which, lifting my hand high above the blood-red pile, and opening wide the palm of my hand, I half brought it down, half let it fall, in a movement, carefully modelled upon what I had seen real butchers do, and, as it hit the slivers of meat, it immediately sorted them into the different cuts. In a butcher's shop, the meat would have been soft to the touch, but, in the game, it was sharp and jagged and cut ferociously, from which it gained an unwanted realism as blood ran out from my hand and stained the stack of cutlets, steaks, chops, kidneys, liver, which I piled up in front of me. And I must now explain, if it is not already apparent, that I knew the differences between the various cuts of meat in just the way that I knew the differences between the various sails of a windjammer, or the differences between the various philosophers of antiquity: my knowledge stopped at the names. I had not the slightest idea what the cuts of meat looked like, or whereabouts in the animal they came from, and, least of all, how they tasted. The beauty of the game lay in its abstractness, and the mysterious skills it kept alive. Another snapshot in my possession shows that, from time to time, I would look up from my work, and, under a mop of dark hair, stare out past the camera, to where the beach shelved steeply away, and where the sea could be heard crashing down on the shingle, sucking it back into its interior, with what was for me deadly regularity. My bleeding hands broke up the monotony of holiday life.

Amongst Allen's miscellaneous tasks, set him presumably by my parents, was that of trying to teach me a number of manly skills, such as carpentry, and boxing, but all ultimately to no avail. I always made an enthusiastic start, and the idea of learning a new subject, and particularly a subject that came with new words, a new vocabulary, excited me. But, in a short while, the excitement deserted me. Fear, fear that my body would fail me, compounded by the further fear that I would not be able to live with this fear, so that my mind would give out even before my body, soon drove out every other concern. Allen told me that, when I was a grown man, I would regret not being able to defend myself. But the appeal fell on deaf ears. I did not particularly want to grow up, and, even less, to grow up to be a man.

Allen, in sharp contrast to my father, who was always scented, had upon him a suffocating smell, which I thought of as the smell of the metal-polish that he lavished upon the headlamps of the car, but which I also identified with the thick white substance that was lodged between his tight-packed teeth, and was held in place by a pale yellow film covering everything to be seen when he opened his mouth. Years later, in the army, this particular smell and this look of the teeth, now mingled with the smell of the rough material out of which battle-dress was made, characterized for me a type of man of whom I was particularly frightened: clean-limbed, robust, staccato in speech, with his secret stack of photographs held together by a rubber band, swift to obey when he thought this right, otherwise keen to take his punishment, contemptuous alike of those who never defied authority and of those who would not pay the price.

I admired Allen most for what seemed to me as a captive of the nursery, as a prince in the tower, the most remarkable of attainments: the places he had been to. While he was washing the car, or changing the sparking-plugs, I would try casually to entrap him in a particular kind of conversation. What, I would ask him, was the road like between this town and that town? – not out of curiosity, but for the pleasure of being able to enunciate the place names, and then of hearing them back from someone who had been there, as though this brought me closer to going there. Once I volunteered to Allen, while his head was buried under the bonnet of the car, that I did not like the road from Cambridge to Ely because of the great fields of cabbages that ran to the horizon on either side. I held my breath, for I had visited Cambridge and Ely only once, and then at dusk, and I longed to return. Allen, who had no conception of my motives, looked at me with scorn, and he then said that there was nothing better than "the sight of good grub growing". I, who had raised the issue in order to hear, coming out of my own lips, the names of two places universally associated with beauty, ran indoors in the wild hope of forgetting the remark, which was like a stinging slap across the face.

Around this time Allen married my nanny, who had been replaced, as far as my upbringing was concerned, by a governess, but who had stayed on to be cook. I was six or seven at the time of the wedding, and I got very drunk on champagne, which was treated as an endearing frailty. To my amazement my nanny was now called Mrs Allen, though, until that moment, I had thought of Allen as a Christian name.

Allen continued to be the chauffeur, and he arrived every morning by bicycle in his cap and his chauffeur's suit, and I retain a picture of him, as the bicycle slowed to a halt, and, with his left foot still planted firmly down on the pedal, he swung the right leg up, up and back over the saddle, and then, for a few seconds, held it stretched out behind him, totally stiff, parallel to the ground, the blue serge held neatly in place by a black bicycle clip, which encircled the turn-up of the trouser-leg. It was only at the moment when the individual spokes on the wheel started to become visible that he brought his right foot sharply to the ground, and ran for a few seconds beside his bicycle, like a trainer with his racehorse. How I loved the majesty of that outstretched leg, held rigid in all weathers: in the soft warmed sunlight of summer mornings, in the grey rain, and when snow lay on the ground and the bicycle wheel drew a dark line through the snow. The gesture was for me godlike in its precision, and how well I knew that its sturdiness was something impossible for my body ever to emulate.

During the war Allen went to work in the neighbouring

aircraft factory, and he rose quickly to become a foreman and then, I believe, a manager. My father, much broken by the war, found the energy to treat the news with incredulity. Allen, he said, was a man who could work well, but he needed orders. On his own, for all his boasting, he could do nothing. Years later, at my father's funeral, Allen railed against him unapologetically, citing his tyrannical ways, his inability to listen to others on any matter, and his insistence upon complete submission. For a moment I thought that Allen had, at least in part, the woes of my childhood in mind. But he was too stern a man to reconstruct the past. Like my father, he would, I think, have called any such reflexion "brooding".

The distance that Allen's manliness put between him and me, and then between me and all men whom I did not in time learn to think of as effeminate, a term of great significance in my vocabulary, was greatly increased by an incident that happened when I was probably ten or eleven, though this book, and my manner of writing it, should make one thing about my life clear: that everything I have lived through either has been completely forgotten or is as yesterday. There is no blue to the horizon of Time.

The incident stemmed from some complaints that my mother made about a small area at the front of the house and to the right, known as the backyard, which lay between the backdoor of the house and a tall wooden gate with blistered paint, leading into the front garden. On one side of the yard was a garden wall, separating us from the next-door house, overhung with tall trees, and, on the other side, the yard was overlooked by the pantry, which was a passage lined with dark cupboards, running from the kitchen to the dining room. The backyard was concreted over, and, though it was ordinarily reserved for the delivery-boys, it was also used by my mother when she had to drive to London to meet my father or a friend, or go to the hair-dresser, and found herself late. Why she was so frequently late is something to which I shall return, but, when she was, she invariably ran across the backyard to her car, and her complaint was that, more than once, having got herself ready to go out, she had been hit by bird's mess as she ran across the backyard. A pair of pigeons had been observed – they had been seen and heard – high up in the trees that overhung the yard. My mother said that she had nothing against the pigeons, but she wanted to know why she should spend so much time on herself if it was all to be wasted. Allen, with unaccustomed subservience, said quietly that he would take care of this. He explained that he had a friend who went out along the hedgerows shooting rabbits on summer evenings, and he offered to borrow the gun, and by midday the matter would all be over. To me, with my head full of historical tales, he was one of the three knights who had barely heard Henry II's angry words than he was riding to Canterbury, having vowed to put an end to the matter. Later that week, so I visualised it, my father, leaning forward from out of the pale leather depths of the rear seat of the car, momentarily put down his newspaper, tapped the ash off the end of his cigarette, and confirmed the arrangement with Allen. Eventually I came to hear of it, though I am sure that it wasn't thought necessary that I should be told.

The news choked me. For I was unwilling to understand how the mere convenience of one person could be weighed against the life of a bird, nor did it seem to me fair that another person should, just for the careless expression of a wish, have to carry such a burden for eternity, and I made up my mind to prevent the occasion. I begged my father to change his mind, I tried to bribe my mother, I prayed to God. As I worked at my lessons in the nursery, I could hear the pigeons gurgling high up in the trees, ignorant of the future, and I refused to allow that their clumsy lives would come to an end so soon. In the next few days I went to the lavatory a great deal, and, night after night, I cried myself to sleep. Then one day Allen must have borrowed the gun. He brought it round strapped to the bar of his bicycle, and all that I stopped were my ears when the two shots rang out at about ten in the morning. I was crouching under the nursery table, with my hands over my ears. I came down some time after the corpses of the two birds had been wrapped in newspaper and thrown into the dustbin, and Allen, who was unsmiling, seemed to swell in size until his frame matched the imagined silhouette of a killer. I was sad, but I could not get angry, because I knew that I was also to blame. If I did not want my mother to bend over me at night with bird shit in her hair, then I too had put my finger to the trigger. I knew that I had grown up a little, and I knew in my heart of hearts – a phrase I loved – that it could only get worse.

The move, to which I now return, was from a house in Weybridge to a house in Walton-on-Thames. The difference was largely one of address. Both places were in suburban Surrey, and, by the time of my childhood, a process was well under way which stripped the names of towns and villages of any clear-cut reference.

For the most part, the towns preserved their centres.

Centre of the centre was the church, standing perhaps on the site of an older building, but the fabric, though covered with creeper, was never more than a few decades old. The body of the church was dominated by a tower made of flint or rough-hewn blocks of stone, and the churchyard was set behind an impenetrable hedge of laurel or yew, filled with dead leaves, and twigs, and spiders' webs. Invariably a bronze plaque, placed somewhere near the west door of the church, recorded the bony features and swelling necktie of the architect, a late nineteenth-century or early twentieth-century revivalist, and often another plaque nearby, with less artistic lettering and without an image, remembered the generosity of a wealthy member of the congregation, a churchwarden, who had "sometime" been a captain in the Indian Army, or had been prominent in the City and a JP, and who had nobly borne the costs of the construction of the building. What most impressed me about these commemorative tablets was the names, and their pure Englishness, evocative of rolling countryside, and hedgerows, and dry walls, and low cloud formations running parallel to the horizon: a world that I knew only from the backseat of a car, and which I first confronted as a wholly aesthetic object only when I read in early adolescence the opening chapters of *The Well of Loneliness*, in which an unattainable English world was suffused with the delicate, foreign love of women for women to act upon me as the purest magic. At home, the few English names I heard were of the husbands of my mother's friends from the stage: a bank manager who fell asleep after lunch in his overheated house with the Sunday newspaper across his lap, or chinless men, younger sons of old families, caught up in financial activities they did not comprehend, and who drifted in and out of trouble with the law.

In the vicinity of the church there would be two or three parades of shops, built around the turn of the century, which took the form either of a low stucco terrace surmounted with a white-washed parapet or of a row of shop windows above which there would be a half-timbered expanse of pale plaster, rising to tall fretted gables. Incised on the stone or on the timbers would be the name of some distant imperial victory, fought under a blazing sky. The name itself would generally be familiar to me from a boy's comic paper or an old illustrated volume, showing hand-to-hand fighting, or cannons firing at point-blank range, but I had no one in my life, an older relation, the father of a boy, a friend of a friend, who could remember the glories of that day, or of any similar day.

At the end of one of these terraces, or standing on an island of grass all its own, there was the one pub that the town possessed, generally a modern, half-timbered building, from which the rancid smell of beer escaped. In our land, the brewers did not go in for the florid, armorial inn-signs to be found in the deep countryside, or in the small winding streets of London. Instead they favoured, as I recall it, a board divided diagonally into red and black, and underneath could be found the name of the brewer. Outside the pub, a decrepit man in a shiny suit, with long wavy grey hair, would be smoking and reading a newspaper, waiting for the iron gate to be unlocked, when he could shuffle into the public bar.

A sight I loved, but which not every town could afford, was the fire station, painted scarlet, with big, folding doors, going up to the ceiling, and, pressed up against the panes of glass, like a dog straining to be let out of its kennel, was the fire engine itself. Some of the crew, in high rubber boots and burnished brass helmets, were standing around the fire engine, like heroes from the Greek myths, and others were, I knew, upstairs, drinking tea and playing cards, but ever ready to slide down the pole, and to find themselves looking out of the rear of the engine as it raced out of the fire station.

Inevitably somewhere near the centre of the town, situated on a quiet patch of grass, which the public was begged to keep off, was the war memorial. In the nearest town, the memorial was composed of a marble base, shaped to my mind like an enormous version of the money-box in which I kept my pocket-money, and mounted on this base was a stone book, left open at a page covered with names: names of the dead, names of the regiments whose badges they wore on their caps, names of the battles in which they fell. In the town that lay in the opposite direction from us, the memorial was a heavy undecorated column, on the top of which an infantryman could be seen, standing at ease against the sky, as the Last Post sounded. A third kind of memorial, not uncommon, was an actual field-gun, now fallen silent, which had participated in some of the battles it commemorated. The thick coat of bituminous paint, which protected it against the elements it had once defied, formed lakes and puddles down the barrel, in which vignettes of the bloody engagements in which it had taken part, where the fortunes of battle had flowed backwards and forwards in foreign mud, were visible to a small child.

At about the time when I came of an age to notice novelty, and no longer assumed that the world as I now looked out on it had witnessed all the events recounted in the history books which I was just beginning to devour, the first new thing to break in upon my vision was the cinema. At one moment the cinema did not exist, and, the next moment, these generally square buildings were all over. Made of the thin, dark red bricks of the period, they were faced with white stucco grooved to look like stone, which, with great artificiality, introduced the bright look of the sea-side into land-locked suburbia. Behind the cinema was the car park reserved for the patrons – "cinema", "car park", "patron", all being new words – but soon there were few more familiar, more welcome, sights than the string of small coloured lights looped over the entrance to the car park, or the two chromium-plated boxes that were screwed to the brickwork of the cinema, and, through the glass fronts of which, when they were not too dirtied by the rain, passers-by could make out from the sepia-tinted stills, the high points in the movie that was currently showing: when one of these shots came up in the course of the movie, a low gasp of recognition was involuntarily released into the crowded darkness of the hall. If the film was a western, or a war film, another form of preview, which I loved, was a sand table that would be set out in the foyer of the cinema, recreating the high sierras and canyons of some unknown land, or the battlefields of Flanders with their water-filled trenches and blasted trees, or the skies above them where fearless aviators were locked in single combat.

In every cinema, a patrons' book was placed next to the kiosk where tickets were sold, and those who signed their names in the book would then receive free a monthly programme, printed in violet ink on shiny paper so that the lettering was always slightly blurred. Each double bill had a page devoted to it, and it was a rule of our family, originating I do not know how, but probably from my mother, who liked rules without reason, that only on a Thursday morning, and then with her permission, and under her direct supervision, could the programme be picked up, and the page turned, turned and then very precisely folded back on to itself. When my mother turned the page of the programme, she let out a low hiss. Ordinarily the programme lay on my father's bedside table, along with the miscellaneous books he brought back from his travels: some Tauchnitz volumes, a work of Freud's in German, a novel by Joseph Kessel in French. My mother had no need for a bedside table.

Half turning the page, or looking round the corner into the future, was, without some very special excuse, forbidden, and not until I was fourteen or fifteen, by which time I was grappling in my mind with the ideas of Raskolnikov, did it seriously occur to me to breach this rule.

For each film, the programme gave the title, listed the characters and the actors who played them, said whether the film was "U" certificate or "A" certificate, and provided a brief synopsis of the plot. I loved the words, "character", "cast", "plot", "synopsis", and I wanted to learn the precise distinctions that they embodied. I did well with some of these words, but with the last of them I made the least

headway. The word itself was obscure, and so were many of
the synopses themselves, particularly so when the film was
"A" certificate, or was judged to be unsuitable for children
to see, for the management went on the assumption that
the synopsis, though it had to be fair, must be suitable for
all to read, with a result that was very far from that
intended. Even as I began to read the three or four lines, I
fell into a state of dread that I had read, or was just about
to read, something that, innocuous enough in itself, would
nevertheless inform me, particularly if I allowed my mind
to wander, of something that I was not supposed to know
about, and, though I had no desire to preserve my
innocence, what I did not want was to lose it through
someone else, and least of all through someone else's carelessness or oversight, for then I would inadvertently be tied
forever to the shame from which I desired to escape.

The regime under which I grew up reserved the cinema
for two sorts of occasion: winter, and rainy afternoons.

Winter came round with its own relentlessness, and it
began on the day when the clothes I had been wearing for
the past few months – aertex shirts, khaki shorts, cotton
underpants – were, without any discussion, taken out of my
chest-of-drawers and cupboard, and replaced by another lot
– viyella shirts, tweed shorts, woollen combinations –
which were stored on shelves of wooden slats, surrounding
a metal boiler held together by rivets, in a small, steamy
room, called the airing-cupboard. At first the winter clothes
were painfully rough against the skin, the one exception
being my balaclava, which, just because it was made out of
the very coarsest wool, had, on the suggestion of some
friend of my parents, and I think it was Lea, Lehár's

favourite, been lined with silk. However one great glory of winter clothes was that, once the sharp smell of mothballs had worn off, they were aromatic to the nostrils, and, as they were laid out first thing in the morning, most power-fully when there was snow outside, they gave off the delicate smell of warmed flannel, which, merging with the smell of eau de cologne, which illicitly I dabbed myself with as soon as my father left the house, stayed with me all day. The end of winter left more to chance than its arrival, and it roughly coincided with the sound of the first cuckoo, and, a week or so later, winter and summer clothes were reversed.

Rain, by contrast, was unpredictable, and it remained all my childhood the object of a deep conflict.

On the one hand, there was the knowledge that only the sight of rain spitting against the windows, or battling with the wipers as they raced across the windscreen, could convert what was a shadowy promise written in violet ink into the warm reality of the cinema. Entry into this reality was gradual, and it was the richer, the darker, the more deliciously oppressive, for the three or four stages into which it was broken up. First, the car had to be parked. My mother, like many drivers of that period, had some difficulty in "backing-back", as it was called, and often I could feel my bladder fill in response to her slowness. Then there was the run across the car park in Wellingtons and a stiff mac, crunching the cinders underfoot as I went, and already feeling that the world in which anything might happen was taking me over. Jumping the puddles, I was a horse leaping a swollen stream as we, the cavalry, moved up into the attack, or I was a steeplechaser taking in its stride a particularly vicious hurdle, or, cut out the horse, and now I was my own awkward self who hadn't seen the puddle, and waded straight through it, or who had seen it but hadn't noticed how deep it was, and I slammed down, first one foot, then the other, to make the water splash up over the top of my boots. For a minute or so, I became the rough boy I never wanted to be. Next there was the delay as the tickets had to be bought, and the small violet or cherry-coloured pieces of paper curled up through the carefully etched slab of steel that lay just the other side of the ornamental grille, and were torn off and handed to us. Certainty descended, and we progressed through the foyer, up the steps, into the cinema itself, unless there was a necessary detour through the long curtains into the chamber grandiosely marked "Gentlemen". My prayer was always the same: it was that we should arrive just before the lights went down, and the torches of the usherettes, flickering like fireflies in the night, were needed to direct us to our seats. For, once darkness fell, couples who had nowhere else to meet started to find comfort in the warm smell of each other, and, for me to be certain that I could withstand the excitement with which the cinema began to creak, it was best to have looked upon the faces of the audience while they were still distinct under the ceiling lights. Indeed I could see no reason why my mother should not imitate the punctuality that my governess showed every Sunday when she took me to church, and why we should not time our entry to perfection so that we would walk down the aisle at the very moment when the organ, which always gave me a headache if I had to listen to it for any period of time, had stopped, and the organist had taken his bow, and organ and organist had descended into some uncertain depths. If only my mother would co-operate with my wishes, then, no sooner would I have been got into my seat, and my mac taken off my hands and folded on a neighbouring chair, than the great miraculous event, half sunset, half sunrise, with the intervening night displaced, would start to unfold. The lights dimmed, a hush, like the end of the day, fell on the audience, and the first titles came up on the screen, and they could, just for a moment, be seen, the far side of the gauze curtains, as clear as pebbles through still water. Then, as the curtains slid open, and the gauze was gathered up into pleats, it was as though a light wind had started up before dawn, and made ripples on the surface of the stream, and now, from one second to the next, as fast as that, the lettering became blurred, until the curtains passed across it, and then, one by one, the words again became legible, and the screen took on the unbounded promise of a book first opened.

All this I longed for, but, on the other hand, and what made for conflict, was another sight, and the deep-seated dread I had of it, and that was that, when, at the end of the film, still blinking at the light, still trying to resolve the loyalties that the film had stirred up in me, who was good, who was bad, and, as a separate issue, which side was I on, I would find myself standing by the heavy glass doors that led back to reality, and, not only would the rain have stopped, but the sun would have come out. By now the water that had clung to the trees, or that had collected on the lampposts and on the tiled roofs and on the undersides of the gutters, would, at first slowly, but with gathering momentum, have dripped through, and lay on the road, where the first rays of pale sunlight hit it, so that, looking out, I could see the tarred surface glint and sparkle in the late, departing glory of the evening. A natural cause of joy to many, this sight stirred in me the deepest, darkest melancholy. Local sunlight after rain had, quite unaided, the power, not just to make my spirits drop – many things did that – but to convince me, beyond anything that hope could counter, that life would never again have anything to offer me. Even today, when in actuality the sheen on a bright, wet surface has more or less lost its terrors for me, I have only in imagination to take myself back in years, and to recall it in the mind's eye, and, in such moments, I can once again understand the full dismal power that the experience had over me. But my inability to convey this terror to others, like my inability to convey the far worse horror of the smell and sight and touch of newspaper, of which more later, has sometimes made me feel a mute amongst mankind. One evening, while I was an under-graduate at Oxford, about the time I first got to know Lord DC, and he had given me the sense, which I had barely had up till that moment, of how easy it might be to talk to someone, the conversation after dinner turned, in a way usual at that period, to the differences between melancholy, and sadness, and nostalgia, and to what Turgenev, and what Jane Austen, and what Hardy, could tell us about these things, and I, after a silence that I had kept for twenty minutes or so, plucked up my courage to bare my soul to the company around the table, and I said that I knew nothing more melancholy than sun after rain on a suburban road. D, who was my host, turned to look at me, screwing his head around in a very characteristic way, and blurted out his answer in a fast, high-pitched voice. "Richard," he said, "I think I see exactly what you mean, and it's fascinating, but really I don't see why 'suburban'. Aren't you trying to be too – specific? I don't see why 'suburban' has anything to do with it. I really don't think it has." At that moment, I believe, though I have not fully appreciated it until now, the certainty that I had had interesting experiences, and that one day I would be able to convey their poignancy in words of great precision, died. Over the years it was to die many deaths, none altogether fatal.

Someone might ask, Why could I not have wanted the rain to come down enough so that I could go to the cinema, but to clear up enough so that, the film over, I would look out on dry streets? I convey nothing about my childhood if it is not clear that I could never have formed such a desire, for I always found one thing worse than having too little, and that was having too much. To a superstitious child, which I was, it was like being God. To a young boy unruly with socialism, which I was soon to be, it was like being rich. It handed life over to boredom.

The sight that so distressed me brought me closer to the sense of death than anything else that I experienced at that time of my life: closer even than seeing, as I once did, from the front seat of my mother's car, around six o'clock on a Saturday evening, a man in white flannel trousers, who had been walking home after an energetic game of tennis, and had collapsed just where the road was crossing an expanse of gorse and fern. At the moment we passed, two ambulance men were drawing a sheet over his face. A tennis racquet lay beside him, out of its press, which, I knew, was the final neglect.

Over the years, sunlight after rain on suburban streets has

been overtaken as an intimation of mortality by another sight. This is the sight at evening of large orange tail-lights, dipping and rising, rising and falling, as the cars and the taxis, one after another, slowly recede down Park Avenue, bumping over the potholes and the large metal panels, past the expensive apartment blocks and their doormen, past the neon-lit coffee-shops where small elderly ladies in fur capes dine early, past the street-vendors and the stores where cheap cigars are sold, until they eventually disappear into the electric blue of the dusk.

The church, the Edwardian terrace of shops, the fire station, the war memorial, the cinema, were common possessions of all towns of a certain size, but each town also boasted something peculiar to it.

Walton-on-Thames had a group of medieval shops, which were famous for the traffic jams they caused in the late afternoon, and their survival continued to hang in the balance. That the thought of their destruction brought scalding tears to my eyes was treated as a sign of my immaturity, and of the fact that, by this time, I had spent too long with my head in a book. At one of these shops, my mother, whom I never knew to buy anything except clothes for herself, bought what she took to be a masterpiece. My father saw that it was a Victorian oleograph of a Venetian painting, and threatened to sue the shop, but the picture continued to hang in the dining room as long as I can remember. My father did not, I believe, care what our house looked like, and certainly he put up with things that, if he had found them in an hotel bedroom he had taken for the night, would have led him to call for the manager. Perhaps, for some period of time, he found my mother's absence of taste, indeed her ignorance of everything, beguiling.

In Weybridge there was a tall column surmounted by a ball, commemorating the unfortunate Queen Caroline. A stone's throw away, there was a village green with perfect grass, sunk slightly below the level of the road, and there, passing by in the car on a Saturday afternoon, I would see Englishmen of a kind my family never got to know playing cricket to desultory applause. A circle of wives gently laughed at the men they had married. Sometimes, at the very moment we drove past, there was a short burst of clapping, and, craning my neck, I saw a man with sandy complexion, who had proved obdurate at the wicket, look round and survey with manly despair the shattered stumps. I felt myself to be observing a small piece of history, in which I had no part.

A mile or so from Weybridge was St. George's Hill, where rich men from the City lived in large, tile-hung houses, brick courtyard opening out on to courtyard, and visible through enormous banks of rhododendrons were garages disguised as stables. This was where, the Thames having been crossed, as we would have to say in Latin lessons, Caesar pitched camp. In winter I would go tobogganing down one particularly steep road, and, in summer, I rose as early as I was allowed, and came on my bicycle in search of arrow-heads and to dig for coins. I found arrow-heads, but no coins.

Hersham had a light-engineering factory, and, now virtually on the main road, there was a large, low, early nineteenth-century house covered in creeper, with stone window-frames against the brick, from which occasionally there issued another nanny, pushing a pram with a coronet and a crest, and once or twice I played with the young girl, who wore, I profess to remember, a broderie-anglaise dress. At Shepperton there was an enormous weir. In the river above it, the water was icily smooth, the colour of crème de menthe frappée, which my mother's friends sometimes drank after Sunday lunch, and, in the river below the weir, where the water seethed with anger, there was a row of large posts, each made of three or four beams strapped together with iron hoops, and bearing the single word "Danger", in large letters, black on white. Men crossed in love had, I was told, thrown themselves to their death in these waters, and I envied them the drama of their lives.

At Lower Halliford, there was a big, rambling hotel, part Tudor, part improvisation out of corrugated iron and ill-fitting panes of glass. It was there that parties of fishermen stayed, and, one stifling August evening, when most likely I was ten or eleven, my father, quite uncharacteristically, proposed that we should go there and dine as a family, perhaps to celebrate the unlikely fact that he was in England at that time of the year. I was given a warm bath, I was dressed quickly, and I held out my hands for inspection, turning them over to display my fingernails. The hotel dining room stuck out into the river on a rickety pier, the mosquitoes buzzed around us, and, as our plates were put before us, my father tapped them with his hands to see if they had been warmed, and, when the water was poured out, he brought his glass quickly to his lips to see if it was iced. How the meal passed, and who spoke to whom, and the measure of my father's disappointment, are things I find it impossible to imagine. What followed an hour or so after I had gone to bed was of a kind that punctuated my childhood.

At dinner I had ordered what was at that time my favourite food: a grilled Dover sole on the bone. Whether the fault lay with the fish, or with the way it was cooked, or with the suppressed excitement inside me, I do not know, but, after saying my prayers and sleeping a short while, I woke up. I rushed myself to the bathroom, and there, crouched over the washbasin, I began a long agonizing vigil. Hour after hour passed: for much of the time my governess, with whom I shared a bedroom, stayed with me, and once my father came in and cooled my forehead with eau de cologne. Craning my head forward, I wondered why, knowing that things would be better if I could stick my finger down my throat, I could not do so: was it the love of life, or was it the lure of death, and why could I not achieve the result I desired by merely pretending that my finger had gone as deep down as I could want? I prayed to God, and promised that, in return for a respite from terror, I would give up this, I would give up that. Never again, as the bath-water grew cold, would I tell myself stories about the courts of distant royalty, which had, I noticed, the power to wrinkle the skin on my scrotum.

Some time in the early hours of the morning, I managed, against all odds, to raise my head, and I suddenly caught sight of the moon, and I tried to offer up my stomach, and the dreadful taste of rotting fish in my mouth and around my teeth, and all my feverish thoughts, to this sudden vision of beauty. To see the moon in her entirety, I placed my forehead against a pipe, and rolled it to right and left, so as to catch now this refraction, now that refraction, as the image passed through the pane of fluted glass, and, years later, during and just after the war, in nightclubs, or bottle parties, or small homosexual clubs where my friends took me, I would, in response to frustration, or uncertainty, or fear, get up from the table where we were sitting, excuse myself from the predatory attentions of the cigarette-girl with her bee-sting lips, and walk falteringly to the lavatory, and there I would rest my forehead against the cream-coloured pipe that brought the water down from the cistern into the lavatory bowl, and slowly rotate my head in that old way, to right and left, from side to side to side. Without benefit of the moon, I sought solace from the cool of the pipe, and from the words of the crooner as they filtered through the flimsy door of the lavatory. On such occasions, a single line of poetry, which had become like a rune for me ever since I first read it at the age of fifteen, appeared in my head, repeating itself over and over again, night after night, frustration after frustration, lavatory after lavatory. "Elle passa sa nuit sainte dans la latrine." It has been my companion, this vagabond line, this present from the voyant voyou, for over sixty years.

What happened with the Dover sole repeated itself with every favourite food of childhood. First, I loved it: then there was one occasion too many, and I was sick all night: then the next morning, I had turned equally against the thing, the thought of the thing, and the word for the thing. The foods were in turn Dover sole; flapjacks, a kind of biscuit from Australia; unripe plums, which I preferred to ripe plums; tinned sardines; fried tomatoes; and, most fallen from grace in that I cannot eat them to this day, sweetbreads.

⌐

The fundamental role that the towns filled in our lives was as the places from which food was ordered and arrived. My mother spent some part of each morning on the telephone to the butcher, the fishmonger, the grocer, the greengrocer, finding out what was in season, how much it cost, whether this was more or less than it cost the week before, how much you got per pound of weight, and how many people a pound could stretch to. Then it would be the turn of the woman on the other end of the line. She would say, "Do you want something really nice and juicy?" or "Do you want something really nice and sweet?" The words "juicy" and "sweet" could be applied to a bewildering variety of things – to cuts of English lamb, to Cox's Pippins, to hothouse tomatoes, to a slab of cod, and to the first consignment of nuts, and to things which, the complaint was, local people didn't appreciate even when Christmas came round, such as Carlsbad plums, and dates which came in boxes with rounded ends, carrying pictures of oases and of *caravanes en marche* – and the question put to my mother was whether she wanted the best. At first she would agree with what was recommended, and then, minutes later, perhaps after a telephone conversation with her mother, would ring back and cancel the order. If my mother regularly complained of the way she was spoken to, I believe that the tradespeople noticed in her voice an absence of that total self-confidence to which they were subservient.

Later in the day the food would be brought to the house by errand-boys on heavy, robust bicycles, the chrome part of which was flecked with rust. At the front of each bicycle there was a large wicker basket, and often another smaller one behind. Suspended from the bar that made a bicycle a man's was a sheet of black metal on which the name and nature of the shop was sign-written in white.

Sometimes, if it so happened that I was taken out early enough on my morning walk, I would come across a whole group of these boys of fifteen, sixteen, seventeen, with their rough skin and their large chapped lips, and their hair clipped to the skin over the ears and high up the nape of the neck, congregated at one or other of their habitual meeting-places. One meeting-place was the dirty patch of grass outside a pub, another one of the large horse-troughs which a benevolent organization had set up at points throughout the neighbourhood, with the name of the organisation and the date incised in Gothic letters the length of the long, granite basin. Here they could stretch their legs without dismounting by resting their boots on the rim of the basin, with the heel lapped by the water. These meetings were a morning council of war, at which the boys compared notes about where they had to go, and who could ride with whom. They worked it out together, though I doubt if all of them could read, and then abruptly, from one moment to the next, they broke up into small detachments, and fanned out in different directions. Standing up on the pedals, their bottoms off the saddle and swaying from side to side, they urged their bicycles forward, swinging now to right, now to left, leaving a track of elongated Ss scorched into the camber of the road. From time to time, they addressed one another in what were to me unintelligible sounds, and they were responded to with other unintelligible sounds or with loud guffaws, and, with much ringing of bicycle bells, they rode always to one overruling end, which was, by all the means at their disposal, to take over the quiet suburban roads, and make them their own. If one of the boys looked up and saw a great cascade of blossom pouring down over a hedge and covering the pavement below with white or yellow petals, or a toy bear propped up against the bars of a nursery window, or a massive dog confined to his kennel, the record of such fragile beauty, or of cossetted childhood, or of strength enchained, provoked storms of derision, and the bicycles raced faster forward. Excitement ran highest, it knew no bounds, when a little distance ahead, steam was observed to rise up slowly from what at first looked like a great plait of brown hair cut off from a young girl's head and thrown down on the road, but was actually a pile of dung, which had been freshly deposited by a dray-horse. At the sighting, the boys braked, and they formed up in a line three to four bicycles abreast. Eagerness was in the air. Like young knights confronted by the defender of a bridge or causeway, they arranged precedence amongst themselves, and then, one at a time, as if vying for the honour, they gathered up their mounts, and charged. As soon as the front wheel hit the target head on, but not a moment before, they jammed on the brakes, and the brown juice spurted up into the air. It coated the wheels and spokes of the bicycle, it stuck to the mudguard and the boy's trouser leg, and, vaporising into an ever finer spray, it covered the basket, and the errands, and it settled on the body of a car parked close up to the curb. Defiance could go no further, and, the victor having quickly declared himself by his stained clothing, the detachment broke up in sudden fear and confusion, and lone boys now pursued their own ways to their own destinations.

Sometimes, around lunchtime, or just after my rest, I would be standing in the pantry, leaning over the sink so as not to spill any of the metallic-tasting tonic that was always prescribed after a cold or flu, using two fingers to press the bib I was required to wear on such occasions against my chest, as I had seen my father do in a restaurant with his napkin, and, as I raised my eyes, suddenly there, not more than four or five feet away from me, I would find myself staring into the watery eyes of one of the boys trudging across the backyard. His casque of hair was silhouetted against a low building, which contained a coal cellar and an outside lavatory that smelled of distemper and carbolic, and which I wanted to be allowed to use, but never was. Much of the fury had gone out of him, and with it much of the fear that he could instil in me. Off his bicycle, on someone's property, which was clearly signed "No Hawkers, No Trespassers", weighed down by his load, the boy shuffled like a prisoner.

Most of the errand-boys held up their trousers with a belt fastened with a massive buckle, and, noticing how the seat of the trousers had invariably been worn thin and shiny, I formed my own explanation. Nightly, when the boy's father arrived home smelling of beer, he would, in a casual tone, ask for the belt, and the boy, for his part, would compliantly unloop it, and, without another word, adopting the position required of him, would count the lashes until his father, telling himself that he had done enough of God's work for the night, tired, and coughed uncontrollably. It was, as I saw it, the good fortune of the poorest boys, who were without any spirit to break, without any fire to put out, and who, for the most part, kept their trousers up with lengths of string, that they escaped their fathers' attentions.

Once, when I was about eleven, and I was walking my dog across an indeterminate open space, where large clumps of blackberry bushes and gorse surrounded a secluded cricket pitch, I noticed a group of boys converging on me. Singly they seemed harmless, but I grew apprehensive as they started to join forces and come closer. Then two boys rushed me. They snatched the beret I used to wear and threw it away, then, seizing my chin, they pulled my mouth open, and filled it with rabbit droppings. For a second or so, I had no idea what it was. "What was it?" I screamed. The boys laughed, and, though I had never seen them before, I felt that they were taking revenge upon me for years of humiliation suffered at other hands. Or perhaps, I reflected, I had something to do with it. In front of my dog, I sat down and cried.

I went to the towns whenever the weather permitted and there was some domestic task that could conveniently be combined with my walk without extending it unduly.

For instance, once a week there were seven ties of my father's, plus one or two black bow ties, to be taken to the dry-cleaner's to be steamed and pressed. I always tried to be the one who gathered up the ties from the stair-rail on which they were set out, so that, running my thumb into the heavy silk of the lining, I could find the name of the shirtmaker from whom they came. For some years I used to think that I would come of age when my ties too were pressed every time I wore them. But, by the age of eleven or twelve, I changed my mind on this subject, and for a reason that was to have far-reaching consequences. For, by this time, I had pored over the photographs of poets and avant-garde composers, and I had noticed that they favoured large loose knots, whereas my father instructed me that a well-dressed man, though he tied his tie at its widest part, pulled it as tight as he could, at the same time puckering it in the middle with the help of his index finger, and then slid the knot up so that it concealed the collar button. It was, of course, only if in life I continued to follow my father's instructions that my ties too would need to be so frequently ironed, and, not only did the photographs I loved tell me not to, but increasingly my deepest wish was to break him too from the habit, even if I had no idea how a flowing knot would look as it swelled under his well-tended double-chin. The reality was that my father had, after all, known poets and avant-garde composers, and, in quarrelling with him, as I did in the early years of adolescence, and bitterly too, I was above all things trying to recall him to a sense of who and what he really was. When I was sixteen, I found the phrase I needed to describe what my father had turned his back upon: it was "the buried life". My father had turned his back on a life he had buried, and, by turning his back on it, he buried it deeper, he buried it from me. I found the phrase in the poetry of Matthew Arnold, which I loved at this stage, and which was one of the few tastes I had that bound me to the "official" culture of the school, and two things made the discovery more poignant. One was that Arnold's poetry was itself the poetry of a buried life, and the other was that, underneath some exterior that I was starting to form, there was a buried life of my own, another "stripling Thames".

Other errands that might be combined with my walk were visits to the chemist's to collect a prescription, or to the grocer's or the greengrocer's or the butcher's to query a book-keeping entry. Tradesmen's books were amongst the first books of which I was enamoured as a child, and they were probably the first physical objects that I saw at short range and regarded as works of art, so that I did not resent the instruction to wash my hands before I touched them. They were about seven inches by four, and their covers were made of board, with a small window cut out of the upper half of the front cover to show the customer's name written in a copybook handwriting. The board itself was of a sumptuous colour, crimson, or olive green, or the very darkest royal blue, and stamped on it was the name and address of the tradesman, and a brief description of his trade, such as "Family Butcher", or "Supplier of Provisions". Below the small window was an emblem of the trade, worked in gold, with a flurry of ribbons, and much tooling. The greengrocer displayed a cornucopia of fruit and vegetables, the butcher a bull unconcerned by death, and I still cannot see a great Renaissance or eighteenth-century binding, ordered for a king or an ambitious prelate, without thinking back to those books whose glow lit up my childhood.

When we arrived at the shop where we were to make our complaint, we entered to the tinkle of a bell, and, if it was the grocer's or the greengrocer's, I would immediately sense a hand reaching down to hold mine. But at the butcher's, not so, for the gesture was primarily to forestall any suspicion that I might pick up something and put it in my pocket. We walked down the varnished floorboards to the kiosk with its dark-wood stain and glass on three sides, and we paused in front of the bookkeeper, who sat behind a small grille with her ledgers, her pen, and a brass inkwell. She opened up, and we placed the book with the offending entry on some sheets of pink blotting paper, which carried a palimpsest of back-to-front writing. A brief conversation took place, which I was not expected to hear since it concerned the frailties of adults. The bookkeeper picked up the book, her lips moved, she adjusted her hairpins, and then she all but invariably pronounced in our favour. Not only was my father's arithmetic likely to be correct, but to question it would sooner or later have meant that we would change tradesmen. The bookkeeper dipped her pen in the ink, corrected the entry, turned the book over, blotted the page, and returned it without a smile. Then she shut the grille with a click. My favourite shops had small brass containers, which carried change on a wire that ran the length of the shop, and, in winter, a paraffin lamp was set out, which smelt of warmed clothing and Christmas.

At the chemist's the routine was in accord with the higher status of the chemist. He was, compared to my nanny, or later to my governess, or, for that matter, to my grandmother, a man of education. We did not go with a complaint. We went to the chemist's solely to collect prescriptions that he regularly filled, and, though he could see us from the backroom where he worked, we were always kept waiting. The clock ticked, and I looked around with fear and admiration until, without warning, a man with waxed moustaches, and wearing a freshly starched white coat, was staring at us through his pince-nez from between the tall coloured bottles on the counter. He held in two fingers a small cardboard pillbox with my father's pills in it. Once a month he produced a bottle of the mouthwash my father liked, which was glycothymolin with a spoonful of oil of cloves tipped into it. The money would be handed over to him, and he would carefully count out the change and hand it back to us on a small piecrust tray of highly polished silver. Sometimes, without expression, he held out to me in the palm of his hand a pink or pale violet cachou in the shape of a star or a heart, which I quickly stuck in my mouth. "What do you say?" I was asked. "Thank you," I said. If I had not already said thank you, it was not that I didn't know that I should. It was fear, fear in response to his impassive gaze, which I could feel penetrating the many layers of clothing that I was made to wear, laying bare the slightest irregularity in my body. It was another variant of the medical gaze, and it too, as far as I could tell, would, if acknowledged, if overheard, cause the very scar it professed to discern.

The long winter when I was recovering from pleurisy, and which covered the period when much of the regime of my childhood years was established, I was taken regularly to a house made of dark grey brick, with gables painted chocolate, and buried in rhododendrons, mauve and crimson, and there I lay under a sunlamp for three quarters of an hour. When I was called in from the waiting room, I took off all my clothes, except my socks, and I did the only two things that I was required to do for myself at home: I folded my clothes with extreme care, and I lined up my shoes side by side. Then I lay down on the sheets, under which I could detect the cold embrace of rubber trying to endear itself. Dr Behr asked me to close my eyes, and he placed over them a black scarf, made of heavy satin, with weights sewn into the ends. Raising the end of the scarf very slightly, I could see Dr Behr take from his desk a large piece of carbon paper, used for taking copies of letters, and, noiselessly approaching the bed, he carefully laid the carbon paper across my genitals. Half way through the treatment, he tiptoed back into the room, replaced the first sheet of carbon paper with a new sheet, and slipped a triangle of Swiss chocolate into my mouth. The taste of chocolate and honey and hazelnut invaded my body, and, lightening the weight of the black scarf, I allowed the eerie violet light with which the whole room was inundated to percolate through my eyelashes. The light, I noticed, was the colour of the small glass probes that my father regularly rubbed over his bald head, hoping they would shock the roots of his hair into life. At last the sunlamp was turned off, and I dressed.

As I was driven away, I looked out of the rear window of the car, and, through the rhododendrons, I could see that the violet light had been turned on again on for the benefit of another patient. I started to think that this treatment was part of some much larger, carefully planned process, in which, at each visit, something would be taken out of the body, so that in time an existence of permanent convalescence would result, in which it would be as hard to be well as to be ill. It was a prospect that for much of the time I welcomed.

The landscape of my childhood was not the neighbouring towns, but what lay in the interstices. Spread out across
what only a few years earlier had been field, or heath, or
woodland, although, in the whole course of growing-up, I
never met anyone who had memories of this land from an
earlier age, was an untidy, unpremeditated criss-cross of
roads, and avenues, and common land, which, disregarding
the older boundaries, established newer distinctions
between town and suburb, between suburb and
country, between subtle shades of affluence, and between
many many different senses of the word "middle class".

If what had been obliterated had fallen victim to neglect,
neglect continued to eat away at what survived. A Tudor
potting shed could be made out in a field choked with
nettles where couples walked their dogs; a milestone by a
busy road, where the dust from cars settled on the blackberries, told the motorist how far it was to Tyburn or East
Cheap; a pair of crumbling eighteenth-century park gates,
surmounted by eagles, marked the beginning, not of a
poplar-lined avenue, but of a street of low terrace-houses,
where I used to go to be coached in Horace and Quintillian
by a man of old-fashioned manners, called Mr Wilson, who
had a shiny bald head like a new potato, and wore a thick
grey cardigan over the waistcoat of his dark blue suit, and
chewed on raisins while we construed, to my unutterable
delight, complex Latin sentences. Outside the room where
we worked, his tall son, who ran a motoring school, opened
the front-door to girls fresh from the tennis club. Mr
Wilson seemed to me at the time of extreme old age, but,

more than twenty years later, when I wrote a review of a book in a Sunday paper, he wrote to me, and asked if I was the boy he had once tutored.

But, if it was only with difficulty that the relics of older habitation survived the indifference of modern life, nature, at least in the short run, thrived on the uneven struggle. It clung to the edges of golf courses, and to the sides of disused clay-pits, and it was rampant in the backwaters of the local rivers, where reeds and waterlilies were the breeding-grounds for swans and gnats. Nature lorded it over low-lying fields, which flooded in winter, so that, as we drove home on an inhospitable Christmas Eve, bowling along an elevated road, the back seat loaded with Christmas shopping, hoping to get home in time for a reading of the last instalment of *A Christmas Carol*, we could see ice stretching away as far as the eye could reach, holding in its embrace tall tufts of grass. But the broadest expanses of preserved nature were the extensive, sandy commons, cut by broad paths, here and there whisked up into dune-like formations, or into hillocks surmounted by a small ring of fir trees and covered with gorse and blackberry and fern, where I would beg to be taken to play what was, from the age of eight or nine, my favourite game. Released from the car, I crawled through the undergrowth on my stomach like a snake, or like an infantryman, flattened to the ground, trying to make my progress invisible. I do not know when I abandoned this game, but one of the most vivid tricks that memory has ever played on me is the clearly false recollection that I have of my worming my way through the bracken, the roots smelling of incense, trying hard not to rustle the fronds and thus give away my presence, and at the same time being in a position to think how striking the resemblance was between my father and the father who appears in the first pages of *Adolphe*, both men being liberal and speculative in their ideas about art and the sciences, true free-thinkers, but, the closer their opinions got to life or politics, the more corrosively conservative they became.

Where, for me, nature survived with greatest pertinacity, and in its most untamed, its most fecund, form was not here but where it required a child's eye, momentarily released from the sense of scale, to discern it: in the ditches that ran along the sides of roads which, though not yet burdened with through traffic, were no longer mere country lanes. Standing on the edge, and looking down into them, I imagined myself on a steep precipice, suspended high over a canyon, where in deep shadow tribes of dwarfs slaved away at trying to extract from the depths of the earth some recalcitrant element, which would make others rich but would leave them poor and broken in body from bitter drudgery. As I was looking down, from one moment to the next a sudden breeze parted the coarse grass and the tufts of dandelion on the far bank of the ditch, the shadow was dispelled, and suddenly vast cavalcades of knights, carrying pennants, poured forth from fortified caverns, and clashed at daybreak in battles that were hard and impetuously fought. All day long, which for me passed in a few mesmerized minutes while I pretended not to hear my name called with greater and greater impatience, the battle hung in the balance, swaying backwards and forwards, favouring first one side, then the other, and it was only when the sun went down, and the canyon returned to darkness that the outcome was clear. It was only years later when, the war long over, I first took in the small copper panels of Altdorfer, in which he represented mêlées of beetle-like warriors locked together in a kind of congested combat, which, if it was ever resolved, would be so, not by the force of arms, but by the sheer weight of armour, so that eventually one side would cause the other side to subside into the earth, that I recognized a vision of life, of battle that is, that barely differed from what had been mine when, a child, I hung over the suburban ditches that ran alongside Station Road or Burwood Avenue, and, out of sheer hunger for imagery and narrative, brought my reading of Froissart and Malory to bear so that I saw what was not there to be seen.

At no time did I like fighting, or any form of roughness – I was a pacifist by taste, long before I was a pacifist through the reading of books – but I loved the thought of battles, and I loved the thought of people who dressed up to fight, just as I loved the thought of people who dressed up to work, or to go fishing, or to take the honey from bee-hives, or, most of all, years later, who dressed up, slightly absent-mindedly, to make love, or to be made love to, and who knew, through all their absent-mindedness, that the uniform of love would stay on until the time had come for them to swoon back on a bank of soft pillows, their mission accomplished. But, in all such matters, I was something of a stickler for rectitude. From an early age, I had collected toy soldiers, and I always insisted that, when I organised them into tableaux, there should never be the slightest breach in the unities of period, scale, or accoutrement. When, at the age of thirteen, I became an ardent pacifist, something I abandoned only when Germany declared war on the Soviet Union, my earlier love of uniforms and armour, of battle honours and heraldry, became a more diffuse aestheticism, while my love of the unities stayed intact in the way I read books, or took notes on them, only to resurface with singular literalness when I found myself in the army, in a regiment, in uniform, in the midst of actual fighting. For, called upon, as I frequently was, to bring down from one command to another, or to take forward to the front, an order of battle that included, say, the temporary secondment of a squadron of the such and such Hussars to the Blankshire Light Infantry, or the creation of a task force composed of two companies of motorised infantry, a battery of artillery, and some flame-throwing tanks, I felt the most intense reluctance to pass on these dispositions. I wanted nothing to do with these inelegant and unnatural monstrosities, and I would willingly have torn up these orders, or at least refused to transmit them, were it not for the penalties involved. It has not been easy for others, such as Dr S, or for myself to recapture the genuine difficulty I had at the time in reasoning myself out of a course of action that would have amounted to infamous conduct in the face of the enemy, and would have led to the most summary of court martials.

In the new emergent geography, railway stations, places of worship, recreation grounds, cottage hospitals, signal boxes, even post offices, started up bearing the names of places that, in some cases, were not even within walking-distance. For instance, from the window of my bedroom, which was at the back of the house, I could, when I was ill, or on a bright summer morning if I had obtained permission the evening before to open the curtains early, look out over our garden, over the wooden fence at the bottom of the garden, over the allotments where, a few years later, I would paint the runner beans in blossom with little hatched strokes in a manner derived from reading Roger Fry on Cézanne, over the railway cutting, marked out by a line of fir-trees, in which for years I saw a line of pirates in cocked hats carrying chests of jewellery, over more allotments, which lay in dead ground, until eventually my eyes took in the parapet of a church tower, with gargoyles at each corner, rising above some old cedars. This was the church where I was christened. An elderly clergyman, called Dr Oxford, a gaunt soft-spoken man, popular in the theatre, known to have been entrusted with the confidences of famous actresses and young showgirls, with a reputation for helping out any pretty woman who went to him with a story of trouble, had come down from London to perform the service. He had done it for my mother's sake, my mother told me, and she also told me that there were not many for whom he would do such a thing. She told me this many times. It had been necessary for him to obtain a special dispensation to officiate in another parish, which was not easy. But he had persisted for my mother's sake. Three years earlier he had christened my brother against the same obstacles. When I was seven or eight, he came down to the house, and now behind pebble spectacles he was blind, and his dark suit was covered with soup stains. I was brought in to be touched by him as he sat on the sofa between two turbaned ladies, who were drinking tea and smoking black cigarettes, and the wintry afternoon sun streamed in through the fawn-coloured net curtains behind them. The ladies had been on the stage with my mother, and one, I fancied, had sat down by the side of a signed photograph of herself in a silver frame, as if this would lead the old blind clergyman to continue to think of her as she once was, with soft, dewy features. She ruffled my hair, and said, without looking at me, "Connie, he'll break some hearts."

Dr Oxford's signature was clearly legible on my baptismal certificate, which had for years hung above my bed, framed in an ugly passe-partout. In the centre of the certificate, there was a large gold cross, and above the cross in Gothic letters was the inscription, which I used to mutter to myself in moments of bafflement, so determined was I to find it an inspiration for my life: *In hoc signo vinces*. When at the age of thirteen, I took the scholarship examination for my school in the great medieval hall, I found myself sitting under a coat of arms, which bore the motto *Will God I shall*, and that too I took for my inspiration in the exam. I said it over and over again, and was convinced that, in its obstinacy, it helped me to keep my mind clear.

The baptismal certificate also had on it the name of the parish. The parish had the same name as one of the neighbouring towns, but this did not mean that the church had been built to serve that town. It had not been built to serve any town, and it took only a fine Sunday morning to make this fact visible. For then you could see a very varied group of people converging upon the church, some walking along the roads, some on a raised footpath, which ran like a causeway across the carefully tended allotments the far side of the railway from us, and it was natural to assume that there were about the same number of people, and of about the same sort, approaching the church from beyond it, and it

was these different groups, rather than the inhabitants of
the town that gave its name to the church, who were its
intended congregation. There were large families, aug-
mented by cousins, herded along by untidy mothers, who
jabbed at their hair with hairpins. There were solitary
widowers with clipped moustaches, who had austere habits,
and were known to dress for dinner every evening and eat
alone under a single, unshaded light bulb. There were pairs
of unmarried sisters who lived together, and they wore pale
grey gloves to carry their prayer-books, and round the neck
a band of black faille with a cameo brooch pinned on to it,
and I was always curious to know how the pin of the brooch
avoided running through the windpipe. There were groups
of young girls back from boarding school, where it was
feared that they had picked up improper habits. Some had
learnt to sway their hips when they walked so that their grey
flannel skirts swirled around their legs, rising a little, falling
a little, and those who didn't do this greeted the sight with
a smile of amused recognition, as though for them too it
signified some special stage of emancipation. The different
groups mostly kept their distance from one another, but
certain families, or couples, invariably associated in some
way with the army, found it unthinkable to adapt their
speed to those in front of them, and would suddenly, as
they bore down on them, quicken their pace, and race past,
muttering a few words, or offering a hurried gesture of
apology. This was not the norm. For the understanding was
that the walk to church permitted, for each age in its own
way, an adjustment of the mind to the decencies of what lay
ahead. Of necessity children did it by letting off steam,
adults did it by allowing their thoughts to be hushed, old

people would do it as second nature. I took the powder with which old ladies swathed themselves to be a way they had of turning their thoughts to death.

It was only as the churchgoers passed through the lych-gate, and they were brought to a halt on the broad gravel path, flanked by laurels and rhododendrons, and over-topped by old cedars, that some general form of sociability broke out. The men raised their hats, the women with their great upturned cheeks veined with crimson smiled. Knighted civil servants and commoners, ladies and the wives of tradesmen, children whose accents were beginning to diverge, acknowledged each other for the few moments before the tumult of the carillon stopped, and the five-minute bell began to toll, at which moment, putting aside their smiles, recomposing their faces, dropping their eyes, they all filed in under the tower along a short stone-flagged passage, with its own smell amalgamated of granite, and furniture polish, and old leaves, where girls of seventeen, eighteen, who knew everyone by name, and whom it was my ambition to ask to play tennis, or to go out on the river in a punt, handed out hymn-books with a quick, passing smile. I barely have to say that no assignations were ever made, and, as we entered the nave of the church, there was always a moment of excitement, which was more real for me than any rendezvous, for which I was anyhow, in every possible way, unprepared, as I looked up at the giant lime-wood figures who balanced on top of the rood screen, enacting the greatest drama that I had, at that age, ever come across. I quickly glanced at the pale carved frame where the hymns for the day were given, and then I was led to what was to be our pew. We did not have a regular pew of our own, and, every Sunday, there was an explanation, or an excuse, delivered in clipped tones, why we were sitting where we were. The organ grew louder, and, as the music swelled, most of the congregation who were not infirm pulled out a hassock, and fell to their knees, and engaged in muttered prayer. Some opened their eyes, and stared up at the pale Crucifixion, and at the toes of the Virgin and of St John as they curled over the wooden parapet on which they stood. Some, I noticed, kept a straight back, others allowed their bottoms to rest on the bench behind them. I spent much time as a child wondering whether these two postures were equally acceptable in the eyes of God, or whether those who slouched without good physical reason might not be required to pay a penalty at some future time, in some future life, at some altogether unexpected moment.

For a child, or for a child such as I was, prayer came easily. There was so much to give thanks for, so much to ask deliverance from, so much that called indiscriminately for both, that, though often tongue-tied in daily life, I found it absurdly easy to put into words that I was sure God could understand the terrors of the night, or the pleasures of food, or the love of books, or the lasciviousness of pictures, or the shame of bedwetting. The only anxiety that communication with my Maker caused was how to avoid having in my mind simultaneously thoughts that I needed Him to know about and thoughts that I would rather He didn't. But what troubled me was how it was that grown-ups, who led organized lives, and read the newspaper, and wore proper clothes, could ever find in a similar way something to reveal, or, for that matter, something to conceal. Indeed why should they think it worthwhile for them to torture their pressed trousers, or to crumple their carefully pleated skirts – objects made, not for kneeling, but for opening the door to guests, or for waiting on a railway platform, or for rebuking a servant or admonishing a son or daughter – when all they would get out of it was a posture for which they, not being children, had barely a use?

Once, it is true, I overheard my father, towards the end of Sunday lunch, at which much vin rosé had been drunk, turn to his neighbour, Bunty H, drop his voice, and advise her how a certain kind of dream could be prevented by crossing one's legs before falling asleep. For years I followed this advice, which I set greater store by because of the way I had come by it, and I spared myself, particularly when I was staying in someone else's house, much embarrassment. But I still had to wonder what value the advice could have had for this neat, middle-aged woman, with her Eton crop, and her black tailored suits, and her perennial Alpine hat, which she wore at a rakish angle, or what lapses it could save her from, or why she would want to control the flow of thought or the rhythm of internal secretions, when, as far as I could understand, her inner life had been, in what I took to be the adult mode, totally turned outwards into such things as her chain-smoking, or the iron grip she had on her charmingly ineffectual husband, who had defied his family to marry her, or her well-known skill at arranging flowers, or her fierce use of the monocle, which she let fall when she laughed, which she did heartily.

79

If I have found it so easy to slide from the geography of my childhood to the sexuality of adults, I excuse myself at this stage by appeal, not to the subtle similarities that doubtless existed between the two themes, but to the brute way they were brought together within one of the great continuing adventures of my early years: the voyages of discovery through my father's books.

It began when, about the age of nine or ten, I looked into a glass-fronted bookcase, and there saw, on the shelf below where my father kept his copies of the German classics, an ancient guidebook in six volumes, dating from the mid-eighteenth century, entitled *The Environs of London*. Bound in leather-covered board, the colour of pale creamy fudge, these volumes soon became my favourite reading of a certain sort. I say "of a certain sort" because, up till then, any book that captured my interest, such as a novel by Scott or Dickens, or by Kingsley or Harrison Ainsworth, or even by the much despised and now completely forgotten Jeffrey Farnol, whose daintiness deeply offended me, I would pick up, and starting on page 1, I would race through it as fast as my eyes could carry me, until some demand, like washing my hands, or getting ready to go out, forced me to put it down, and any other way of reading would have seemed to me to be as bad as, in fact as exactly like, driving through a town or village without catching its name, hence without being able to write it down, so that I had no way of feeling that I had actually been there. What made for a new sort of reading was to open the book at random, to read one page, and then perhaps the page before that, and then the page before that, or to leap a whole volume ahead and read a batch of pages, sometimes too fast to take any of them in. It was called, I soon learnt, "dipping into" a book, and it seemed not to matter that, when I had to put the book down, I couldn't, on coming back to it, always find where I left off, nor that I often found myself reading the same pages more than once, and with the sense of learning something new.

Why initially I found *The Environs of London* such a rewarding book to dip into was because every place that I had ever gone to on my walks, every place that I had ever driven through on the weekends with my father at the wheel, every town or village whose name I had ever seen on a signpost, or read on the front of a bus, or noticed as some-where where shops, or garages, or estate agents, had another branch, could boast of its own entry. Each entry had the same structure. It began, immediately after the place-name, with a reference to the seat of some baronet, or of Mr so-and-so, a captain in the yeomanry, and it then went on to talk of the village itself, and the agricultural improvements that were under way, and of the tablets that were to be found in the old church, and, if it was a locality of sub-stance, to the coaching inn. Woodcuts, some of them imperfectly printed, and with a great deal of air around the subject, showed parkland, and bridges under construction, and thatched cottages strung along a country road with a woman carrying a child on her shoulder staring out, hollow-eyed, at the traffic that never passed. I read all such entries with avidity, and I soon found myself encouraged to daydream about Captain so-and-so's dinner parties, or about meeting the daughter of the house out riding on her pony, or sometimes, when the weather was icy, and I found joy in the way in which the frost loosened my permanent catarrh, about being a ploughman turning the long hard furrow. But soon I found that this invitation to casualness in my reading had another and more disturbing source, and this was the growing sense that, though every place I was reading about shared its name, altered perhaps by a minor difference in spelling, with a place I knew, they could easily not be the same place. So much had happened between then and now that the similarity in name could be no more than a coincidence massively repeated. Time, about which my neighbours in church sang so lustily, carried away, not only its sons, but also its places. It was, in part to acknowledge, in part to ward off, this conclusion that the habit of dipping into, dipping out of, the old guidebooks had its share of appropriateness.

And it was to a somewhat analogous conclusion that I found myself drawn when, now about twelve years old, adolescence pricked me, and I started to explore another, and what might have been expected to be for me a totally inaccessible, section of my father's books. Inaccessible, for it was only a few years earlier that I had, for about six or nine months, of which more later, suffered from such an intense fear of heights that I could not walk down stairs, and instead had to be carried down in what soon became, through the intensity of my sobbing, a state of total exhaustion. How was it then that, one early afternoon, I took advantage of the overcast weather outside, and of some preoccupying event in another part of the house, and, pulling one of the wooden bar-stools that my father had introduced into the house up against his bookshelves, at first cautiously, then less so, hauled myself up until I was half-standing on the seat, and my hands were beginning to explore the rock face of books? An explanation is called for, but all I can say is that I knew that, if only I straightened myself up, and continued my ascent, I would find something that would fill a need in my mind, and that it was this knowledge, this need, that drove me forwards.

At first I had to satisfy myself with the books on the right hand side of the shelf where my fingers were straying. Here were the memoirs of a few dandies of the turn of the century, Frank Harris and Boni de Castellane, and a copy of the commonplace book of the mysterious "Comtesse Diane", but it was the books on the left hand side of the shelf to which destiny was leading me. Slowly I crossed my right hand over my left hand, and, after the first happy encounter, nothing was ever the same again. I recall to this day the promise that a delighted boy made to himself that, whenever he was alone in the house, or could be certain that he would be undisturbed, he would return to these new pleasures.

I kept my promise, and my new discoveries did not disappoint me. Bound in exotic covers, one in the most delicate mauve paper with silver lettering, another in Satanic black, another affecting the objectivity of a scientific text, their meaning only partially buried in a foreign language, these books offered me, as I clung to my inadequate footing, waiting for a door to open, or a floorboard to creak, all the stolen pleasures of instruction, and delight, and adventitiously the lure of danger. Two volumes that I took down most frequently, and which gratefully opened at the page at which they had last been shut, were a French translation of the *Kama Sutra* in a copy given to my father in 1907 by Percy Pitt, a violinist, I believe, with copious endnotes by a Docteur Garnier of Marseilles, an international authority on degeneracy, who listed with great precision the diseases that followed on each specific form of self-indulgence, and *Le Vice et l'Amour*, a book in bad condition from having been read too often, which left tell-tale stains of black on my hands from the cheaply dyed binding. A work more unapproachable by me, partly through the unbearably coarse illustrations, partly through my almost complete inability to read German, was *Sittengeschichte des Welteskrieges* by Magnus Hirschfeld, inscribed to my father "von Ihren Kurt Weill", dated September 1934.

If, as I knew, these books were for grown-ups, the question was how this phrase was to be understood, and the understanding that I settled for was that grown-ups could read them with impunity because, for them, there was no danger that these books could represent, there was nothing left in the grown-up mind for them to arouse except a kind of detached amusement, something that produced a slow, abstracted smile, and the wafting of a cigarette-holder across the open page, like a censer rocked before the altar of a religion that the world had outgrown. There was, in my imagination, no similarity between the fevered state into which these books threw me and the worldliness with which one of my father's friends, or, for that matter, my father himself, would turn the pages, each time running his forefinger lightly down the outer edge of the page. The need out of which I came to devour these books, which no more entered into this other reading of them than the routine with which my father started to order in a restaurant – first interrogating the waiter whether there had been any special delivery of plovers' eggs or of white asparagus, and then always settling for the same thing, which, I believe, he had concocted (potted shrimps rolled up in smoked salmon with small triangles of thinly cut brown bread) – was in fact motivated by hunger.

Sometimes, when I was engaged in this illicit reading, my whole body shaking, I would try to envisage what my father would say were he to discover me in flagrante delicto. His first reaction would, I knew, be mockery, but I suspected that his second would be to insist that I didn't understand what I was reading: it was "beyond" me, and I came to the conclusion that there would be more truth to this than he knew. For, if certain words, which he could enunciate with a slow urbanity, precipitated me into a mild delirium, there must be some discrepancy between what they had meant to me and what they now meant, which in turn was not what they had once meant to the grown-up reader. And it was this shift in meaning that in time I came to think of as in every way comparable to the change in reference that, I had already concluded, had overtaken the place-names in the eighteenth-century gazeteer, making it such a poor guide for a curious child trying to get around the paved roads of his suburban world.

⁀

The house we moved from was called "Upton Pyne", the house we moved to we called "The Mask".

The name "Upton Pyne" appears on my birth-certificate as my father's address at the time, and I keep my birth certificate in a small tin attaché case, of which I am very proud, which has been painted with a decorator's comb in big brown and ochre whorls. One bright morning in New Delhi, having been lent by the High Commissioner a large limousine to go where I wanted, I could think of nothing that I wanted to do more than to get for myself a piece of the tin luggage that I had seen, often covered in burlap to protect the delicate paintwork, stacked in large piles on railway platforms with the cows wandering between them, or else carried aloft on the head of a grey-haired woman or a meek unshaven clerk. My driver shook his head in disbelief. I was persistent. Then reluctantly he drove into one of the popular bazaars, hooting people out of the way until gradually we were brought to a standstill by the crowds of shoppers, and beggars, and animals. I got out, bought my case, and now, when I have it open in front of me, and am leafing through an old engagement-book, and come across a forgotten name or a block of unidentified telephone numbers, I am very soon brought face to face with my birth certificate, which is tucked into one of the slots inside the lid, and on it I see the words "Upton Pyne". With time the impact has lessened, but I still ask myself how anyone could have formed an attachment to this name. Did it please through a euphony, audible to others, but in which I cannot hear the merit, like an aria by Bellini? Or was there at work in its formation an association to some early moment of happiness, or to an encounter late in life, which, if I knew about it, would make a difference to how I heard the name? Or was the name an invention, dreamt up for its utter fancifulness in some distant hill-station, or on the banks of a turgid African river, at a time in life when the rhythms of the English language, overlaid with too many commands barked out, were half-forgotten? And what could the person have been like who, so seized with the name, had warmed a poker, and then, not once but twice, had burnt it into a small rectangular piece of plywood, letter by Gothic letter, and stuck one piece to the front gate, and hung the other over the very front door from which this memoir set out?

As to Upton Pyne – the house, not the name – everything that I now know about it I learnt from later walks, or from very rare visits to other children who lived nearby.

It stood at the T-junction where a long, straight road, with a row of telegraph poles which emphasized its straightness, ran into a broader, leafier, avenue with larger houses, which curved gently three times in the course of a mile. The straight road had metalled pavements on either side, while the avenue had wide paths with grass verges, and here and there an oak tree or a beech spread its branches across the road. When I fell off my bicycle on the metalled road, the graze was surrounded by an angry bruise: when I fell off on the sandy path, specks of earth worked their way under the broken skin, and came off only with the scab.

There were houses along one side of the avenue, and on the other side there was for most of the way a strip of mixed woodland about twenty yards deep running back to the edge of the railway cutting. When the express train for Portsmouth or the West Country raced by, a large cloud of smoke billowed up with the whiteness of cotton wool, and for a few minutes it blotted out even the tallest trees, until it shredded away, and there were revealed, first, the branches of the fir trees with little bits of smoke sticking to them, then the outlines of a small wooden hut, and finally a row of beanpoles set up in a clearing in the trees. Over the years the bigger trees pushed their roots outwards, and these lay across the path like great bundles of knotted arteries in a medical illustration. On a Saturday or Sunday morning, in all weathers except rain, well-dressed children in chocolate-coloured velvet caps rode their ponies this way, and cries of warning or fright would go up as the riders suddenly found themselves trapped in a sea of roots, and the mounts had to be brought up sharp on the rein. In the autumn, the smell of bonfires permeated the area with a heavy dry smell, which reminded me of illness, and of the small red cardboard boxes, with, on top, a flat wick, like a ribbon, sticking out, which were called *Incense de Bruges*, and which, on my father's insistence, were lit, in the morning and at bedtime, after I had been sat on the chamber-pot in my bedroom, or, as it was romantically called, the sick-room. The long fingers of earth that lay between the roots, and formed the divisions of a casket, started to fill up with beech-nuts, and pine cones, and sodden leaves, and, for a schoolboy sometimes aspiring to be ordinary, joy of joys, red shiny conkers bursting out of their pale green armour.

On the opposite side of the avenue most of the houses lay behind a carefully tended hedge of box, or yew, or holly, which rose up into a high arch of solid leaf as it cleared the imposing brick piers from which the iron gate was hung. Generally a paved path led up to the front-door, but, where the owner was apprehensive of a fall in winter, the paving-stones had been replaced by gravel. I can think of only one house in the avenue that was without a hedge, and it stood, not at the level of the road, but at the bottom of a small dell, and at road-level there were low wooden posts, cut square and with the sides chamfered, and slung between them a chain of alternating links and spikes. Then the ground fell away sharply, with a path that twisted down to the house, which on the ground floor was made of brick, and, on the upper floors, there was harling washed a pale lemon, with the ever-popular mullioned windows and a mansard roof pierced with *yeux-de-boeuf.* There was a time when I used to go to this house and play with a boy named Michael. I remember nothing about the boy except that, for some forgotten reason, he was someone whom I wanted to know before I knew him, and so our friendship seemed to me always something of a miracle. Mostly what I remember about going to the house was being given biscuits in the shape of animals with hard coloured icing, and the taste of the biscuits blended with the smell of ivy and the rotting wood of silver birches that were soft and spongy to the touch. Next to the house was an empty lot with a sign nailed to a tree, saying "For Sale". In spring and early summer, the earth was carpeted with primroses, bluebells, violets, and cowslips, which sprouted through the dark, rotting leaves. Much despised, but to me the headiest of flowers, was the convolvulus, which appeared and disappeared in the undergrowth, and ran wild along the hedges of the neighbourhood.

Most of the houses along the avenue were lived in by noisy, easy-going families, large enough to ensure that there was at least one child whose birthday fell in dry weather, so that there was a party in the garden. Trestle tables were set up, and large tablecloths laid, and tea was served. The guests gorged on cakes, and jellies in stemmed glasses, and small torpedo-shaped rolls filled with fish paste or hard-boiled eggs, and they pulled crackers and wore the paper-hats that fell out of them, and of which I hated the smell with a ferocity that staggered the grown-ups. After tea there was a treasure hunt with clues buried in the lavender-beds, or in the hollows of trees. Races were run, and often the father had a starting pistol, which he fired into the air. Children dressed as cowboys or in brown beaded shirts stalked each other amongst the fruit-trees or around the large clumps of pampas grass planted in circular beds cut into the lawn. One side walked slowly with bent knees, and often a finger against the lips in warning to the world, and we came to know of their prey only when screams went up as they were discovered and thrown out of their deep hiding-places. As the sun started to go down, or in high summer as the heat of the day abated, the figures of nurses appeared along the periphery of the garden, holding walking-shoes and satchels and other reminders of reality, and there would be sudden tears or bursts of temper.

My own knowledge of parties was largely second-hand and obtained through the thickness of a hedge. My parents knew no other parents, my nanny knew only a few other nannies, and in consequence I was seldom invited. But when I was, and the acceptance was sent off, and my clothes were laid out – generally a shantung shirt, a straight red silk tie, and dark blue or dark grey shorts – and I was washed and dressed, the excitement would likely get the better of me, either before I arrived, or on arrival as teams were being chosen. I would be sick, or I would burst into tears, or I would wet myself, and I would be taken home, sad and shaking. At the age of ten or eleven, I formulated a principle against friends. Friends, boys in the real world, with their interests in games and dirty jokes and lavatories, represented for me a dilution of the universe of the imagination, peopled by historical figures or the characters of Scott or Lamb's *Tales*. I said once to my mother as we drove to see a matinée of some play by Shakespeare, "I think that having friends is a weakness." She did not find this declaration worth a reply, and I sat on in silence, judging that this was not the stuff of which conversation was made.

Not all the houses in the avenue were possible venues for children's parties. Some, the largest, with the most intricate Tudor-style bricklaying on the high chimneys, and with stucco work showing cherubs holding up scrolls, and with wisteria curling round the bow windows, belonged to rich widows or spinsters, living alone or with companions whom I would sometimes find myself standing next to in a shop, also querying a bookkeeping entry, but more imperiously.

A sure sign of such habitation was the sight at mid-morning, or earlier in summer months, of a chauffeur, young and good-looking, or elderly and pink-faced, wearing a peaked cap, and dressed in a grey uniform and leggings, standing outside the house by the side of a big, well-upholstered car. To pass the time, he smoothed his moustache with the back of his hand, he adjusted the muff that protected the radiator against the frost, he put one foot on the running-board and brushed away the dust on first one, then the other, turn-up of his trousers. In cold weather he wore a belted raincoat over his uniform, and, to warm himself, banged the fist of one gloved hand into the palm of the other. In summer he could be seen slowly swaying from side to side, and someone alert, as I preternaturally was, to the signs of vanity, would recognize that he was try-ing to catch his reflexion in the satiny bodywork of the car, just like the young shopgirls whom, twenty-five years later, I used momentarily to fall in love with, as they raced through the bustling arcades of Milan or Bologna, darting looks to right, to left, catching admiration from passers-by, but seeking, not that, but their own image in any reflecting surface.

The straight road that ran at right angles to the avenue by the side of Upton Pyne was another story. It started off, not grandly, but favourably, with houses behind hedges, small houses, small hedges, but it changed character about a hundred yards down, where the church school stood on the left. The school was made of grey brick with lancet windows running high up into a steep gable, and it was surrounded by an asphalt playground. One dark evening I was driven there, wrapped up in scarves, and I was expected to rehearse the small part I had been given in my Sunday-school Nativity play. I had been somewhat looking forward to the event, and I hoped to use my theatrical background to some good and lasting effect: I would make an impression. It was cold, there were scrubbed boards, to which I was unused, and, though I tried to feel, beyond my own pettiness, the solemnity of the occasion, I was frightened by the smell of old rag, which came out of the hissing tea urn, and by the black night that pressed itself against the lancet window. I made an excuse, and I was driven home, not to return. Soothed by the warmth of the car, I insisted on stopping to buy an historical novel with my pocket money.

Next along after the school, there was a low terrace of villas, each with its own potted plant behind the lace curtain, and in the middle of the terrace was a lone monkey-puzzle tree. At this point, the road dipped slightly, and ran ahead to meet the main road that connected the centres of Weybridge and Walton, and along which buses ran. I was not allowed to walk this last stretch, but I remember, one autumnal evening, seeing in front of me in this no-man's land large-breasted girls in school uniform leaning against a fence and laughing, and the pavement marked out for hopscotch, to this day the obscurest of games, and little boys kicking a football in the gutter. I sensed the premature flowering of love.

Immediately before the corner, there were a few miscellaneous shops, which I knew only from coming at them from the opposite direction, of which the most important to me were a shop that did bicycle repairs, which reverberated with the sound of air and the noise of tyres being bounced on the wooden floor, and, on the corner itself, with two stone steps rising sharply to the door, a newsagent, crowded with an assortment of goods selling for a penny or tuppence – bars of chocolate, daily papers, wooden rulers, packets of envelopes, plain and airmail, comics, and thick black coils of liquorice. The shop sold bottled drinks and ice cream in the summer months, and, as autumn drew in, fireworks appeared in the window: squibs, and rockets, and Catherine wheels, and Roman candles, encased in paper wrappings decorated with tiny silver or gold stars.

Just behind the row of shops, and to be entered only from the road that united the two towns, was a sloping expanse of grass, which straggled upwards towards a wooden fence and a row of fir trees. Near the entrance, on a concrete slab, was the gun that commemorated the war. This was the recreation ground, or "the rec", as it was commonly called. The grass was poor everywhere, but there was one particular patch, where the ground flattened out, where it was permanently singed. This was where the bonfire was set up each year.

As the year decayed, and the fog from the river started to form haloes round the lampposts, people would arrive on foot or by car carrying, dragging, old bits of furniture: broken wash-stands, lavatory-seats that had come unglued, sodden rolls of carpet, old cushions, old deckchairs, mattresses with their insides falling out. They came with bundles of newspaper, and leaves and twigs in large garden-bags, and plywood boxes, and, as best they could, they flung them up on to the pile, which grew daily. Every town had its own bonfire, and one evening, as a treat in which my father generally co-operated, I would be driven round half a dozen or so of the local towns, looking with admiration and amusement at what other people had found to throw out, but never with the eye of a neutral, for the bonfire was an event that evoked the most intense local loyalty beyond anything else that the year called for.

As November the 5th drew close, a very carefully dressed mannequin would be prepared, wearing a black morning coat and sponge-bag trousers, grey gloves for hands, and, if one could be found, a top hat on his head, and he carried himself with an air of gentle resignation. On the day itself, the guy would be lifted up, and placed on top of the bonfire. If there was any suggestion of excessive dampness in the air so that the wood might not kindle, a clerk from the council would come round in the late afternoon with a workman carrying a ladder, and, climbing up to where the guy sat, would empty a whole canister of petrol on to the twigs around him, and then, as a final homage, he doused the finery in which he was dressed. At seven o'clock precisely, a higher official, wearing the insignia of office, would appear, and, in front of the crowd that had already assembled, he applied an enormous taper to the nearest inflammable object. As the wood started to crackle, a cheer of a military kind went up.

People of all types, all ages, stood around, gossiping by the light of the conflagration. There would be old, weather-beaten men in blue striped suits with their grandchildren. Ordinary fathers in deerstalkers crouched down as close to the fire as they dared, and, holding their sons firmly between their knees, tried to make men of them by getting them to hold out a sparkler and light it from the glittering flames, and then whirl it round and round in the heated air. There would be more affluent families half in, half out of, large cars, the men seated at the wheel, small children running round in circles or gloating over a picnic hamper, the women leaning back on their shooting-sticks. Parents and children shared tea from a Thermos flask.

Going to the bonfire meant for me staying up beyond my normal bedtime. Invariably I slept in the car on the way there, not from tiredness, which I would not have revealed, but from fear. If momentarily the large rockets exhilarated me as they raced up into the sky, I was also frightened. I was frightened by the quiet, relentless roar of the flames, I was frightened by the great gusts of smoke that swept up from the bonfire every time the wind changed, I was frightened by the many white faces of the spectators as they laughed and shouted, like the crowd in Jerusalem baying for the death of Christ, but most frightening of all was the thought, which entered my head as the flames reached the guy, and they started to burn his clothes, and he dropped his head in final despair, that, at that very moment, a soul was breathed into his dying body. It arrived just in time to suffer the final agony as the carcass twisted and turned in the hot blackness of the night. I could not believe that there was not one other person in that crowd who did not secretly, shame-facedly, but somehow, share that thought.

Back home, because of the lateness of the hour, I did not have to have a bath. Instead I was made to stand in front of the gas fire in my bedroom, and was washed down in warm water with a large floppy sponge, but, when I was rushed to the bathroom to brush my teeth under a naked light bulb, the sight outside the window of the very night, and the very stars, under which the guy had eventually expired, re-awakened my fear. I longed to confide my doubts, but, though I formed the words, nothing came out. As always at home, I said nothing of what was on my mind, and I knew that to grow up, really to grow up, was not to do all the manly things I so much dreaded: it was to be able to break silence.

By the small hours of November the 6th, the bonfire could be expected to have burnt itself out. The objects that had escaped the flames, and the empty casings of the fire-works, and the charred sticks from the rockets, and the circle of burnt grass, marked the site of the evening's delirium. As the days shortened, the winds of early winter that blew along the Thames valley picked up the ash and the leaves, and drove them across the deserted slope of the rec. They settled against the wooden fence, or formed piles of rubbish under the scruffy hedge that screened the ground from the road, or collected on the base of the field-gun, and they remained until the rain came, and then they were washed into the earth. In spring, boys came out and ran round the track, and, in early summer, nets were set up for cricket, and young men arrived from a surveyor's office, or from serving in their father's shop, or from the school where they taught, and they practised their strokes or their spins until the light failed and play seemed dangerous. Then they left for homes of which I knew nothing. There was a period when I thought of such homes, with tennis parties, and girls dropping in, and the telephone ringing, and no books, as an escape from my own postponed existence.

The other side of the main road there was a well-known hotel, and there another form of life began.

Along the road itself, there were white palings always freshly painted, and the lodge gates were half-buried in clumps of rhododendrons, and massive poplars and elms and horse-chestnuts blocked the public view. Someone standing at the highest point of the rec could have made out, through the trees, luxuriant in summer, bleached in winter, only the blue of a further horizon.

The hotel itself, a large Italianate building of yellow brick with parapets and broad steps leading up to the entrance, had been built on the site of a palace where Charles II, later a hero of mine, had passed the summers in indolence. A formal garden was laid out with urns and geraniums and beds of lavender, and the original glory of the place survived in a stand of enormous cedars of Lebanon, whose branches, sweeping right down to the ground, invited even the most nervous child to climb them, and in a grotto with broken shells and porous lava, which I found once, so that I felt I was at the birth of time, and then never again.

I was first taken to the hotel about the age of seven or eight during one of the severest winters of my childhood. A backwater of the Thames had frozen over, and large families in brightly coloured woollen hats and scarves had come out to skate or throw snowballs. I remember only the cold that hurt my sinus and the wool that rubbed my skin, for this was before the silk was sewn into my balaclava, and I cried from the pain as though I had fallen into a nest of stinging nettles.

In my growing years, I went very often to the swimming pool of the hotel. Sometimes I went with my parents and friends or business associates of my father – foreign actors, *diseuses*, dancers, composers of music for cabaret, theatrical agents from Central European capitals – and we sat on deckchairs, and waiters in white jackets with epaulettes served us tiny, triangular sandwiches and tartlets filled with overpoweringly sweet jam. Once we went with Conrad Veidt, and his cavernous eyes were recognized. Sometimes I went with my school on hot mornings just before lunch to swim. At a later age, around the time that I was working for a scholarship, I was allowed to go by myself on my bicycle. I took *Wilhelm Meister* with me, and when, from time to time, I put it down in order to rest my eyes, I would suddenly feel commanded to climb up to the top diving board and dive off, even though I had never learnt to dive, and, if water got up my nose by mistake, I started to drink it in, believing that I should get death over quickly.

Accompanied or unaccompanied, I was always alone. The sun in my face, the constant splash of the fountain, the cries and snorts of the bathers as they dived and surfaced, and, coming from a distance, from the alley of poplars that marked the perimeter of the pool, the laughter of brothers and sisters as they ran barefoot on the hot concrete of the curling-rink – all these things served to isolate me, to cut me off from their actual sources, to immure me within myself. At first, this sense of isolation allowed me to get on with what I was doing: wondering what Mignon could have looked like, following the lives and loves of the characters in an Aldous Huxley novel, for a long time exemplary works for me, struggling to compose verses in which I pinned down an impression of the moment in language at once modern and melancholy. Periodically I looked up from the novel I was reading or the penny notebook in which I was writing, and I concentrated on the girls of fifteen, sixteen, seventeen, always older than me, back from boarding school or Switzerland, downy-skinned, fair-haired, freckled, plump around the breasts, wearing bathing-suits ordered from London stores by their parents, and with rows of gold bracelets and bangles round their wrists, which rattled as they shook the water off their skin and hair. One of them might be standing under the high diving board, one arm abstractedly embracing the chromium-plated frame; another would put now one foot, now the other, into the water, pulling it back with a look of horror at the cold, and then, the next moment, would dive into the pool as though it was the most welcome of temperatures. A third would be constantly preoccupied with her hair, and with hairpins, and slides, twisting a strand round her finger, examining it with the utmost care, perhaps trying, as if it were a scientific experiment, to split it all the way up without breaking it off. Oddest for me was the way that one of these fiercely independent girls, after swimming enough lengths, or having talked to enough boys, or in desperation over her hair, might give up, and go over and sit with her mother and father, who, one reading, one knitting, or both staring ahead, seemed to be expecting her. In a flash, she became the little child, the apple of her parents' eye, and, in that materialization, was, I knew, as far out of my reach, as far beyond my ken, as she had ever been when she was the big-breasted grown-up, distributing her favours, Messalina-like.

But if, just for one moment, there was a sudden burst of sunlight in my eyes, or the warm, inviting smell of the silver teapot drifted over to me, or I allowed my vision to slide out of focus so that I now saw two of everything, or, as years before, standing on the edge of the ditch, I turned a deaf ear to the voices around me, in that moment of distraction one of these fabled creatures, her skin glistening with tiny bubbles of oil and water and sweat, would take advantage of my momentary absence. She would float across the narrow divide that separated us, and slip into my fevered mind, and there take up her place, abstractedly, without curiosity, wishing to know nothing of me, prepared to show me nothing of herself, but as unmoveable as someone who, having lost her way, was determined to stay the night, and in my bed.

If that same evening, as I was undressing, while it was still daylight and the birds were singing hard enough to crack the windowpane, I felt within me a certain restlessness, I knew that it came, not from myself, but from this truant from the pool, now cut off from home, from name, from flesh. Distracted herself, she distracted me, though it was only some years later, with the first stirrings of desire, that I had to ask myself why this half-turning away from me had such a power to torment me.

⌒

The move to The Mask was a move to a larger house, but, having described it as a move to a house of my parents' choice, I must add that I do not see how either would have made such a choice. I cannot imagine my father looking at an empty room, or at a garden with the grass uncut, and thinking, "I like that." What I can more easily imagine is his staring for a few moments, one hand resting in the other behind his back, and abruptly saying to my mother, "I'll leave this to you," and then walking back to the car, and saying this, not because he trusted her judgment, but because he was not disposed to tax his any longer. He was saving it up.

As to my mother, one of the strongest memories I have of her is of a late afternoon, after riding, or on being collected from school, going with her to a nearby town of some size, where, in the marketplace, behind iron-railings, there was an ominous block of dark grey stone on which the kings of Wessex had been anointed: it was said that you could still see where the stains of the oil had poured off their heads. We would park outside a small dress-shop, which was ahead of its time in that its owner ordered dresses from Paris. I sat on a hard chair, while Suzy, a vivacious woman, thirty or somewhat more, with pretty earrings, smelling of cigarettes, brought out dress after dress for my mother to try on. Each new dress she held up for inspection, tucking it under her chin, or breaking its fall by draping it from the waist down over the back of a small sofa, and she would say, "I think this is going to be perfect for you," "I had you in mind when I got this from the collection," "I've been keeping this one back for you," or, as we came to the end of the line, "This, Connie, is you." Sometimes my mother rejected a dress out of hand, but, if she didn't, and tried it on, she was always, when asked whether she liked it, less than fully positive, though to different degrees, and in consequence the dresses were sorted into rejects, probables, possibles, and those which needed to be tried on again. I remember one particular dress vividly, made of very fine, very dark blue cashmere, with a little sprig of daisies woven on to it, and underneath the daisies the word "marguerite", spelt with a small "m", had been handwritten in pale blue wool. Every so often, I would pick up a dress out of the pile to which it had been assigned, and examine with great care the stitching, and how the shoulders were cut, and how the buttonholes had been made, in an attempt to see whether an incontrovertible way of reaching a decision could not be thought up. For a period I wanted to be a dress-designer. After an hour or so, my mother had settled for three or four, which she would take home on approval. If in the car my mother did not start to regret one in particular, she would be in high spirits. She would say to me conspiratorially, which I loved, "Don't say anything to Daddy about this." She would add,

"I can never make up my mind," and further add, "You know me." The truth is that I didn't: but I knew that she couldn't make up her mind.

Rarely did my mother talk about the one occasion, decisive for me, on which she had made up her mind. When she did, she would say, "I could have married many people," or "Many people wanted to marry me." And then she was likely to add, "And I could have done much better for myself." It was an odd thing for her to say, since she cared so little about doing well, let alone better. After my father died, leaving precisely £186, she felt that she must find work for herself, and only one test counted: whether what she did would bring her into contact with people who would admire her. Of the various possibilities of marriage that she had foregone, she always turned to the son of the Dutch Ambassador, and sometimes she showed me photographs of his house in The Hague, and of his Hispano-Suiza, and of herself in a long fur coat and boots, leaning against the bonnet, and laughing with her large grey eyes. The sticking-point, she explained, had always been her mother, and this was where my father won. She could have married only someone who could accept her mother, which my father could. She spoke to her mother on the telephone perhaps twice a day, and they met frequently, but, as I recall things, every conversation, every meeting, was a quarrel, and they quarrelled as two people might who truly hated one another. My father accepted his mother-in-law in that she could come to the house whenever she or my mother wanted, and he paid all her bills. But they found nothing to say to one another.

The Mask was the house where I grew up. It was the house where I learned to read and write, where I had many childhood illnesses and came to love them, where I acquired certain habits of religion and day-dreaming, which were of enormous importance to me, and where adolescence struck me. It was where I discovered, first-hand you could say, how much the larger world around me was changing when, one morning, I looked out of the window of what was still called the nursery, though I was now seventeen, through the bars, which no one had thought of taking down, and I saw very clearly, barely above the trees, two aeroplanes locked in a dogfight, until abruptly one disengaged, as if bored, and dived to the ground in a thick cloak of burning oil. This was June 1940, and, a month or so later, we left the house, never to return. Now, when I think about the house, I do so largely with incomprehension, and with affection reserved for three small areas. Once when I returned, and looked at the house from the outside, it looked smaller than I remembered it, and once larger.

The first area was a square of asphalt laid out in the back-garden immediately behind the garage, which was the site for a game, which consumed some of my later childhood years, from seven or eight onwards. The garage had large double doors, front and back, and, when the back doors were opened, the car could be driven out on to the asphalt and washed. A tree with stalks like bamboo drooped down, and in summer its branches were heavy with long pendulous blossoms. For weeks on end, or so it seemed, I stood at my post, racket in hand, hitting a tennis ball against the chocolate-coloured doors. I would count the rallies, and, memorizing them one day to the next, always tried to do better. The sun shone, butterflies fluttered between my racket and the flower-beds behind it, and the only sound besides that of ball on gut was the occasional fall of water as a pipe discharged itself into an outside drain. At eleven o'clock precisely, I was made to break off, and drink warmed orange juice out of a Bakelite cup with a blurred mottled pattern.

I do not know how I started this game, nor do I know whether the aim was to improve my tennis, since I do not believe that otherwise I played tennis. However, I soon used the game as a way of taking control of my life yet-to-be. Each rally corresponded to some broadly defined ambition, in which I would succeed only if I kept up some unspecified number of returns. Sometimes I let myself be distracted from the purpose for which I was playing. This was when my attention was caught by something like a boil, formed where the paint had blistered, for then all my skills would be directed towards hitting the blister and breaking it. Sometimes it broke only on the second, or third hit, and then there would be a long, orange-looking streak where a secretion from the blister ran down the exposed wood, and mingled with the brown paint. The sight of the secretion held me in a faintly excited state for most of the day. Years later, on another tennis court, placed behind some early-nineteenth-century stables, I wagered the whole of my uncertain love life on victory or defeat at the hands of the Russian mosaicist, BA, and won.

What I did on that asphalt patch, what thoughts passed through my head, what skills I gained, how what was universally referred to as my "highly strung" temperament fared, were not matters of any concern to those who looked after me, and this was because, in staying out-of-doors, I obeyed the only clearly moral rule that was truly enforced in my childhood: that was that I must always be out in "God's sunshine". There were few enough days on which it shone, and to lose one of them was wicked.

At some moment my mother bought a small car of her own, a Morris Minor, and the garage had to be extended, and my square of asphalt was rudely incorporated. In compensation I was given what was called a Kum-Back. Two upright posts, steadied by guide-ropes, were joined at the top by a cable, from the mid-point of which a tennis ball hung down on a long piece of elastic. It was not the same thing at all. It was a toy, it had a silly name, it attempted to control the number of things I could do, there were no blisters to pierce, and now I had to hit the ball away from the house, or towards the bottom of the garden. In revenge, I recruited all the skills I had at my disposal into devising a stroke, which, after four or five attempts, would break the elastic, and the ball would fly free, and, if it did not sail over the fence, it would come to rest amongst the waxy-looking foliage that crept up the bank that marked the end of the garden. When this happened, I had to ask permission to walk on the earth, and generally, if there had been no rain the night before, and I promised to walk on tiptoe, permission would be forthcoming: it needed only a call to a first-floor window. Bending over, I would run my fingers through the dark-smelling vegetation, pretending, as I did with most of the most ordinary activities of childhood, that I was practising some very ·special skill of the hands or mind, like dowsing for water, or picking a lock, or shearing sheep and getting the clippers to swerve round the testicles. If it had rained recently, and the earth was muddy, then there was a different routine to follow. I went to the back door, knocked, it was unlocked for me, I walked through the scullery, then the kitchen, I went into the cloak room, and either put on a pair of galoshes over the shoes I was wearing or changed into Wellingtons. Then I walked back the way I had come. Twice a week, the linoleum in the kitchen and the stone floor of the scullery were washed, and opened sheets of newspaper were put down on the floor until it was dry. I walked slowly, followed by eyes that made sure that I did not step off the paper, and, for my part, though the smell of newspaper nauseated me then as much as it does now, I twisted my glance downward so as to catch sight of the faces of the famous and the notorious of the time: aviators, film stars, the bemedalled victims of political assassination, share-pushers, fire-raisers. But I never wanted to walk so slowly, or to look so hard, that I might learn something that I didn't want to know. Back in the garden, the mud meant that I was no longer allowed to let my fingers run wild through the undergrowth. I had a stick put into my hands, and I was instructed to prod the earth in a systematic fashion until I eventually met resistance, and the missing ball rolled out of its hiding-place, down the bank, on to the lawn. Many years later, as an adolescent, I found a sentence in an old euphuistic translation of *Daphnis and Chloë*, which I forever associated with the swelling bank. It ran, as I can best recall, "The Venus of the garden was all gone, and nothing remained but the lutulent soil."

The second area for which I felt affection, but here I was

most like any ordinary boy of my age, was the upstairs lavatory. It was where the passage on the half-landing turned.

Until I was thirty or so, I experienced life, in my own case, but even more so with others, as traversed by a series of boundaries, which, once crossed, could never be uncrossed, for their passage left an indelible mark: some knowledge was acquired, some experience gained, innocence lost, a new shamelessness entered into. One summer's night, sitting in a shabby club in Crawford Street, frequented by young burglars and male hustlers, of a kind where for many years I felt much at home, I watched two unshaven men play cards on a table laid with newspaper. Their eyes followed one another with deep suspicion, and they looked up only when a young, white-faced girl, fitted out in an overcoat too large for her, drew up a chair, and, putting down a mug of fresh tea on the newspaper, handed over some pound notes. They said something to her, and she, who had looked tense and vulnerable, suddenly let out a loud, coarse laugh. It was her first night "on the game". During the worst days of the war there were young officers whom I had trained with and then lost sight of, and who reappeared in France or Germany, suddenly materializing in a sun-drenched field that stank of dead cows or in a small mud-filled copse where all the branches had been broken by shellfire. By the time I saw them, they had already survived their first patrol, or their first battle. They had a look of greyness around the eyes. They had received, and passed on, orders to kill, and it would never be the same. Or, my second term at boarding school, there was a small, slender boy, endowed with magical prettiness, dimpled, lightly freckled, a Ganymede, who, every evening, as we congregated round the kitchen steps to put in special orders of eggs, would be encouraged by his circle of admirers to masturbate at night. He smiled elusively, someone whispered something in his ear, he seemed not to listen, and then, one Wednesday, the rumour passed round the ancient hall that, for the first time, he had come, and there was boisterous delight amongst his well-wishers. He had crossed his Rubicon.

In my own case, a painful number of such transitions were connected with the loss of faith, but the earliest, which was different, I experienced in the upstairs lavatory. It was when, for the first time, I was allowed, not just to go to the lavatory alone, but to leave it alone. Up till that moment, I had been required, when I was ready to do so, to get off the lavatory seat, hobble to the door, open it, and shout "Ready". But, if the sweeper was being used, or worse the Hoover, I could not be heard, and, though I felt ignored, I had, as for much of my childhood, my own resources.

My father, who was not a tall man, had legs short for his size, and he had had a footstool made, painted white, with a cork top, to ease the situation. My father sat there and smoked, but, when I sat on the lavatory, and put my legs up on the stool, I was a king, King Canute, or a great prince, though also a bard. The stories I told myself were of tournaments, and of knightly encounters in which the combatants were represented by the tassels at either end of my dressing gown cord, which I bashed together until the cleaning outside stopped, and help was on its way, and then one of the combatants took off his helmet, and capitulated with honour. Sometimes, not often, I told myself stories of shipwrecks, and other disasters at sea, which tracked more closely the movements of my bowels.

But one evening I was taken by surprise. I was told that I could clean myself, that I would be initiated into the mysteries of how, and that from that time onwards I would be on my own. First, I was asked to observe how the roll of lavatory paper was divided into separate sheets with perforated lines between them. Then I was instructed how to hold the roll, and that I must first tear off three sheets in one, then fold them so that the fold ran through the middle of the middle sheet, and then I wiped myself. Then I folded that whole piece in two, and wiped myself with it a second time. Then I tore off just two sheets, and folded them along the perforated line, and wiped myself with them. When I tore off two sheets, there was no second folding, no second wiping. I was to go on using just two sheets until I was clean, and I was shown what a clean piece of paper looked like. Then I stood up, and, for the first time in my life, I could take it on myself to pull the chain: it was my decision. If I did, I mustn't pull too hard, or too gently. I could, if I liked, turn round, and watch the paper go down the lavatory, and in Australia it would rotate the other way.

This small incident was probably the single greatest increase in personal responsibility that my childhood had in store for me. It is what I think of when I hear moral philosophers discuss responsibility.

The third area of the house for which I felt affection, though it was very rarely that I visited it, was a small low cupboard, which could house two small children, though I doubt if it was big enough for even one adult, and it was behind the dark chocolate-coloured panelling on the staircase where I had overheard the conversation about ears. The door to the cupboard was flush with the panelling, and only a small keyhole with a small key in it gave away its existence. When children, invariably friends of my brother's, visited the house, I pointed out the cupboard with inordinate pride, and, sometimes, to my brother's embarrassment, gave a brief demonstration of how to get into the cupboard and out of it. Getting in required a leg-up, and then something of a leap, and getting out was, like everything connected with climbing down in childhood, worse. Later, getting into the cupboard became for me the first of various things that I thought of as a time machine, which could transport me to a medieval, or a Tudor, or a Jacobite past. Later I thought of riding, then later of reading, as also time machines.

At the bottom of the stairs was the hall. It was the room that the front door opened into, and it was also the most used room of the house. Most of the furniture was ugly, and it contained my father's books and pictures. The dining room and the drawing room both led off the hall. For many years I was taken down to the drawing room every evening to practise the piano, which I hated, and I hated it particularly at the beginning of the week: my fingernails were cut every Saturday night, and it was only by Tuesday or Wednesday that my finger-ends had regained enough insensitivity for me to bear to hit the keys. On Sunday afternoons, when my father was in England, he used the drawing room to entertain his friends and business associates, speaking in French and German, sending out for more coffee, until the room came to smell of eau de cologne, and Turkish tobacco, and Sunday newspapers. At about half past four, my father and his friends returned to the dining room for tea, and my father refused to spread jam on bread in the English style, but ate it out of a small spoon. In the week the drawing room smelled mostly of camphor, which arose out of a small glass-topped table containing some icons and some silver trinkets which the camphor was supposed to prevent from tarnishing.

Off the hall, between the drawing room and the staircase, was the cloakroom that I have already mentioned. It was small, lit by a very low bulb, and I did not feel affection for it, but it may have had an ominous influence in the formation of my emotions. There sight was replaced by touch, and touch not only proved a frail method for the identification of objects, but it in turn was supplanted by smell. Groping behind a thick cotton curtain, I found my hands closing in upon coats hanging from a hook, boots that stood on the floor and sagged, or mysterious attachments to the Hoover that felt like parts of the body. Sent there with a precise order for something with which to protect myself against the elements, I inevitably came back with the order less than completely obeyed. The sharp smell of the rubber had allied itself with the formlessness of the shapes to confuse me, and confusion had turned to intoxication, and intoxication to disgust. A titter of laughter, which I took as punishment, greeted me on my return from the shades.

If my early childhood was largely housebound, or barely extended beyond what I could cover in my daily walks, experience enlarged as I grew older, eleven, twelve, thirteen, and several new kinds of activity, all pursued on a Saturday or Sunday, led me to the very confines of Surrey.

First, there was riding, which started from stables on the northern slopes of the North Downs. Mounting our horses in some small cobbled yard, no sooner had we left behind the sharp smell of horse-dung and of sweat-filled saddle and blanket than we found ourselves traversing a startling variety of countryside. We walked our horses along narrow paths that encircled steep hills covered with thick pine forest: we galloped across the sandy expanse of Newlands Corner from which we could look across to the prosperous fields and villages of the Weald: we trotted downhill into the lush Tillingbourne valley: we paused to survey flocks of sheep and their young in lambing time. Each change of scenery brought with it its own historical time. Knights in armour lurked in the shadowy gloom of the fir trees: a detachment of Cromwell's Ironsides, out foraging, disputed with us the great clumps of broom and blackberry, from which famous views could be obtained: entering from one end a village high street, which was low down by the water-meadows, we had reason to suspect that, barely an hour before, a notorious highwayman had waved goodbye to his moll with the black beauty spots, as he rode out the other end with total impunity: an old-fashioned carriage, abandoned in the shade of a giant hedge of blackthorn, with the horses enjoying the shelter of a spreading oak, was that out of which the young squire, carrying his snuff-box, and giving a hand to his bride in taffeta, had just stepped down to admire the baby lambs.

The one sight that lowered my spirits was a bleak expanse of common land that we cantered across on our way back, arriving there on wintry Saturdays as dusk was falling, and there goalposts had been set up, and men in striped shirts, with muddied cheeks, struggled with one another in stupid manly competition. My dreams deserted me. I was no longer riding with Prince Rupert's men, I was no longer out to apprehend the fiercest of the century's gentleman robbers, I was no longer curious to see who was challenging all comers at the ford across the river Wey. I was a 1930's schoolboy looking out at a man's world.

Secondly, there was an odd group of activities – gymkhanas, treasure hunts in cars, local pageants of the kind celebrated in *Between The Acts* – which required maps, and which invariably took me to the southern edge of the county. They were organised by people who not only knew, they themselves came from, places I had never heard of until that very day. Gymkhanas took place in open fields with ropes set up to divide the spectators from the competitors, and there were tents where refreshments could be bought, and announcements over the loudhailer told us where in the programme we had got to. They were events without mystery, which took place in full daylight. Treasure hunts and pageants, by contrast, were headier events, often protracted into summer dusk, and sometimes the names of the places where they occurred – Abinger Hammer, Blackheath, Friday Street, the Silent Pond, Waverley Abbey, of which so little was left – were impressed on my mind only the next morning by the shadowy recall of walls of ancient brickwork and cascading foliage, and by the sharp sting of gnats. I remember vividly a picket-fence on a high ridge, half-buried in ferns, the wooden slats greyed by the rainwater that had dripped through the trees, and covered with pale green lichen.

Thirdly, and most precious of all for the immersion in the past that it offered me, was the pursuit of old coins, which was something that I embarked on through the sheerest chance, when the owner of a small toyshop offered me for next to nothing a commemorative silver coin struck in favour of Queen Caroline. It showed an image of the queen, and, on the reverse, a cushion on which a sceptre rested, and the edge was delicately milled. My hands quivered as I held it. The quest for coins took me to antique shops in ever remoter villages where, by the age of twelve, I proved, both in my knowledge of the subject and in my capacity to drive a hard bargain, at least a match for the melancholy owner of the shop, who would go into his backroom, and return with a collection of small square envelopes. Each envelope contained a coin, and there was a description of it, written in a curate's hand. "I don't know if this would be of any interest to you," the man would say, taking the coin out of its envelope, and rubbing it between thumb and forefinger. I sat down at the table, and he handed me over a magnifying glass. "I've had them a long time," he would say of things he had shown to no one before, because no one before had been interested. He and I formed a strong attachment.

By the time I was fourteen, my collection of medieval, Tudor and Stuart coins was substantial. It numbered about a hundred coins, which ranged from Norman pennies, then worth little more than a modern penny each, to some rarities, like a Richard III groat or a cunning Charles II forgery, about which I consulted the British Museum. My father meanwhile had bought for me a miniature eighteenth-century chest of drawers, about eleven inches high. I lined the drawers with baize, and laid out the coins from William the Conqueror to George IV, where I stopped.

I kept in a separate cardboard box a few Greek and Roman coins, great hunks of ancient metal, the by-products of my real foraging.

꒐

The name of our house, "The Mask", derived from the symbol of the stage, was suggested to my father by an old friend, an actor, a matinée idol of the period, SH. During the First War, my father had become the manager of a touring company that entertained the troops. H was the lead, and, in several plays lying between farce and musical comedy, my mother played opposite him. I learnt the names of two of them: *Cash on Delivery*, and *Potash and Perlmutter*. H was an actor famous for his charm, often drunk on stage, and, when he was drunk, he forgot his lines. Drunk or not, he deftly adjusted them so as to propose assignations with his leading actress. Unexpected references to times and places caused momentary surprise to those who, sitting in the front row of the stalls, tried to follow every inflexion of the dialogue, only to give up.

H was my godfather, though not actively so. When I was born, a telegram arrived from Australia saying "Cap following". This was interpreted as saying "Cup following", but nothing followed. Nor did he make any effort to see me, though we did meet once or twice in my father's office, or in a theatrical restaurant, like The Ivy, or the Moulin d'Or, or Romano's.

Another side to H was H the author, who had to his

credit half a dozen or so edificatory manuals written for the benefit of a certain kind of young man who figured prominently in successful English comedies of the period and in the novels of P.G. Wodehouse, but who possessed, as far as I know, no existence in social reality. H advocated a brisk, debonair manliness, which, he claimed, could best be maintained by the love of Empire, by the avoidance of effeminate company, or what he called the "limp-wristed", and by the love of a young, healthy woman. My father owned two of H's books, but I do not recall his pressing them upon my attention, and the first occasion on which I really confronted one of them I was in a peculiarly susceptible state.

As a child, I had been diagnosed as having flat feet, and, over several years, was subjected to one regime after another, all of which had, more or less, no effect. In my first year of boarding school, the school was asked if I could be permitted to continue with a new form of treatment, which seemed to offer better prospects, and which consisted in my putting my feet in an enamel bowl of warm water, through which an electric current was passed, and the arches would be galvanized into life. Permission was given by the school, a physiotherapist was found nearby who did the treatment, and once a week I visited her in an old-fashioned mansion flat near Caxton Hall, into which the daylight barely penetrated. I regularly arrived early, and I used to turn the pages of dog-eared copies of magazines devoted to nursing and child care. Then one day I looked on a small shelf, and there I found a book by SH. When the physiotherapist came to call me in, she found me so engrossed in the book that she told me I could bring it in with me, if I liked. My nervous state was due to the fact that the habit that I had developed, which, it must be said, was widespread, of waiting ten minutes or so after lights out, and then standing up on the head of my iron bedstead, and talking in a whisper over the high wooden compartment with the boy who had the next cubicle, had the night before taken a new turn. The boy with whom I had these conversations, which sometimes extended for a couple of hours, had recently come to intrigue me with his small head, his large mouth, and his extreme cleanliness, and curiosity and eroticism had been creeping into our conversations, which had been about loneliness and the structure of the body, more or less in equal measure. Then suddenly, from one moment to the next, just as I was pleading tiredness, he offered to slide out of his cubicle and get into my bed. Would I like that? It was a proposal, and I was enchanted by its sheer directness, which was in sharp contrast to anything that I could have managed with my own mixture of hunger, fear, and procrastination. Within a minute he had arrived, wearing his heavy dressing gown, which was school uniform, and, pulling it apart in a casual manner, lay on top of me, and, within three or four minutes, by which time the smell of toothpaste, which had so enchanted me when I was standing up, had begun to offend me, I had asked him to leave. The next day at the physiotherapist's, as the water in the enamel bowl grew cold, I felt vulnerable to H's invocation of the clean life, and his denunciation of weakness, degeneracy, and the fruits of forbidden reading. I started to think that there might be something to be said for knowing that, the first time I sat beside a girl with long blonde hair in her sports car, and we stopped the car at some famous "beauty spot", and looked out at the view, there were no evil practices that I had to confess to her. But this thought brought me up short. Things were not so simple. What were the chances, I asked myself, that I would ever find myself in such a situation, and might not the chances be increased if I were the kind of person who had such things to confess to? I started to feel bad that, the night before, I had turned down a spontaneous gesture of friendship. The physiotherapist noticed that I was disturbed, and, in the quiet tones from which I have always had most to fear, she suggested that I put the book down.

Many years later, my mother asked me if I would drive her out to Kew on a Sunday afternoon, and visit Lady H, as she now was, for SH, long dead, had been knighted for playing Scrooge every Christmas for nearly half a century. We arrived, and, in the hall of the small house, Betty H, the daughter, dressed in a tartan skirt, asked us not to stay too long. Her mother tired easily, and she was about to celebrate her hundredth birthday in two or three weeks' time. My mother said that she understood, but also said that she was very good at making people laugh. We went in, and a very frail woman, sitting in an armchair, dressed in royal blue, greeted us. "Do you remember Connie?" Betty asked. "Of course, she does," my mother said.

I had had high hopes of this occasion. I had, I think, had higher hopes of it than of any event involving my mother in my adult life. I thought that there would be talk between Betty and myself, between my mother and Lady H, between Lady H and myself, between three or four of us at one time. It would be conversation. Lady H would tell me something of her past, I would mention someone I knew which would make her look with her old eyes into mine, my mother would pause, and look at me, and say, "I never knew . . . ," and "And when was it that . . .?" and "It's so amusing . . . ," and "Remind me of . . ." – things that I had never heard her say. From then onwards we would be friends.

It was not to be. My mother talked for two hours without interruption. She told stories of herself and the bus conductor, of herself and the man who sat next to her in the bus, of the woman who came up to her in the street and thought that she must be someone famous, to which she said that she was. She reached back into the past. She told how Chaliapine had said that she was beautiful, and how she was the only person who had persuaded Diaghilev to come on to the beach. She explained how she began the story of her life when she talked at her local church, "I say that I was born with a full head of hair, and I was christened in water brought from the Jordan." When she had finished one lot of stories, she began all over again. "I've not changed, Elalaine, have I? Betty said that you might not remember me, I told her you would."

At last the warnings about tiredness were listened to. We got up to go. "Don't hurry me," my mother said, "Elalaine is interested." I held the cold metal of the car keys against my wrist to remind me of the external world. In the car, my mother thanked me. She then told me that I had been very silent. "Elalaine and I," she said, "had a lot to talk about. A lot to catch up on." After a while, she said something of a kind that I had never heard her say before. She said, "If God had wanted me to relax, He would have made me differently."

Lady H never lived to see her hundredth birthday.

CHAPTER TWO

My Families

One morning, over two decades ago, in the course of what were to prove for me ten very consequential days teaching in Boulder, Colorado, I had the distinct feeling that I was about to start work on this memoir in earnest. The desire to write it had been with me for a year or so, ever since I had reluctantly abandoned another project, which was a novel about life in the servants' hall of a large Irish country house, upon which the Empress Elizabeth of Austria, the wife of Franz Josef, descends with her own retinue, including courtiers, grooms, ladies' maids, and her favourite "pilot" in the hunting field. The novel would tell of the carnival that followed, servants aping their masters, mistresses corrupting their maids, and the seed for it had been sown in a bookshop where I had leafed through a popular biography of the Empress, which contained in a paragraph or so a description of her visit to Ireland. When I gave up the project, I had already written many, many pages of my book, articulating certain characters and certain events, such as the dyspeptic housekeeper with her strong lesbian proclivities, the brutal stable boy who takes a young recruit under his dubious wing, the rather priestly agent who procures young housemaids at country fairs, and, all the while, there is the building of a railroad, which, at first the destination of light-hearted outings, becomes more and more ominous as it approaches the park gates. I had started on this work in a motel outside Fargo, North Dakota, where paper clips lay concealed in the cheap floor-to-floor carpet, and there was snow outside, and I abandoned the work abruptly because I recognized that to complete it would have required too much dedication, too much copying from one notebook to another, too much sad, wilful invention. And I had other work to do. However, in the intervening period I had made little head-way with the memoir, and the desire to write it had remained inside me like a benign lump. Now it seemed to be growing.

The truth is that, with a kind of refined cruelty towards myself, I had, in the writing of the first paragraph in which the early fall is recounted, set myself a task that lacked all rationale, except that it blocked all progress. For I had decided, though without full consultation with the side of myself that would have to do the work, that each sentence, beginning with the first sentence, which was three words long, would be one word longer than its predecessor, up to the moment when I trip, and then the words would stream out, one tumbling over another, like a body in free fall. I soon saw that this device was pointless, in that the ear, which is sensitive to the greater structural complexity of the sentence, has no way of taking in mere changes in word-length, but I could think of no way of accommodating to this criticism. I discussed the matter with the person who most encouraged me in the writing of the memoir, my great friend SS, and I asked him if he could find any justification for the labour that I had imposed on myself. He laughed as he used to, slightly choking on his laugh, and encouraged me to break my vow, but it turned out that I could not: as a result, I was set back some twelve or fifteen years.

On the morning in question, I had returned from breakfast, which was eaten communally, I had made a telephone call to the south of France, and I was sitting in a spacious room, which was in shadow from some large, sweet-smelling trees outside. A notebook lay open in front of me, and, sensing that I needed to be careful not to allow work to become drudgery, I freely let myself listen to the conversation beneath my window, where a tall blond boy and a tall blonde girl were playing frisbee on the grass dappled by sunlight. The temperature was in the upper 80s, but it was dry and pleasant, as it is in the Rockies, and the morning and the lawn outside and the whirr of the sprinkler started to approximate to what I have called a place of repose. Out of nowhere boredom threatened, and I became more convinced than ever that I should concentrate on the conversation outside: the only way that I could continue to work on the open page before me was to be partially distracted from it. I told myself that, if I listened hard, I might learn something. Or, if that was hoping for too much, I might hear something with which to amuse my new friends at lunch, or on the afternoon's drive up into the mountains. Reasons to listen, to overhear, propagated.

The conversation started in a desultory way, and it never lost a certain abstracted quality even when the two players began to take a heightened interest in each other. The girl asked the boy where his parents came from. He told her. Was that where he had been raised? she asked him. Then the boy asked the girl where her parents came from. She told him. Was that where she had been raised? Then she asked him where his parents had gone to college, then where they had gone to graduate school. They had gone to the same college, and then they had gone on to the same graduate school. Then he asked her the same questions. Where had her parents gone to college? They had gone to different colleges. Where had they gone to graduate school? They had gone on to different graduate schools. The frisbee flew backwards and forwards once or twice, in silence. It rose up towards the topmost branches of the trees so that it came briefly into my field of vision, and it fluttered down. The boy, who had evidently been taken aback by the girl's answers, was now concentrating harder on his game. He did so for a rally or two, and then he suppressed his bafflement no longer. "In that case," he asked her, "how did your parents ever get together?"

What the girl said in answer to the boy's question I do not know. She replied in lower tones than I could catch, but I knew that, whatever she said, her answer would not have had for me the interest of his question. How, I had so often asked myself, did my parents ever get together? Did they get together? Would they ever separate? I have often said to friends, with more than a touch of bravado, that, as a child, I longed for my parents to separate, but it has probably been no easier for me to grasp the notion of their separating than it was for them to grasp that of their getting together. And I have never wanted to deny that, had they separated, I would have been tormented by that too.

My father and my mother were very different.

So were my father's family and my mother's family.

If jointly they brought it about that I grew up in England, they also ensured that I didn't grow up English. I did not have an English name, I did not have cousins, I did not belong to a social class, and, for most of the time, I did not think of myself as English, nor did I want to be English. For some of the time, I thought of myself as something else, something I wanted to be. When I was a fervent reader of the Waverley novels, I thought of myself as Scottish. For a period in the army, when words like "boche" and "hun" and "kraut" floated around freely, and particularly, I remember, in the heat of a battle in front of the city of Goch, which had been a medieval town with walls and turrets, I prided myself on being German. But, ever since I had, around the age of eleven or twelve, come across the phrase "a citizen of the world", that was my favourite way of thinking of myself. I have always detested patriotism with a fierce hatred. When I heard the phrase, "My Country", tears came to my eyes, tears of shame, tears of anger. At school we all – that is, my group – loved to quote Dr Johnson's famous saying, "Patriotism is the last refuge of a scoundrel," but I thought that I had a special reason for loving it.

My father's family was a German Jewish family, the first known Wollheim being Jacob Salomon Wollheim, who was born in 1745 and died in 1811, living all his life in Breslau, now Wrocslaw, where he was, as the name indicates, a wool merchant. In the course of the nineteenth century, as the wool trade suffered an economic reverse, various Wollheims moved westwards: to Hamburg, to Berlin, to Konstanz, and some to America. Some of the Wollheims were rich, some very rich, and some not at all well-off. My mother's family, or families, came from the West Country, and for centuries they were poor peasants. When they ceased to be, it seems to have been their downfall.

I do not know a great deal about either side of my family, and, as a child, I knew considerably less. Nor have I thought it proper to do any serious research for the writing of this memoir, and for a period I even plotted to recapture the ignorance of childhood, but I rejected this. Grown-up ignorance is not the equivalent of childish ignorance. What I can say is that everything that I do know now I know by chance.

Ignorance is one thing, error is, of course, another. There was error as well as ignorance in my childhood views about my families. My grandmother, my mother's mother, told me that her family was Irish, and came to England to avoid famine: my father told me that his family was Sephardic, and came originally from Portugal. Both were wrong, and, while the matters on which they were wrong might seem insignificant, and probably are, they both, I am sure, tinged my childhood perception of myself.

I imagine that the earliest Wollheims benefited from the social emancipation that occurred at the end of the eighteenth century to emerge from a secluded Jewish world.

The most colourful member of the Wollheim family was undoubtedly Anton Edmund Wollheim, the grandson of

Jacob Salomon, and eldest child of Hirsch, or Harry, who had moved to Hamburg as a self-styled banker, but, more accurately, was a lottery-collector, and there he married Hindel, or Henriette, Goldschmidt. Anton was a scholar, a journalist, a playwright, a novelist, a dramaturge, a diplomat, a poet, and twice a soldier, and knew, in some serious sense, thirty-two languages. For what I write about him, I depend upon two brief biographical sketches, each just a few pages long, copies of which were given to me by my cousin in South Africa.

Born in Hamburg in 1810, he was educated, first in Breslau, then in Hamburg. At the age of 18, he entered the University of Berlin to study Philosophy, Philology, History and Politics, and the degree of Doctor of Philosophy was conferred upon him in 1831 for a thesis on certain Padma Purani manuscripts. The next year he went to Paris as a

journalist, and there he fell in love with a beautiful girl, the daughter of a Portuguese officer, and, to please her father, he joined the Portuguese army. Civil war had broken out, and Wollheim fought for the liberation of the country from the absolutist regime of Dom Miguel, and for the restoration of the young Queen Maria and her father Dom Pedro. In the course of the war, he was wounded several times, and, as a reward for his courage, he was promised the hand of the Portuguese girl. The victorious liberal regime made him a Chevalier, and the suffix "da Fonseca", which I assume to have been the name of his betrothed, was bestowed on him and all his siblings and their descendants. He converted to Roman Catholicism, which he practised all his life very devoutly. However, before they could marry, his betrothed suddenly died, and in 1834 he returned to Hamburg. There he started a literary journal called *Kronos*, he translated poetry from the Scandinavian languages, and he started on his career as a playwright with a drama entitled *Don Sebastiano*.

Shortly afterwards, Harry Wollheim died, and Anton Edmund moved to Copenhagen, where he embarked on cataloguing the Sanskrit and Pali manuscripts in the Royal Library. It was as a scholar that he attracted the attention of King Friedrich VI, who appointed him to his private cabinet, and sent him on a personal mission to the Prussian Crown Prince. The mission concerned the notoriously complex Schleswig-Holstein question, on which he may have been one of the three experts to whom Palmerston famously referred. While in Berlin, he was lured into accepting a position as a linguistic expert at the Russian Embassy in Persia. The position did not materialise, but

Anton, who had had to resign from his Danish appointment, stayed on in Berlin, where, amongst various literary activities, he wrote and produced a play called *Andrea*, based on the life of Massena, the Napoleonic Marshal, and embarked on a major programme of translating a number of European classics, including Florian's *Wilhelm Tell*, Voltaire's *Charles XII*, and Tegner's *Frithiof's Saga*. By 1838, Wollheim was in Vienna, where his diplomatic skills led to an introduction to Metternich, who employed him in various political roles. Personal liking seems to have entered into it, but the two men were so far apart in their political outlooks that, after two years, Wollheim left the service of Austria, and returned to Hamburg. There he married Dorothea Leffmann, and, in the same year, he accepted the post of *Dramaturg* at the Stadttheater, and thus started on what was to be, in a life of improvisation, the most continuous thread: that is, a long-standing, much interrupted, connexion with the Hamburg theatre. Two more of Wollheim's own rather belated Romantic dramas date from this period: *Raphael Sanzio*, and *Die Rosen in Nord*. At this period he made some contribution to the libretto for *The Flying Dutchman*.

In 1849 Wollheim left Hamburg for Berlin in the belief that his linguistic gifts should be rewarded with academic employment, and that he was worthy of a major chair at a great university. But, after a brief spell at the University as *Privatdozent* teaching Oriental languages, it became apparent that he would not get a Chair, and he abandoned the project, and went to Paris, where he resumed his literary and scholarly pursuits, including translation from the Scandinavian languages.

With the fall of Metternich, there was a more politically congenial atmosphere in Vienna, and Wollheim spent the years 1852 to 1858 in the Austrian service, and was entrusted with various diplomatic missions to France and Italy.

In 1858 Wollheim returned to Hamburg, and his great theatrical opportunity came when that year he was made Director of the Stadttheater. Under his aegis, there were remarkable initiatives. Wollheim engaged the two great actors, who were also fierce rivals, Emil Devriendt and Begumil Dawison, and his achievement was to stage the first production of Goethe's *Faust*, Part II, to which he had given much thought over the years. He devised a season of Schiller to commemorate the centenary of his birth, and Offenbach became the favourite element in the repertory. But, for all the esteem that attached to his period as Director, it was not a financial success, and Wollheim was compelled to resort to ignoble ruses to draw in the public: he put on a parody of Wagner's *Tannhäuser* immediately after the real thing, he inserted acrobats between the acts of *Minna von Barnhelm*, and he brought trick riders on to the stage. None of these devices worked, and finally in 1861 he resigned, but not before having written an eloquent pamphlet, in which he argued for an adequate civic subsidy for the theatre, quoting what was already enjoyed by the theatres in Berlin, Munich, Stuttgart and Karlsruhe.

In 1862 Wollheim returned to Vienna, where he worked as a political columnist, and in 1863 he wrote three pamphlets on some of the outstanding political issues of Europe: "*La question italienne*", "*La question danoise*", and "*Bundesreform*". He was a diplomatic delegate to the

Congress of Princes at Frankfurt-am-Main. However, there he quarrelled with his superior, and in 1864 he left for Paris where he once again engaged in a startling diversity of literary activities before returning to Hamburg in 1868. This time he founded his own theatre, the Floratheater. It was the same story. Despite elaborate productions of international drama, of German and Italian opera, and of his own special favourite, the ballet, the theatre lost money, and failed.

In 1870 Wollheim returned to Berlin, where he became *The Daily Telegraph* correspondent. Almost immediately war broke out, and Wollheim joined the German Army, and served in the headquarters of the Grand Duke of Mecklenburg-Schwerin. When the Germans set up a provisional government at Rheims, Wollheim was made the editor of the *Moniteur Officiel du Gouvernement Générale*. For his services in this role, he was awarded the Iron Cross, and the Order of the Wendish Crown. After the war he became attaché at the German Legation in Paris, but, in the summer of 1872, while he was visiting his dying wife in Hamburg, he was abruptly relieved of his post. He took revenge by writing a two-volume work of diplomatic memoirs entitled *Indiskretionen*.

Once more Wollheim was involved with the Hamburg theatre. He was artistic director of the Zentrallhallentheater, but it was his last venture, and, within a year, it too had collapsed under a burden of debt.

The last decade of the Chevalier's life was spent in Berlin, and it is treated as a period of decline, though these were no less evidently years of amazing literary productivity. During this period, he produced a free translation of the Chinese play, *The Chalk Circle*, he wrote an autobiographical novel, *Don Lottario*, of which three volumes appeared and more were promised, he wrote a large history of Scandinavian Literature and a volume on the national literatures of the Orient, he completed his translation of Camoen's *Lusiad*, and he published a book on marine trade, and a German-Portuguese and Portuguese-German dictionary.

His wife had died in 1873, and in 1876 he married a young woman, the Gräfin Romanowski, who was said to be "of somewhat doubtful reputation", and this lost him money and friends. As is the way of the world, well-wishers, worried by what he had done to himself, decided to desert him. He was by now entirely dependent on his first cousin, Caesar Wollheim, who, on one view, continued to stand by him, on another view, gave way to censoriousness. He died in pain and poverty in Saint Hedwig's Hospital, Berlin, October 1884.

Whatever may be the quality of Wollheim's literary output, its volume is remarkable. He wrote 17 scholarly works, 60 works of a literary or belletrist kind, and 12 sustained political essays. The languages he knew were German, Old German, Portuguese, Spanish, English, Icelandic, Faroist, Danish, Swedish, Dutch, Latin, Classical Greek, modern Greek, Russian, Sanskrit, Pali, Hindi, Gypsy, Kairi, Javanese, Malayan, Makaffarisch, Dajakisch, Old Persian, Persian, Afghan, Arabic, Hebrew, Turkish, and Chinese.

It seems to have been a matter of general agreement that there was a discrepancy in Wollheim's make-up between the outer and the inner, between his appearance and his true nature, though there were various ways in which this was described. Paul Wittko, the chronicler of the Hamburg theatre, wrote, "This man of almost remarkable physical ugliness was basically a worshipper of every form of beauty on this earth." Theodor Fontane, who knew him well, and has left a brief biographical sketch, put it by saying, "When one looked at him, one saw pure Wollheim. When one heard him, he was wholly da Fonseca," and he goes on to explain himself: "It certainly could not be claimed that Wollheim was a handsome man. He possessed such genuine and pronounced Semitic features that all who had an eye for such matters could not fail to notice it." This, for Fontane, stood in direct contrast to his high intelligence and his remarkable gifts. For others the contrast lay between his extreme aestheticism, which expressed itself in a manner described as "limp lassitude", and the vigour with which he defended himself when anyone was misguided enough to tease him, or take any liberties with him.

Anton Edmund was not the only Wollheim in the nineteenth century to embrace Christianity. In South Africa in 1986 I met Oscar da Fonseca Wollheim, then in his early eighties, once a schoolmaster, then the member for a coloured constituency, and, on its abolition, a formidable opponent of apartheid, and the founder of the Institute of Race Relations. He told me that his grandfather, also Oscar, a nephew of Anton Edmund, was already a Lutheran by the time he emigrated to South Africa in the 1840s. Another brother of Anton Edmund, Hermann, produced a son who was an admiral in the German navy, which indicates a measure of assimilation.

The Caesar Wollheim who, according to Fontane, continued to support Anton Edmund, even though he disapproved of the marriage, was the child of Scholem Wollheim, another son of Jacob Salomon, and he justified his name by becoming a great tycoon in the early days of industrialization. My father spoke of Caesar Wollheim as owning most of the coalmines, canals and shipping in Silesia. More recently I have been told that he secured his fortune by endowing most medium-sized towns in Prussia with a gas-factory on condition that they burnt only the coal from his mines. A half-brother of Caesar Wollheim's kept alive the spirit of adventure by emigrating to Mexico, where, having changed his name from Moritz to Mauricio, he became the first Ambassador to Japan.

Another descendant of Scholem Wollheim was the painter Gert Wollheim, who, with Otto Dix, was a member of the "Mama Rot" circle in Düsseldorf in the early 1920s, and then the Junges Rheinland group, and was an active member of the Communist party. I once sat next to a man at lunch in Los Angeles, who asked me whether I was related to Gert Wollheim. I said that I had never before met anyone in a position to ask me that question, and that the answer was Yes. He invited me next day to see his two paintings by Wollheim, which harrowed me.

⌐

My great-great-grandfather was Salomon Marcus Beer Wollheim, who was born in Breslau in 1791, and was either a son or, more likely, a nephew of Jacob Salomon. Hanging in the very room where I am now writing these words is a pair of portraits by an unknown Breslau master, and I believe them to be of my great-grandparents, and I was frequently told that the husband died at the age of thirty-seven, leaving behind twelve children, the last one posthumous. In point of fact, he died at the age of forty. The wife has the fine, beautiful, mournful eyes of George Eliot or Virginia Woolf. She is elegantly dressed, and her right hand plays with a crucifix, which hangs down from her necklace. The man, whose portrait is far inferior, as well as being in less good condition, has a long, bony face, a dead white complexion, small eyes, big ears, and a look of nervous, thin-lipped resolution: he is wrapped in a coat with a broad fur collar, which I still own in a much decayed form. His name, Bezaliel, which could be spelt Bessalie, with or without an accent on the final "e", derives from Bezalel, the only aesthete referred to in the Bible, the artificer of the Ark of the Covenant, and it was a not uncommon name in my father's branch of his family until it was abandoned on the grounds that it brought the bearer bad luck in the form of great ugliness. I imagine that the comparative poverty of my father's immediate family was brought on in part by the large number of children that his grandfather left behind.

⌒

The only European member of the Wollheim family I ever knew was a worldly man of letters, called Hans Feist-Wollheim, a grandson of Caesar, who, trained as a doctor, never practised. He was a friend of the Hofmannsthal family and the Mann family, and he was Rilke's tenant in

Munich when Rilke withdrew to Muzot. He tried, as far as I can see, to make himself indispensable to people, but, when he turns up in memoirs, as he does in those of Cocteau and Thomas Mann, he is invariably referred to with a note of exasperation. He and his brother, Ernst, had been brought up in a large house in Wannsee, where his mother collected porcelain and Old Masters. In 1934 or 1935, the Nazis came to the house, and arrested Ernst, a poet, and physically very delicate. Ernst was denied permission to take his overcoat with him, and died overnight in his cell. Despite this Hans continued to occupy the house in Wannsee, from which he attempted to negotiate the sale of his mother's objects. Finally, in 1939, he despaired, and, wrapping a few paintings inside his trouser legs, he took the train to Switzerland, where he lived between Zurich and Geneva. I had met him once as a child, and on Christmas Day, 1946, I arrived in Zurich from Paris unannounced, and invited myself to stay with him over New Year's Eve. Except for two days, when we went to Lucerne to interest a Swiss shoe manufacturer in buying a Cranach or a Lancret, Hans spent most of his mornings and his evenings on the telephone in protracted conversations with émigré women of title, Viennese or Hungarian. Might they like to meet for lunch, or for coffee, he asked, and, in long, old-fashioned German sentences, the voice slowly rising and falling, he arranged and rearranged the calendar of his day, endowing every invitation with a sensuous yearning. Procrastinating, or rebuffed, as the case may be, he returned the telephone to its cradle, and, leaning back against the stiff wooden chair which he, this sybarite, preferred to all others, he completed the next stage of his dressing. He slowly tied his shoelaces, or he inserted his cufflinks into his white shirt, or he carefully knotted the heavy black satin tie he invariably wore. His lips moved as he prepared the cadences for the next conversation, and then he slowly leant forward for the telephone. But Hans's life had not passed in indolence. He gave me a copy, inscribed to "my dear cousin", of *Ewiges England*, an anthology of about five hundred English poems, selected "from Chaucer to Eliot" with a refined modernist taste, and he placed opposite the English text his own translation into German verse. The volume carried an epigraph by Hamann, and it was dedicated "*Dem Friedensland der Berge*". In his day Hans had translated Cocteau, Pirandello, Croce, and Christopher Fry.

Hans was attentive to the *petits soins*. The day before I left for Italy, he said that I must come with him to the railway station, and there meet the Countess S, who wished to entrust me with something for her son in London, whose name was familiar to me as a great collector of Old Master paintings and drawings. We met on the platform, and Countess S, whose creamy complexion entranced me as she looked at me over large furs, handed me a soft parcel, which, when opened in an icy cold flat in Princes Gate, was found to contain three pairs of thick British Army socks. Next Hans turned his attention to my journey to Italy, for which he felt that I was unprepared. He learnt that I had £5 on me, and he arranged that a chiropodist would get on the train at the last Swiss stop, take the £5 from me, then a colleague of his would board the train at the first stop in Italy, and hand over to me the equivalent in lire. Thus armed, I would leave the train in Como, ask for the Palazzo

Manzoni, and stay with two very old ladies, great-nieces of the writer. The house – for I obeyed Hans's instructions to the letter – was filled with mementos of the great man, and folio editions of *I Promessi Sposi* in imposing bindings were set out on medieval lecterns. The three of us dined at a round table, over which there hung an enormous Venetian glass chandelier with many brackets. As the snow fell on the cables high up in the mountains, the light from the chandelier sunk to a faint glimmer, and our conversation, conducted in stilted French, came to a halt. Then the light returned, and we resumed the conversation.

In the week or so that I spent with my cousin in Zurich, sharing a large bedroom which had pale varnished floorboards, and views over the snowy gardens of the neighbouring villas, he told me that he had always found my father impatient, and asked me if I had "the London taste", meaning, Was I homosexual? Though not homosexual himself, he thought of England affectionately as the land of homosexuals, and, when I answered No, he contemplated the answer, and said, after a while, musingly, "You might be." In turn he talked to me of his mother, an eccentric overbearing lady, who had refused to let the Kaiser see her china collection because he had once visited a Jewish family that she thought of as upstart, and used to tell her children that synagogues were places where one caught germs.

As for my father, I never knew what religion he was brought up in, though I believe that he was educated in a

Catholic school. At some point after he came to England, it would have seemed to him inevitable that he should behave as a member of its established church. He was married in St James's, Piccadilly, and sometimes he accompanied me to church. How deep this went was not a question that either of us was disposed to pursue, though for different reasons in the two cases: I because, though, when I went away to school, I encountered boys who were Jews by religion and were thus, like Roman Catholics, excused from going to Abbey, it was not until very much later that I knew of the Jewish religion as a serious possibility of belief; he because his real views were those which he exposed to me only when, after having insisted that I should have a religious upbringing, he took me, by now sixteen, out to supper in the restaurant of the Savoy, told me that all religion was folly, asked me if I had read Freud's *The Future of an Illusion*, and suggested that I should.

As the Thirties deepened, and anti-Semitism swept through Central Europe, my father spent a great deal of time and money in getting not only his own family, but friends and acquaintances, out of Germany. At the same time, partly in response to my questions, partly to make his position clear, he insisted that to classify people as Jews had no basis in scientific fact, and that doing so was all but invariably the first step on the way to persecuting them: persecuting them, humiliating them, imprisoning them, and – though I don't remember whether his foresight went as far as this – exterminating them. He held that to classify oneself as a Jew was just as vacuous, just as dangerous. He once recalled an incident in Berlin when, as a young man, he had asked a Berlin policeman the way, and the policeman had said, "Why should I tell a Jewish dog like you?"

My father's family, as well as converting to Christianity, also married Christians, and the result, or so my South African cousin told me, was that, despite the Nuremberg Laws, some of the family were treated as Jews, some as Gentile. The consequences were even more arbitrary than the labels. For, whereas my father's sister and her son Hans, who had been crippled by malnutrition brought on by the Allied insistence on reparations, having fled Germany in the mid-1930s, were rounded up in Holland during the war, and sent back to die in the gas chambers in Auschwitz, Oscar told me that a fairly close cousin of his, a much less close cousin of mine, a nephew of the admiral, had been permitted, under the race laws, to practise as a doctor in Berlin. However, at some late moment in the war, he was denounced, not for being a Jew, which he wasn't, but for lack of enthusiasm about the war, and he too went to Auschwitz. He went, not as a prisoner, but as a doctor: that is, to work under the terrible Dr Mengele. This he refused to do, and he also ended in the gas chambers. Later I learnt that this story was not altogether accurate, but close enough to the truth to make the point that there were many roads to extermination.

My mother's family was altogether different. Both her father's family and her mother's family came from the West Country, and both had lived close to the soil. I have come to know more facts about them than I ever expected to, for reasons which I shall explain, but I have almost no awareness of what they, or their cold, rain-sodden lives, were like. As a child I knew almost nothing about them, and it did not occur to me to be curious.

My mother's father's family was called Baker, and the Bakers can be traced back to the muster roll of 1569. They lived between two villages on Exmoor, Swimbridge and Filleigh, one of which belonged to the Russells, the other to the local grandees, the Fortescues. Being on the bottom of the social ladder, the Bakers are hard to trace. In 1768 they emerge from obscurity when James Baker, presumably of Swimbridge, married Thomasina Downman, for the Downmans were socially superior, which is registered in the fact that she could write and he could not. Thomasina's mother was born Margaret Yeo, and the Yeos, who were to be found in the area for as long as the Bakers, were tenant farmers, and over the generations a Yeo turns up as church warden, or the local schoolmaster. James Baker lived to the age of 88, and his wife to the age of 99, and they had ten children. Two of these children bore the same Christian name, something familiar in rural life, which signifies that the elder of the two children had died before the younger one was born. One of the daughters of this marriage, Hester, repeated the misalliance, and married another Baker, Richard Baker, this time it seems of Filleigh. A son of this marriage was William Baker, my great-grandfather, who was born in 1807, worked as carpenter and mason, and died in 1848 "of pneumonia at harvest time". William Baker had married in 1835 Eliza Keeble, a noteworthy happening, for Keeble, unlike Yeo, Downman, Baker, is not a local name: it comes from Suffolk. It is possible that Eliza Keeble arrived as a nurse or housemaid with the new vicar, who also came from Suffolk. William Baker and Eliza Keeble did not prosper; at any rate, his second son, William Henry, my grandfather, was born in the workhouse at Barnstaple in 1840. One story is that it was through the good offices of the Fortescues that they escaped from the workhouse, and were accommodated in some almshouses in Filleigh.

In about 1857, my grandfather arrived in London, most probably with his elder brother, Robert. Legend has it that they walked from Devon. Then a few years elapsed in which my grandfather's movements are hard to track, but from which he emerged a fairly rich man with useful connexions, of whom Lord Ailesbury seems to have been the most enduring. During this period, he attended the Working Men's College to continue the education he had started in his village school, and he joined a militia regiment, which was probably associated with the College, and in which he rose to be a colour-sergeant. A photograph of this period is in existence, but I am told that it is hard to make out from the uniform the exact regiment to which he belonged. In 1863, while still a young man, he married. His wife was Lucy Mildenhall, who also came from the West Country, and together they had six children – four daughters, and two sons.

By the 1870s William Henry Baker and his younger brother Dick were established as licensed victuallers, and as such they embarked on what was to become a highly profitable kind of career in late Victorian England, in which none did better than they. The vast rambling pubs that made late Victorian London a city of palaces were not, as one might have thought, the work of the brewers, who were loath to get their money tied up in such ventures, but of speculative builders who had some connexions with the wine trade. William and Richard Baker met this description, and, by the 1880s, they had built, or re-fashioned, the Angel, Islington, the Cock, Highbury, the Victoria, King's Cross, and the Falstaff, East Cheap. Over the next fifteen years, the two brothers and their joint venture, Baker Brothers Limited, engaged in complicated business deals, which meant that they owned now this, now that, set of properties. In the late 1890s, they engaged in the most grandiose of all their projects. Abandoning the pub architects, Saville and Martin, to whom they had been loyal, and who worked in a flamboyant style, a mixture of Italian and Flemish mannerism, they took on a more sophisticated architect, Walter Emden, and they used him to redesign the north side of Leicester Square in the form of two massive and ornate buildings conceived on the contemporary French or German model, part hotel, part brasserie and café: these were the Queen's Hotel and the Hotel de l'Europe.

Meanwhile my grandfather had embarked on what was for him another career, a second life. In 1875 he joined a City volunteer regiment, the Honourable Artillery Company, and I possess a damaged photograph of this immensely attractive man in what I am told is the uniform of a trooper in the Light Cavalry section, which had recently been formed. In 1881 he was commissioned as a lieutenant, and he rose a rank every other year, from lieutenant to captain, from captain to major, within a period of some ten years. When he retired, he was appointed a colonel of the regiment. He owed his success, it would seem, to two things:

his brilliance as a horseman, and his great administrative abilities. In a limited way, he anticipated the later re-organization of the British Army on the Prussian model.

Sometime in the early 1880s, my grandfather left his wife, and, a year or so later, he set up a new establishment with my grandmother, whom he never married. My grandmother, who, I have always assumed, met my grandfather through being a barmaid in one of his pubs, was young at the time, but certainly more than sixteen, which was what my mother claimed for her. I knew her well when I was a child, and she told me that, once, at Ascot, the famous Prince of Wales smiled at her from his coach, and, as Princess Alexandra turned to smile too, the porcelain that was spread finely across her face cracked. My grandmother retained a very faint Somerset burr. In 1884, when their first child, a son, was born, they were living at 27 Ingrave

Street, Battersea, but later they moved to 44 Gordon Square, and from there eventually to Cavendish Square. Meanwhile Baker's estranged wife occupied a house in Cumberland Terrace, Regent's Park, and he went there every Saturday morning to administer punishment to his sons for any misbehaviour that was reported to him, or to reward them with sixpence for good behaviour.

In the late 1890s my grandfather developed trouble with his heart, and my mother would tell me that, while he lay ill in bed, his coachman laid straw in the street outside in order to attenuate the fierce roar of the horse traffic. Later he was ordered to take an ocean voyage. He sailed round the world, and he wrote letters back home to his second daughter, Floss, and to my grandmother, whom he addressed as Dollie. Those to his daughter are lively, informative, describing what he saw and the people who entertained him: English people at Monte Carlo, an American admiral, the Governor-General of New Zealand. Those to my grandmother contain no news, and are full of injunctions about when to write letters and where they must be addressed: they are letters to a little girl. When my grandfather returned home, he seemed well. He went down to shoot with Lord Ailesbury at Savernake, and, a week later, he attended a banquet of his old regiment: he arrived home late, and his manservant, going in to wake him next morning, found that he had died in his sleep. According to my mother, he often read throughout the night, and for this reason he and my grandmother slept in different rooms. He read mostly the Bible and Tennyson.

My grandfather died in June, 1900, and, six months later, Baker Brothers sued for bankruptcy. It was the end of the great period of affluence for the London pub and the London pub-owner.

My grandfather was hard-working, self-disciplined, self-educated to a high degree, and something of a dandy: he knew, but probably not well, dukes and lords, and he regularly went shooting in Kent with a friend who had grown rich by being the principal importer of ostrich feathers, which he alone knew how to dye a singularly dark

glossy black. However my grandfather did not follow the lead provided by most Victorian Englishmen who, starting from extreme poverty, attained considerable wealth. When he left his first wife, he did not try to improve his position by a better marriage. He did little to educate his sons, though he did something about his daughters, nor did he instil in them any of the various marks by which a second generation could be recognised: the desire to make more money, a sense of social position, a love of the arts, or even a taste for gentle dissipation.

In one respect at least my grandfather approximated to the stereotype of the self-made Victorian man. He was secretive. Almost all the facts that I have just recorded about him I learnt only when I was in my mid-fifties, and then through a strange coincidence. A first cousin of mine, daughter of one of the legitimate children, who had been christened George Frederick Napoleon, appeared in my life, and everything she told me, of which her existence was not the least, found me unprepared. What she told me she knew, of course, from her own family, but, when, intrigued by our common grandfather, she tried to add to her stock of knowledge, and to write his life, she was confronted by a wall of silence which he had constructed around himself, and, though she found out a lot, she could find out next to nothing about what she ardently, and I to a lesser degree, wanted to know: the kind of person he was.

⌐

My grandmother, Augusta Mary French, was born in the village of Weston Zoyland, on the edge of the famous battlefield of Sedgemoor, in 1862 or 1864, the fifth and youngest child of John French and Mary Pester. The date on the birth certificate is 1862, but in the census of 1871 her age is given as 7. It was the name French, which she claimed was really spelt "ffrench", that led her to believe that her family was Irish. She talked of her father as a schoolmaster, and he is described as such on his marriage certificate, dated 1850, as well as on her birth certificate twelve years later. On the 1861 census, and in the Somerset directory for 1866, he is recorded as a shopkeeper, but, in the country, these two occupations could readily go together. His father, also John, was a mason, but his wife's father, William Pester, was a wheelwright, which was a superior rural occupation. The Pesters came from Devonshire: from a small village called Rose Ash, near South Molton, not far from Baker-land.

Nothing is really known of my grandmother's life before she set up house with my grandfather. Though I saw quite a lot of her, I have little conception of her character. She had, as I recall it, a warm nature, though when she was with my mother, it was the warmth of bad-temper and irritation.

My grandmother was not, even in the most attenuated sense of the term, educated. She knew nothing, she read nothing, and she displayed no interest in, nor did she have any understanding of, others. I never met a friend of hers.

Once I was taken to visit her surviving family: I met her sister, my great-aunt Rose, who was dressed in black taffeta, and did not treat my grandmother with great affection, and Aunt Rose's daughter, and her husband, who was called Delver May. They were farmers, and lived in what I took to be a late eighteenth-century house in the middle of Weston Zoyland, called Colyton House. In the afternoon I was driven in a pony trap across the land they farmed, desolate fields separated by wide ditches called locally "rhines", a fact which struck horror in the Duke of Monmouth when he learnt of it on the eve of battle while comforting himself and his companions with the words of the old fortune-teller, who had foreseen that he would die only on the banks of the Rhine. The pony, a fast trotter, brought us back past the church with its famous wooden roof, where, after the bloody defeat, Monmouth's men awaited trial and summary execution in terrible circumstances. When I returned to the farmhouse, I disgraced myself by falling into a tank of cow-dung, and then getting drunk on elderberry wine. I was probably eight or nine.

My father, Eric Wollheim, was born in Breslau on December the 13th, 1879, the son of Eugen Wollheim and his wife, who was his first cousin, but whose name I do not know. Indeed I know of the name Eugen only because my father used to recall with such delight that, when he visited St Petersburg before the Great War, he was called Eric Efgenovich.

I knew two facts about my father's childhood. One was

that his family doctor was the doctor of Friedrich Lassalle, the famous socialist, and enemy of Marx, who, born in Breslau in 1825 of a rich Jewish family, had died in a duel in Geneva in 1864. The other was that, when he had to walk to school through the bitter cold, he prepared himself by swallowing a mouthful of goose fat, and wrapping a sheet of brown paper across his chest under his shirt. I possess a photograph of my father and his elder brother and his sister, taken in 1884 by the photographer, G. Mandel, whose address is given as Neue Taschenstrasse 5, Breslau. The two boys have close-cropped hair, they are wearing wide white collars, short double-breasted jackets, dark pleated skirts like kilts, and knee-length boots; the girl wears a slightly feminine version of the same clothes. I scarcely ever heard my father talk about his siblings. Just before he died, he decided to correspond with his niece, whose name I remember as Ilse de

Neschelski, and who lived in Santiago de Chile.

When I was a child, my father preached to me a doctrine of total obedience to one's parents. Our first quarrels, which began when I was fourteen, were about pacifism, and, after one such quarrel, which involved my leaving the Training Corps at school, he sent me a letter, which he had dictated to his secretary, and in which he said that he expected me to write to him, and say, "*Pater peccavi*". But he also made clear to me that this subservience was required of the young only so long as they lived under the same roof as their parents, and were supported by them. Accordingly, if one wanted freedom, one should aim to leave home as soon as possible. I believe that this was what he did himself. He went to the Gymnasium in Breslau, and then, without going to university, he left Breslau, indeed Germany. I do not know whether the incident in Berlin with the policeman played any role in his decision.

My father's first move, on leaving Germany, was to Paris. This was in the very late 1890s. After a childish desire to be a woodcutter, and wear a green jacket with wooden buttons, my father formed two ambitions: one to be a lawyer, the other to be a theatrical impresario, and, either through force of circumstances or through choice, he became an impresario, and to this he brought two qualities. He had great natural powers of discrimination – he loved, in no matter what area, to discern fine differences of quality – and he possessed a mind of a distinctly legal cast. In Paris he joined the Marinelli agency, and in 1900 he came to England, perhaps to open, certainly to run, their London branch, and this he continued to do until 1911, when he opened an agency in his own name with an office in Charing Cross Road. On arriving in England, he went to live in Brixton, but, by the time the war broke out, he was living in the Adelphi, then one of the glories of London. He once described to me the rooms he occupied, with, over the fireplace, what he referred to as a Fragonard. One Sunday morning, years later, we were walking to the station, and he started to wonder what had happened to the Fragonard, as though he had not thought about it in the intervening decades. He was much like that about things that he had once owned, or thought he had. As he was dying, he started to think about a triangular plot of land high up on the slopes of Montmartre, which he had been given in partial payment of a debt, by his friend Lartigue, the owner of the Café des Ambassadeurs on the Champs Elysées, who also had a share in the casino at Biarritz.

Around 1905 or 1906, with a recklessness of which I otherwise never saw a trace, he threw up his career, and went off to the south of France to attach himself to one of the most famous courtesans of the period, La Belle Otéro. He was in his twenties, she was eleven years older, and I have no conception of their life together, how it began, what it was like, why or when it ended. Was he her lover, was he her *homme d'affaires*, was he the butler, did he merely stand outside the iron gates to catch a glimpse of the famous dancer as she strolled amongst the bougainvillea and the myrtle? In the early 1970s, I wrote to Sir SS the writer, whom I did not know, asking him for any recollections he had of my old friend AS, who had, I knew, at one period been extremely close to his brother. Sir SS replied in a very guarded fashion. He talked of AS's shyness, and of his deep appeal to all, and of the colour of his eyes, and what ES-W had said about them, but assured me that A himself had never been "that way", and then, in a postscript, changing the subject, he added that my father

was "quite a friend" of his in the "far-off days" of the ballet, and regularly put him and his wife in an empty box. He went on, "You will not mind my saying that Diaghilev, whom I was very fond of, told me of your father's friendship with 'La Belle Otéro', but I never liked to broach this subject even in the box at Covent Garden." I thanked him for the information about AS, and then, after ten years of mulling over this postscript in its beautiful handwriting, I wrote to him again: Could he tell me exactly what it was that Diaghilev had told him? He replied courteously: he wished that he could, but he couldn't, his memory was gone, he could not even place the incident I was referring to. My father had for years a secretary, Miss Udale, thin like a stick, with a row of large amber beads, which she fingered nervously, and a strange quavering high-pitched nasal voice. She had total recall, and I believe that, in some pages she wrote about my father after his

death for her own benefit, she described the year or so he spent with La Belle Otéro. I think that she also attributed to him an affaire with the exquisite dancer Adeline Genée. When I tried to get hold of Miss Udale, she was dead.

My father listed in *Who's Who in the Theatre* a number of artists whom he brought over to England before the 1914-1918 war, either as the deputy of Marinelli, or in his own person: they include Sarah Bernhardt, Madame Réjane, Karsavina, the Zancigs, and Leo Fall, as well as the first production of Max Reinhardt's *Sumurun*. All this was interrupted when the war broke out. My father, who was by this time a naturalized subject, but had been declared medically unfit to serve, was not safe from the obloquy that fell on everything German. Dachshunds were kicked in the street, and my father, some time later, discovered that he had been reported to the police for signalling to enemy aircraft. Eventually he was asked by SH, of whom we have already heard, to be the manager of a theatrical company that would tour the armed forces. It took him through the war, and it played a part in my coming to be.

⌒

My mother, Constance Mary Baker, was born on March the 9th, 1891, in 44, Gordon Square, the daughter of William Henry Baker and Augusta Mary French. Snow was on the ground, and it took one of the housemaids a long time to walk across the square through the heavy drifts to rouse the doctor who was to deliver her. When my mother's birth came to be registered, her father's name was given as French, and her mother's name was given as "French, formerly Baker". The same had been done when my mother's brother was born, and these foolish deceptions had to be corrected by deed poll in 1901. A few years after my mother was born, my grandfather moved his second establishment to a flat in a mansion block at 4,Cavendish Square, where he had a bath with a shower, a novelty which, according to my mother, he showed off to all the guests who came to dinner. This, and the careful way he arranged a rose in his buttonhole every morning, were the only specific memories she had of him. But she told me that he loved her to the point of idolatry: I know enough about a father's love for a daughter to believe that.

My grandfather's death in 1900 was a turning-point in the lives, certainly in the fortunes, of the second Baker family. One of my grandfather's legitimate children came round to Cavendish Square, and made off with what he could. My grandmother's possessions, when I knew her,

were meagre, and all that she inherited from Colonel Baker was a small oil sketch by Maclise, which hung in our dining room, and a cheap oleograph by Marcus Stone, showing a young wife who has been ruined by her husband's gambling, and who turns to the spectator for sympathy. My grandmother and my mother moved, first, to Arundel Mansions on Notting Hill, then, in further reduced circumstances, out to Flanders Mansions, near Turnham Green underground station. In her father's lifetime, my mother had gone to school at Queen's College, in Harley Street. When they moved away from Cavendish Square, she went to the convent of Our Lady of Zion on Notting Hill, then to a boarding school at Petersham, at the foot of Richmond Hill, in a house where Dickens had lived.

By this time, the family affairs had further deteriorated through my grandmother's marriage to a man called Dr George Howell, who was a mining engineer, and was said to be involved in potentially lucrative oil explorations in the Caucasus. The name of Prince Dashkov was frequently flourished, much to my father's irritation, who hated references to titles. Outwardly the model of lower-middle-class respectability, a pillar of Welsh non-conformity, who played the organ in chapel on Sunday, short, with a bowler hat, pince-nez, a worn dark suit covered in stains, watch-chain and fob, spats, a grey moustache full of spikes, and constant clearing of the throat, Uncle Pops, as I was expected to call him, was in reality a total rogue: a swindler, a pathological liar, most likely a bigamist, and who certainly managed to make off with whatever money my grand-mother still had left to her after Ernest Baker's depredations. For the first sixteen years of my life, Uncle Pops intermittently lived with my grandmother. It was bad when he left, probably worse when he returned.

In 1909, my mother had money enough provided by her father to be sent to a finishing-school in Paris, 24 Boulevard d'Inkermann, Neuilly, and it was there that she visited her last museum, and did her last reading. My mother would often say to me, "I'm not a great reader," and sometimes she would say, "I'm not really an intellectual." The facts that she was referring to were these: that, in Paris, she bought her-self copies of Racine, Corneille, and Molière. I still possess them, inscribed "Connie Baker Paris 1909". Most of the pages are uncut. After Paris 1909 my mother, to the best of my knowledge, never read a word. She never opened a book, a newspaper, a woman's magazine, or anything that I ever wrote. In addition to the pale yellow volumes of the French dramatists, I have inherited from her an album of miscellaneous postcards in various shades of sepia. They show Old Masters from the Louvre, the murals of the Pantheon, the great public buildings of Paris, works by artists such as Carolus Duran, Comerre, Henner, and Bonnat, and the great figures of the French stage, such as Coquelin aîné, Bernhardt, Réjane , and Augustine Orlhac, all striking histrionic poses. Once, in my childhood, an emancipated woman called Beatrice Wanger, from a Hollywood family, with whom my mother had kept up a correspondence since their days together in Paris, came to the house. As I recall the day, she brought with her a greater intensity than my mother could tolerate. The reunion was not the success of which my mother felt so confident.

On the completion of finishing school, a family council decided that my mother should become a milliner, and an opening was found for her in an establishment in Paris named Louise, which, rumours say, doubled as a high-class *maison de passe* patronised by the Prince of Wales. However, my mother was determined to go on the stage, and she returned to London, and entered the Academy of Dramatic Art, as it then was. She finished her course, she adopted the name "Constance Luttrell", which reminded her of the West Country, and sometimes induced in her fantasies of noble birth, and she joined the Gaiety Theatre, not as a chorus girl, but as a showgirl, an all-important difference. The outward difference was that chorus girls moved, and showgirls did not: inwardly it was a difference in respectability. Gaiety girls of both sorts were much courted, and much taken out by what were called "stage-door Johnnies", who spent large sums of money, first on bribing the doorman to deliver flowers and a note to the girl of their choice, then, if the note was lucky, on buying the supper that

TO UNDERSTUDY MISS ELLALINE TERRISS.

MISS CONSTANCE LUTTRELL

this precipitated. My mother found a supporter, protector, attenuated lover, in the powerful figure of C.B. Cochran, a school friend of Aubrey Beardsley, who ruled the entertainment side of the London theatre for nearly fifty years. Late in life, my mother told me that she never "went all the way" with Cochran, and asked me, "Do you understand?" as though the secrets of sexuality were known exclusively to a generation that professed to have little use for them.

My mother, by this period, was inclined to turn herself

into an actress proper, and her chance came in 1914 when the war broke out, and, through Cochran's intervention, she was invited by SH to act opposite him in a theatrical company that would play to the troops. The arrangement lasted four years.

My parents were married at the beginning of 1920, in St James's Church, Piccadilly. My mother was a woman of great beauty with strong bones, and deep-set eyes. My father was good-looking in the only way that I have really been able to think of men as good-looking: he was well-dressed. They spent their honeymoon at Gleneagles Hotel, in the Trossachs.

On the eve of her marriage, my mother was told by her uncle of her illegitimacy, and she went to my father, and

was prepared to release him from his engagement vows: an idea that my father, who did not even understand her scruples, dismissed as ridiculous. My mother brought as her dowry a dog, her mother, and, on and off, her brother, who represented the decline of the Bakers in a striking fashion. Uncle Ted, who was an exciting figure in my early days, almost entirely because he had travelled to so many places, was, as he liked to put it, "a rolling stone". For some reason, he had, when he was young, discarded the name Baker in favour of that of Barrington, though he sometimes returned to Baker, even to Baker-Baker, and sometimes adopted another name, also beginning with B, which I have forgotten. Destined for the Navy, he passed out as a midshipman, and early on was involved in a mutiny, in which a cruel captain is said to have been left on a desert island. For this he was obliged to leave the Navy, according to one view with, according to another view without, a court-martial, and he joined the Merchant Navy, where he acquired a knowledge of wireless and telegraphy that was in excess of what was required. He spent many years in the East, and he had tales to tell that sounded as though they were out of Conrad or Lafcadio Hearn, whom he claimed as a friend, and he used to upbraid my father with the narrowness of his cultural horizon. My father regarded him as a disreputable drifter, and avoided speaking to him, even at the luncheon table. For a number of years, Uncle Ted lived in a single room in the area of Paddington with a fortune-teller, named Madame Tsa-Tsa, and his only steady job was to act Father Christmas at Harrods. When he came down to lunch, he would ask my father if he could "help" him with the train-fare back to London. His one long-term plan was to build a motor boat in which he would sail round Britain, being continuously photographed for a tabloid paper. The boat, or some version of it, was built, and, the first day in the water, it sank or caught fire.

My grandmother, when I first remember her, lived on Beulah Hill, Norwood, in half of an early Victorian house, made of creamy grey brick with a large bow window, and wisteria clinging to the wall. I used to be taken there and played in the garden. At some moment, Uncle Pops moved in with her, and the news was that my grandmother had had a nervous breakdown. All her hair fell out, never to grow back, and to recuperate she went to a nursing home at Broadstairs, which my father paid for. I remember being once taken to see her. The nursing home was a large building, painted white with dark tile-hanging, and we sat in the garden, which was high up on the cliffs, and had Devonshire tea with splits and clotted cream and jam. My grandmother was reminiscing about the West Country, when to our horror she swallowed a wasp, which had settled on the jam. The wasp stung her on the back of the tongue, which swelled up, and we were led to believe that her life was in danger, but a doctor, who was on call, came round, and injected the tongue and got rid of the swelling. My grandmother was wearing her new wig, and, on top of it, a hat, which, as far as I can recall, she was, from then on, never without. She was generally dressed in brown, and she wore layers of very loosely knitted cardigan. She carried around with her wherever she went a large tapestry bag with a tortoise-shell clasp, and in it she kept her knitting and her thick wooden knitting-needles. From a very young age, I used to imagine with great vividness the intense pain that I would feel if my testicles were caught in the bag as the clasp closed over it.

When my grandmother left the nursing home, she didn't return to Beulah Hill, but took a flat at the top of a Victorian house in Surbiton. Occasionally I would go and stay with her overnight, and I used to glorify these visits to myself by pretending that I had run away from home to stay with a poetry-loving aunt. A few years later, while my brother and I were waiting in the car outside the house she lived in, he spotted a sinister man at the window, and he called him Boris Karloff, after the horror-film actor. Uncle Pops had moved back in, and he stayed with my grandmother until they died within a few weeks of each other just after the war. My grandmother was aged 86. When my mother came to die in 1983, she was aged 92. They were a long-lived family.

After my parents married, my father made two decisions. He decided that he and his family would live in suburban Surrey, and he decided that my mother should leave the stage. I believe it to be clear that both were bad decisions.

I have set out the considerations that led my father to choose the suburbs of Surrey, but a more particular reason for the choice of Walton-on-Thames I discovered one Sunday on a walk with my father. For, as we passed a pair of crumbling lodge-gates, and looked down a straight avenue of bedraggled trees, about a hundred yards long, which led in to a copse, above which could be seen a small clock tower, he told me that this was a house he had rented for several years for his parents before the Great War. According to an inscription incised into the lodge gates, the house was called The Wilderness, and it looked like an illustration to one of Maupassant's short stories about Normandy. His parents left Breslau, and must have led a somewhat incomprehensible existence, far from their friends, and not close to their son. They kept horses, and my father came down at weekends, and rode. At the beginning of the war, they went back to Germany: they lived through the war, and the hardships of the post-war period, and both of them died in 1927, I believe. My father visited them most years, and once took my brother to see them.

As to the decision that my mother should abandon the stage, there were several possible reasons for this. My father might have feared her failure, he might have feared her success, he might have wanted her at home. Years later, my mother openly resented the decision, and in retrospect it was easy to see that it meant two things for her: it meant that she had to think of new directions into which to channel the enormous energy with which she had been endowed, and it also meant that she had to think of a new way, or new ways, of getting praise. The discharge of energy and praise were the two overwhelming needs of her life, and her misfortune was that, after she left the stage, she was never able to find any means of satisfying them jointly. She devised some sort of solution for each: neither was adequate in itself, and they defied co-ordination. They pulled against one other.

For praise, my mother came to depend increasingly upon herself. If sometimes the words came out of the lips of others, it was because she forced people to say what she made it so clear she wanted from them. "You have to agree that . . .", she would begin, or "You have to give it to me that . . .", and then it would turn out to be her originality, or her courage, or her independence, or her sense of humour, that we were being asked not to overlook. As to a way of consuming her energy, my mother – and I do not know how early it was in her married life that she thought it up, or why – hit upon something the ultimate appeal of which may very well have been that in itself it meant nothing to her: it was cleaning the house. She devised a system, which was no ordinary system, and it must be understood that, throughout the period when she put it into practice, there were always two or three servants in the house who could have done, or could have shared, the work. As things were, their presence did little except to endanger my mother's system, but that, as we shall see, was not, from her point of view, so obviously a disadvantage.

At about nine o'clock in the morning, by which time my father, if he was in England, had left for London, my mother would put on an overall, she would tie a spotted scarf around her head, and she would start on her daily routine. She would begin with her own bedroom. The door would be shut, the readily moveable furniture would be put together somewhere in the middle of the room, and all the windows would be thrown open. Then, with a duster, she would brush the dust off all the tops and all the surfaces. When she was convinced that all the dust had been got out of its hiding-place, and had settled on the floor, she would first use the sweeper, or the Ewbank, with its beautiful picture of a lion in a roundel, to remove the top layer. Then there was the dust that had sunk into the pile of the carpet, and for this she relied on the vacuum cleaner, or Hoover. Any residual dust, which had not fallen on to the floor, or had fallen on to the floor but had not been sucked up either by the sweeper or by the vacuum cleaner, would probably have floated out through the window. The room was now clean – cleaned and clean – and so my mother felt at liberty to open the bedroom door, and start on the next task, which was also the biggest, for it took in, first, the corridor that curved round past the lavatory and the airing-cupboard to the bathroom, next, the stairs, which descended to the hall, and finally the hall itself. From her point of view, all this formed a single, though not a simple, unit: it was not simple because of the twists and turns within it, but it was a unit because there was no internal door that could be shut, and thus seal off one part of it from the rest, with the consequence that there was no way of stopping the circulation of dust or germs. Accordingly, once my mother had persuaded herself of two things, one was that all the doors opening off the landing and the hall were shut, and there were ten in all that had to be checked, and the other was that all the windows were open, the same sequence of duster, sweeper, and vacuum cleaner, was reapplied without there being any natural break, or any way of storing what she had done.

And it was here that the system was vulnerable. So long as my mother was still at the stage of cleaning her bedroom, alternatively once she had got past the landing, stairs and hall, and was cleaning either the dining room or the draw-ing room, there was comparative immunity: nothing could go deeply wrong. But what could only too easily happen, and, if it did, would nullify everything that my mother had done up till that point, was that, while she was working on the large unit, someone in one of the first-floor rooms who hadn't noticed the stage she was at might unthinkingly open a door. And, when I say "open a door", it was enough, on my mother's calculations, for it to be opened the merest crack for the dust, the germs, to be able to creep back, and for my mother to feel, no, for her to know, that her work was ruined. Within minutes, she had carried her three aids, the duster, the sweeper, the vacuum cleaner, right up to the very top of the house, to the small, linoleum-covered land-ing outside the boxroom and the maid's room, which, in the ordinary course of events, was not in her sphere, but was left to the maid to clean, but not so when there had been a violation of the system, and what she was now called upon to do was to set the process in motion from the very beginning, indeed from a point earlier than that at which it had started. By this means, my mother's day was set back by something between an hour and a half and two hours. The hairdresser in London, or a friend whom she had arranged to meet for tea, or my father who had booked a table at the Savoy Grill for lunch, had to be informed, and the day re-organised. This happened about once every two or three weeks, and it was this that was the cause of my mother's frequent latenesses, which in turn led to her running across the backyard where the pigeons were waiting for her.

I have said that the ease with which my mother's method of house-cleaning could be set back, and most likely by someone she might have expected to help her, was not necessarily a deficiency in her eyes. For what any such reversal made entirely clear was that it was a matter of decision, a matter of her decision, when her work was finished, and she could stop, and run her bath, and get dressed, and enjoy herself. It was her word, nothing else, not the evidence of the eyes, not the touch of the finger – though my mother loved running her finger along surfaces – that counted, and that she liked. The fact that failure deprived her of pleasure, that it sent her back to the Hoover and the sweeper and the duster for another long period, did not much matter to her so long as failure was hers to adjudicate. It would be hard to exaggerate how readily pleasure could recede as an aim in the life of this woman, who, in company, presented herself as a dizzy hedonist, a huntress after pleasure with not another thought in her head.

My mother never felt called upon to account for the routine in which she was so inflexible until one day there was a new arrival in the house who very much had her own idea of things. This was the new governess, and I shall, in due course, explain the existence of governesses in my life. In fact I had two, and it was the second, Miss King, who was the important figure in my upbringing. But it was the first who, out of the blue, brought my mother's system of cleaning the house into question. She was French, she seemed to me of a very great age, she had grey hair in a bun, and eyes that did not focus, and her name was Mademoiselle de Saint-Germain. Before coming to us, she had worked, evidently for many years, as a governess in a Prussian family. I do not know how she was chosen. She was immediately besotted with the older of my mother's two dogs, Toto, the bad-tempered Pomeranian, who had been with my mother when she was on the stage, and was now eighteen. Next to Toto, Mademoiselle de Saint-Germain loved me, or at least my convalescent state, which she took with the utmost seriousness, which pleased my father.

Within a week of arrival, Mademoiselle had laid down a special procedure that had to be followed every morning before I went for my walk. My brown tweed overcoat was laid out, and, by its side, two scarves. First, I put on the woollen scarf, which was folded across my chest. Then I put on my overcoat, which was carefully buttoned up to the top. My silk scarf was then placed in my hand, and I was instructed to put it across my mouth if the wind blew. Then Mademoiselle brought out a box of big safety-pins, and she put one safety-pin by the side of each button, driving it through the thickness of the tweed: this, she explained to me and to my parents, was a wise precaution in case, while I was out on my walk, the thread on one of the buttons should break, and the button should come off. Then I put on my woollen gloves, and I was seemingly ready to go out. But Mademoiselle was not. There was something she had to do. At every meal she pushed part of what was on her plate to one side uneaten, and, as soon as the meal was over, she set up the mincing machine, which she had confiscated from the kitchen, and passed the left-over part of the meal through the mincer. She then divided the mince into three lots, and, to my anger and disgust, she wrapped up each lot in a piece of paper that she tore out of one of my notebooks. What she had to do before we could start on our walk was to go back upstairs, and fetch these three packages, which she put in the pocket of her threadbare moleskin coat. These packages were then to mark the stages into which our walk fell. If Toto walked to the first curve in the road without stopping, she was rewarded with one of the packages, which was put down on the pavement, and opened up. If Toto walked to the end of the road, which was the most that could be expected of her, she was given the second package, and we then turned back, and Toto would then be given the third package at the turn in the road just before our house. Meanwhile Mademoiselle was on the constant look-out to detect, on my behalf, any change in the wind. As soon as she suspected that the wind was about to blow in my face, I was made to take the silk scarf out of my pocket and hold it tight across my mouth: then I had to turn round, and to walk backwards down the road until the wind dropped.

That Toto was always one of the trio considerably cut down on the distance we walked, but this was not an objection in Mademoiselle's eyes. On the contrary, it fitted in with all those ideas of hers which were fairly soon to bring her into collision with the way the house was cleaned. For, in opposition to my mother, and ultimately to my father, Mademoiselle believed that it was the out-of-doors, the air that came from the trees and the green things, the fresh air to which so much of my life had been sacrificed, that was the danger: it was the source of disease and ill-health. In consequence, when she cleaned the rooms that were her preserve, the nursery and the night-nursery, she began by shutting the windows, and then she opened the door on to the corridor, even if my mother was in the course of cleaning it. When my mother objected, she formulated her opposition thus, "Madame, you believe that the germs are inside, and must be swept out. I believe that the germs are outside, and must not be let in." My mother loved these words, and she repeated them on every possible occasion, to me, on the telephone, at lunch to my father's friends, and she always put it as follows: "Mademoiselle said, 'You believe that the germs are inside, I believe the germs are outside'." My mother always quoted the words as Mademoiselle had used them, and she never adapted them grammatically to herself as a speaker. She never said, "I believe the germs are inside, but she, Mademoiselle de Saint-Germain, believes that the germs are outside."

My mother's failure to state her own beliefs, and her insistence on preserving the actual words of Mademoiselle as though they were mere speech without anything behind them, would not have attracted attention from a grown-up, but to a child, whose head was filled with the idea of religious faith, my mother's insistence upon the use of direct speech seemed momentous. What, according to my mother, was really at issue between them? Did she believe in the germs that she spent so much of her life trying to eradicate, or did she not? Did it, or did it not, matter in her eyes that someone disagreed with her, with what the woman hath said? When someone disagreed with her, was it, or was it not, important for her to persuade this other person of the error of her ways? For me these were the issues, as simple as that, but my mother evaded them, just as she evaded the issue of religious faith itself, and she continued to put her trust in phrases like, "I do what I do," "That's what I'm like," "You can't change what a person's like." I do not know that I wanted to change what my mother was like, or at any rate not until many years later, by which time what I really wanted was to change her for someone else, but I wanted to know, because I needed to know, why it was that what my mother

spent so much of her life doing was so important to her.

And yet I continue to give a misleading impression if I make it seem that my mother regarded cleaning the house as this much, or that much, more important than other things that went on inside the house. It was alien to my mother to have a scale of things. What she thought, and required us to think, was that cleaning the house was serious, and nothing else was exactly that, and the way in which its seriousness showed itself was that it did not require an argument. What my mother did every morning was not something that might have to be altered or revised because of some discovery about the direction in which germs flowed, and, if, in a way, this offended me, it did so in some measure because I too, in some part of my mind, had a view that was beyond discussion. This was my fear that, if things went on as they were going, my parents would go to eternal damnation. – But I anticipate. For my religious certainties rose to such peaks of anxiety only a while later.

Mademoiselle did not last long. The ways parted, and, if her task had been to teach me French, it would be closer to the truth to say, not that she failed, but that she never, as far as I was aware, embarked on the task. I remember only the four frequently intoned words, "*Gargarisez comme il faut.*"

Mademoiselle de Saint-Germain was succeeded by Miss King, who came from York, which won me over, not only because it was so far away and to the north, but because it had city gates which preserved their medieval names. Indeed no sooner had she arrived than she hung up a water-colour of Boothgate above the pitcher and slop-basin where I had to wash when it was thought unwise that I should brave the chill of the corridor and go to the bathroom. She had spent a few years at the Château de Joinville, a name I knew from Froissart, where she had been a servant of sorts, perhaps even a governess. She wore a brooch with a painted cameo of the château, and it was the only ornamentation that she allowed herself. Her father, who was dead, had been a shopkeeper, and her aunt, called Olive Groves, sang operetta, and could sometimes be heard on the wireless in a concert with the BBC Light Orchestra. Miss King was gentle, helpful, and she wore shoes with holes in the soles because, as was discovered only years later, she sent her wages to the missionaries.

Miss King was really "chapel", but she accompanied me to church, and she encouraged me in my zeal for the Book of Common Prayer. She got me to learn the Gospel, the Epistle, and the Collect for each week, and, when I went into my parents' bedroom to say good morning, I recited one of them – and I do not remember whether this was her idea or mine – to two bewildered people. Apart from religious belief, she had a general commitment to self-improvement. On our walks, she carried around with her the three thin volumes of Hugo's German course, one of grammar, one of exercises, one of answers, and she kept them very neatly covered in brown paper. On the brown paper cover of one of the volumes, she had written in ink the two letters, **u p**, and I begged her to tell me what they meant. Sometimes, on one of our walks, I would break off from the fantasies I poured out to her, I would turn to face her, and I would threaten to make her life a misery with my persistent questioning until she confided the answer to me. She held out for two or three years, in the course of which time I made many bold guesses. Finally one day she relented, and she gave me the answer: she had written **u p**, in order to tell herself which side up the book should be. I was dumbfounded. This explanation had never occurred to me, and I could not decide whether this did, or didn't, show that I was totally stupid.

If Miss King was proper and could be disapproving, it never led her to protest against the unbridled eroticism of the stories with which I deluged her on our walks. Perhaps my anatomical ignorance imposed so many barriers between my meaning and what I actually said that she never understood me, or perhaps it was her ignorance, which I suspect was even more profound than mine, that had the same ultimate effect. But I cherish the belief that she had a deep tolerance for life, and also some sense of the love I bore her. I do not recall that we ever quarrelled, or that harsh words passed between us, with the possible exception of the occasion, which I shall later describe, when she was instructed to skip parts of Scott that were thought unsuitable for her to read out to me.

The most powerful moral lesson that she imparted to me was a disapproval of divorce. She thought divorce evil, and she taught me to avoid getting physically close to friends of my parents who had been divorced. I was led to avoid films in which divorce figured, and ultimately films that had divorced actors in them. I never felt that she had the same disapproval of irregular liaisons, with which life around me pulsated. I say this, not on evidence, but for the flimsiest of reasons, which is that when, years later, I read the story of Caroline of Ansbach's last hours, and how she told George II that he must remarry, I felt, in a matter of seconds, completely sure that Miss King would, across the centuries that divided them, have approved of his tearful reply, "*Non, non, je n'aurai que des maitresses.*" It became dogma for me to believe that this strange, pasty-faced woman with the chilled features and the dripping nose, whose face has almost completely faded from my memory, who read to me the Waverley novels without any partisanship for Roundhead or Cavalier, Crusader or heathen, accepted all kinds of feeling that she herself had never experienced, or ever wanted to. She left us about the time I went to boarding school, aged thirteen, and she briefly worked for the family across the road. Then war broke out, and, as soon as it did, she joined the women's army, the ATS, and it is said that, within its ranks, she had a new lease of life, and found happiness. There is no one whom I have ever wished a better life.

Miss King read me, over the years, Scott, and Dickens, and Kingsley, and Harrison Ainsworth, and Charles Reade, all in a monotone, which I loved, and which friends of my parents who came to the house on a Sunday and overheard mocked. Her own taste was, I believe, for books slightly more edifying, and I know that she had great admiration for a novel called *John Halifax, Gentleman*, which she read to herself several times over, and which I take to have been a work of some bleakness. It has a north-country setting, which I knew was significant, but I was never allowed to read it. Morality or virtue could also be A certificate.

Miss King saw me through, though in a certain way she was also responsible for getting me into, what was the single most turbulent episode in my childhood. In retrospect I see that it threatened my somewhat insecure balance of mind. It began one afternoon when I went with my mother to a dog-show on "the roof-garden" of a department store in the biggest local town. I do not know why we went there, but it is possible that my mother was "showing" her Pekingese called Tutti, as opposed to Toto, the Pomeranian. As we arrived at the dog-show, we bought tickets, which also entered us for a raffle. At half past four, the various shows stopped, and a voice through a megaphone announced the draw, and I, as the youngest person present, was called up to take a number out of a top hat, and a few moments later I found myself the winner, and a young fox terrier was put in my arms. An envelope came with him, and in the envelope was his pedigree, which was very distinguished, and that may have been his undoing. To the best of my knowledge, I had never particularly wanted to have a dog, but now I had one, and in circumstances I saw as miraculous.

The dog came with the name Nobby or else I was readily persuaded to call him Nobby, and his earliest days I do not recall, except that, for a reason that will be fully apparent only at the end of this memoir, I refused to let him be fed on a sheet of newspaper. Nor would I listen to the idea that, when I took him out for a walk, which I did often, at first exclusively on the lead, but gradually letting him off for longer and longer periods, I should carry a folded newspaper, and strike him on the nose if he did not keep by my side: it was, I thought, advice of the utmost sadism. Sometimes he would accompany me on my bicycle, keeping up with me, and looking at me as he ran by my side: it was very beautiful.

Then one day things took a different turn, and my life darkened. It was late afternoon, and I was taking my dog for a walk along a stretch of sand, and gorse, and blackberry bush, which started almost at the end of our road and extended for about three miles along the side of a road at right angles to ours, which carried some traffic. The area was called the Black Fence because, for its total length, there was, about two or three hundred yards back from the road, thus enclosing the area, a corrugated iron fence, about ten feet tall, cut into spikes at the top, and painted with tar. The other side of the fence, there was an as yet undeveloped area called Burwood Park, overgrown with spruces and sycamores and occasional stands of fir, from which the smell of fern and decaying wood exuded. To this day I remember every inch of the Black Fence, every path, every bend in every path, every patch where the roots of trees erupted, every stretch where the trees grew together and blocked out the light, every mound and every bank of sand, every silver birch, and every small oak tree, and every likely

source of blackberries, and this knowledge has been kept fresh in my mind because of the way in which images retained from many walks have formed the involuntary backcloth to much thinking in my mind, particularly of an abstract kind.

Evening was descending, and I called Nobby to put him on the lead, when he and I simultaneously noticed signs of movement in front of the gorse bushes and along the sandy paths. The earth started to quake. I had probably never been out in this area so late in the day so that I did not immediately recognize what was going on, but the dog did. The rabbits were coming out of their warrens, so that just as I leant forward to snap the lead on to the collar, he put his nose to the ground, and ran. He ran, and I ran after him, shouting his name, and, to my amazement, he paid no attention to me. Then, about fifty yards ahead of me, he swerved, and headed towards the Black Fence itself, and arrived at it just where the bank on which it was set had started to erode. There was a gap beneath the corrugated iron. The dog flattened himself like a hamster, scrambled under the fence, and was lost to sight. My reaction, which showed that the influence of Miss King had not fallen on stony ground, was instantaneous, and I dropped to my knees and prayed. The good prayers that I said nightly, my hands clasped, my feet in my tartan bedroom slippers, knowing them by heart and reciting them always word for word the same, except that in the prayer that began, "God bless Mummy, Daddy, Grandma . . .", a name could be inserted without harm, were, I recognized, useless on an occasion like this. Whereas ordinarily when I prayed, I did not think that it would be appropriate to keep the Almighty waiting, and felt improvisation to be impious, now, on my knees by the side of the Black Fence, I knew that all that counted was the sincerity of the soul in despair, and what poured out of my throat was a torrent of cries, promises, pledges, and all the strangulated evidence of despair, rebirth, a second conversion if need be.

Half an hour later or so, Nobby returned, and we went home, he chastened and I grateful, and I believe that, on this first occasion, I never conceived that there would be a repeat of the event. My prayers, I thought, had been listened to. However, over the subsequent weeks and months, Nobby's disappearances became ever more frequent, the time of the day at which he was likely to run away always earlier, he needed less and less provocation. Soon he would disappear as soon as we left the house in the morning, and he would take longer and longer to come back. Then he stayed out overnight. Then he was missing for two days, three days. One night he was returned only through a call from the police. And when he did come back, he was wounded: he had wounds on his body, on his head, around his throat. After a while, he returned with wounds that had had time to go septic, and he had to be taken to the vet, and the wound cut open, and the poison drained. The prayers that I cried up to heaven grew more and more exalted, ecstatic, pentecostal. More and more of my life passed out of my own hands, and I abdicated it to the service of God if He would look on my plight with favour. Tears stained my words, and my frame shook convulsively as I made vows that would, if I had really got the measure of what I was saying, have turned me into a monk, a nun, a eunuch. I had, without observing the strangeness, modulated from being a child dog-owner to becoming a religious fanatic, and, for the first time, I formed an attachment to my poor dog. I fell in love with him and with the misery that he caused me, and I failed to distinguish between them. Each time, on first returning, he looked wild, and something across the eyes reminded me of the errand boys, but, after a while, he had settled in, calm returned, and I came to believe, like a mistress, that he would never leave me again.

One day Nobby came back from an adventure that had lasted three or four days. He was emaciated, thorns and burrs were stuck to his coat, his eyes were large and terrified, and his throat had a deep gash, from which yellow pus seeped out. I took him to the vet, who observed my look and my uncontrolled sobs, and he kept him in overnight, and the next morning gassed him. My prayers had found their limits: I could not bring him back to life, and, I suppose, slowly some kind of sanity dripped back into me. I could never bear to hear any criticism of my dog. What I do not recall was what I did in order to re-establish my relations with the Almighty on a less delirious plane. Had I asked too much of Him, or had He, in letting me down, taught me something?

When, many years later, Dr S suggested that Nobby's wounds were sustained in fights over female dogs, and that this was an early attempt on my part at once to deal with, and not to deal with – that is to deny – the facts of sexuality, I was surprised. There was no suggestion in my dealings with my dog, of that overheated, orchidaceous world which I by this time had come to associate with sexuality, or the world of my father's books. Rather I thought of

Nobby as mysteriously involved with some part of the animal kingdom that was lower than that to which he properly belonged: in the hours of darkness, he had, I imagined, battled with foxes, and bats, and hedgehogs, and he had done so out of some blind attachment to ferocity and destruction, which he tried to keep from me. As luck would have it, the fights in which he was engaged were presided over by an Almighty God, who for a while controlled the outcome in my favour, and then He could, or would, no longer.

Before the epoch of governesses, I had had a brief spell of school. It lasted four and a half days: Tuesday, Wednesday, Thursday, Friday, and Saturday morning. It was, I believe, in the autumn after my fifth birthday, and the school was a local school, which my brother had just left in order to go to a boarding school on the South coast. It was called Ropers, presumably after the owner and headmaster. It was in Weybridge. On the third day of school, which long remained in my mind as the exemplar of what it was to learn something, we were asked to bring in an orange, which we were to think of as the earth, and turning round the orange on its axis would allow us to understand many of the marvels of life: how sailing boats disappeared over the horizon, why we didn't fall off the earth, and why people in Australia did not stand on their heads.

Saturday was a half-day with lessons coming to an end at twelve or half past twelve. We packed our small attaché cases, and waited on the pavement outside the school as if at a bus stop for parents to come in cars to pick us up. Seeing my mother drive up, and wishing to make her think that I was at ease in the school, or just wanting myself to feel at ease, I gave the boy standing next to me a tap on the arm. It was meant to be no more than a friendly nudge, as if I were saying, "I know you, remember me?" but I miscalculated. It was as if I had challenged him to a duel, and, within a few seconds, the whole group of boys turned into a wild contorted mass of flailing arms, and book-bags, and satchels, overflowing the pavement and spilling out into the road. Most hands were pointed at me as the bully, the troublemaker, the fist-fighter. I scrambled into the car, and by the time I reached home, I felt feverish.

I have no direct recollection of what happened next, but I later learnt that, over the weekend, my temperature mounted and mounted, and on the Monday or Tuesday I was diagnosed as having pleurisy. Ice packs were put on my forehead, and I had the strange sensation of my thumbs growing to some enormous size. The curtains were drawn with a narrow crack of light at one end, and I believe that they were not opened for several weeks. Trays appeared with soup, and barley water, and calf's foot jelly. Large vases of carnations stood on the bamboo chest-of-drawers: smoke from the little container of *Incense de Bruges* curled up into the ceiling: and there was a great deal of sweating, and changing of pyjamas, and rubbing of eau-de-cologne on my body. My father brought back from London a special bedside table of a kind used in hospitals, with a stand that went under the bed, and the table itself went over the bed: a wheel and catch allowed the table-top to tilt so that reading in bed, when I was allowed to turn on the light, became a luxury. The table was my favourite companion for many years, and I still possess it. Twice a day, then just once a day, the table would be cleared, a square dressing would be laid out, and a tin of pink paste, called anti-phlogiston, which had been heated in a saucepan of water on the burner next to the gas fire, would be opened, and the contents carefully spread with a knife on to the dressing. My nanny would touch her cheek with the paste to make certain that it was not too hot, and then I would be asked to open the front of my pyjama jacket, or to pull the jacket up over my head, and the poultice would be carefully strapped to my chest or across my back with bandages aromatic with the mild, woody smell of recuperation. For much of the day I listened to books being read to me or to the purr of the vacuum cleaner. I would doze off, and wake up, and the light had started to fail. I luxuriated in my new-found weakness, as other boys might delight in their new-found strength.

Pleurisy turned out to be only the first of a series of illnesses, which occurred with no more than brief intervals between them, most of them normal childhood ailments, but assailing me with excessive ferocity, and with a frequency out of the ordinary, so that I had measles three times, which I was told was a record, as well as a threat to my eyesight. During one of these bouts, the curtains did not open for four or five weeks.

The most constant witness to my illnesses was the family doctor, Dr Barclay. I call him the family doctor, but he was in effect my doctor. My father had his German doctor, but, for the first seventeen or eighteen years of my life, I do not remember that either my father or my mother spent a single day in bed ill. There was my brother with whom I might have been expected to share Dr Barclay, but either my memory is defective or he was not much of a patient. Dr Barclay was a man in, I imagine, his late forties. He had dark, glossy hair, carefully brushed back, a jet black moustache, small eyes, a freckled skin, and a soft Highland accent. On my father's instructions, he came to the house whenever my temperature reached 100. Within a minute of the front door opening for him, he had bounded up the stairs with the same élan with which, a bare hour or so before, my father had raced down them and out of the house. There was a tap on my bedroom door, the door opened, Dr Barclay's head appeared around it, a few steps were taken across the room, and he dropped down on the bed beside me, and, allowing his legs to swing loose for a moment or two, he pulled a thermometer out of his breast pocket, checked that it was shaken down, put it under my tongue, and fiddled with the stethoscope that he wore round his neck. Automatically I opened my mouth, and said, "Arrrh", and a shiny spatula held my tongue in place. Dr Barclay was confident in his judgment, and he was knowledgeable in what he prescribed, and, just before he left, he could always spare a glorious minute or two to discuss with me what I was reading. His truly momentous role in my life was to insist that I should at the appropriate time read the Waverley novels. He would say when.

For all the speed with which he came and went, Dr Barclay always looked around him for something in the way of paintings or furniture to admire, and he was famous in our area for the many codicils in his favour that old ladies attached to their wills. Some years later, I was back in his company when I read *Mrs Dalloway*, and I came across the

famous Harley Street specialist, who, as he descends
the eighteenth-century staircase, absent-mindedly taps the
panelling to see if it is genuine. Dr Barclay did not live at
that Olympian eminence, but he was keen to learn the ways
of the world in so far as they had evaded him, and my father
introduced him to his tailor, who made the tight, dark blue,
double-breasted suits that from then onwards he always
wore, the blue emphasising the black of his eyes. – My
father liked introducing people to his tailor, and the only
time I went there, which was in later life in order to get a
dinner jacket I had inherited altered, the cutter greeted me
suavely, and said, with the slightest bow, "I remember your
father very well. He did us the honour of introducing to us
Monsieur de Diaghileff."

During the lengthy period of convalescence from
pleurisy, and the later illnesses, my father insisted that I
should observe what he regarded as appropriate caution.
My temperature had to be down to normal for twenty-four
hours before I could get out of bed, and I had to spend at
least another twenty-four hours, but preferably forty-eight,
indoors before I could go out. I was not permitted to drink
water from the tap, and by my bedside was a bottle of
Vichy-Celestins, which, with its curious fishy taste, always
made me thirstier than before. I was apprehensive that one
day my father would think that I was old enough to take
my temperature, as he did his, in the anus.

School was out of the question, and it was this that introduced the regime of governesses, which lasted, I am
inclined to think, about three years, and I went to school
again only when I was about eight or nine, and even then
Miss King stayed on. I do not believe that Miss King

obliged me to follow any particular course of studies, but we slowly worked through the few school-books she had with her, some of which she ordered specially from Hachette, and some of which had seen use at the Château de Joinville. When I had mastered one book, I went on to the next. I recall with delight the principal French reader we studied, with its chilly grey-blue binding, on which was superimposed a kind of Gothic tracery. Each lesson in the book was completed by a little story, in which some historical character inevitably acquitted himself with verve. What was called for from the protagonist was either a great act of courage or the witty overcoming of one of life's difficulties. The *dramatis personae* whom I can recall included the Chevalier Bayard, *le roi Dagobert* and St Eloi, Voltaire and his valet, la Pucelle, and Bertrand du Guescelin. When Voltaire's valet stopped cleaning his master's shoes in the winter, saying that they would only get dirty as soon as he went out in the rain, Voltaire stopped buying him food, and, when the valet complained, he was told that, if he was fed, he would only get hungry again. When St Eloi upbraided the good king for having so many mistresses and told him to remain faithful to his wife, the king asked the saint what his favourite food was, and, learning it was partridge, fed him partridge day after day, until the saint cried out, "*Perdrix, perdrix, toujours perdrix.*" I liked the idea that life could be mastered so effortlessly, and these little moral stories almost reconciled me to growing up. There was also somewhere in the middle of the book a full-page illustration of Delaroche's *Assassination of the duc de Guise*, which suggested to me that death was a kind of falling over. Another favourite book of the time was *Little Arthur's*

History of England, which celebrated the lives of sad princes, and famous kings, and scheming ministers, and from which I learnt a great deal, but mostly I learnt something that it did not set out to teach, which was how easy it was to be altogether passed over by history, and to lead a life that would pass into nullity.

I have referred to some of the routines that convalescence precipitated: putting my shoes neatly side-by-side when I undressed at night, the weekly cutting of my fingernails, the piano lessons, my nightly prayers, and taking shelter from my mother's cleaning of the house. But there is one routine, more directly connected with health which I have not mentioned, and this was the weekly giving of a laxative. My father took Epsom salts daily with breakfast: my mother took a weekly dose of a thick cream, made from paraffin, called Kayleenol, but I was not allowed to use either of these, though I didn't at all mind their taste. Instead I had to take every Friday night, on going to bed, two teaspoon-fuls, poured out from the bottle, of a thick mixture, which was dark brown, but, as it lay in the spoon, was edged with a purplish black, which was called California Syrup of Figs. The taste was heavy, sickly, morbid, and the smell completely portended it. Having to take the medicine from a teaspoon was a peculiarly cruel part of the ordeal, because it meant that, after the first teaspoon, when I closed my mouth to raise the saliva to rinse it clean, a stern voice said, "No, we've not finished yet," and I was expected to stand perfectly still, with my mouth left open, while the second teaspoonful was poured out up to the rim, and then tipped into me. Though I was told that I would get used to the taste, it in fact got worse every week, until a moment was reached when the mere smell was so overpowering that I started to rebel. I screamed, I sobbed, and many times someone would be brought in to hold my arms. If, as became increasingly frequent, I was still struggling after ten minutes, the dose would be put off to the same time the next day, Saturday, and then, if there was enough rebellion on Saturday, matters would be postponed to Sunday. One week, the fight continued until Tuesday, and on Tuesday, when whoever was administering the medicine was momentarily out of the room, I tried to climb between the bars that were still on my bedroom window, and throw myself to the ground. I believe that this was the culmination, and that, from then onwards, some better way of ensuring "regularity" was found. Meanwhile the curious colour and texture of the medicine became fixed for me in a thought, which I found very hard to shake off for many years. The very hue and tonality of California Syrup of Figs seemed to me to be exactly reproduced in certain effects of the setting sun, and I came to the view that the sunset originated in God's dipping His thick fingers in the medicine bottle, and then smearing them across the evening sky. It was a kind of divine finger-painting. Sometimes I see a penumbra of California Syrup of Figs across the cheeks in Giotto, or wherever the shadow of Byzantium falls across Italian painting.

Much though I loved the condition of being delicate, it was from out of these years that there was born a certain fierce love of freedom, later to be reinforced by other forms of confinement I endured, so that, when I first heard of the now extinct Tasmanian Devil, which was so committed to its personal liberty that, when its foot was caught in a trap, it would bite through its leg in order to free itself, I felt an affinity with this otherwise unlovable animal. But it would be wrong to think that the passion for freedom was my constant companion: it had to be aroused by something in a book, or some incident I watched, as when the gypsies would be cruelly brushed aside as they tried to sell bunches of heather, or increasingly by some reflexion I made upon the world, and then my passion could not be extinguished. The upshot was that I was stubborn, but also indecisive. When I look back on my war years, I have to give thanks that I was never called upon to be a leader of men in battle. I know that I would have had many innocent lives on my hands, as did others.

Eventually – and I do not recall the stages to this decision – it was thought that I was ready to go back to school, and, some time after this, a school was found for me. It was called Burwood Park School, and it was in a mid-eighteenth-century house, surrounded by the parkland where Nobby first escaped, which was of a not very interesting kind. There were flat expanses of grass with sparse woodland, some of it now encroached upon by development: rambling mock-Tudor houses, with imposing rose-gardens. Only the lake at the back of the house, surrounded by thick woods, which was to be a forcing-ground for my early emotions, retained its beauty. Most of the classrooms had high chimney pieces, made of coloured marbles, with classical friezes, and, though I was in no clear position to appreciate them, they and the long parquet floors filtered into a sense I had of airy elegance such as I did not know from reality. The school was mixed in sex, and was progressive in outlook. In front of the house was a large wooden sign, which indicated that the school belonged to some benign organisation, and it gave the patron as "The Rt Hon The Earl of Iveagh, K.G." I hoped that the Earl would turn up in his Garter robes.

I remember just two things about the education the school provided. One was the maypole set up in front of the house, which was the setting for very elaborately choreographed dances, with names deriving from the ancient English countryside, which sometimes required us to work as an ensemble, but quite often there were two partners, or four soloists, who danced while the others looked on, and the record of these individual performances, we could then observe, was preserved, high above our heads, in the abstract patterns woven by the different coloured ropes that the dancers had clung on to as they circled, now round the pole, now round one another. My other recollection, which is equally sweet, is of learning Latin. First we learnt a paradigm: say, the present tense of the first conjugation. Then little slips of paper would be handed out, with the first person, present tense of a new verb, and we would take it in turns to get up and to decline the new verb and to act its meaning. Within my first week of school, a little slip saying *aro* was put on my desk, and, benefiting from a recent holiday on a farm, I got up and steered an imaginary plough round and round the other desks, occasionally clucking to an imaginary horse, pulling now on this imaginary rein, now on that, thus avoiding a series of imminent collisions, and, all the while, I recited as I went, *aro, aras, arat, aramus, aratis, arant.* School too could be, like the cupboard on the stairs, a time machine.

The second school I went to, when it was decided, much to my regret, that I had outgrown Burwood Park School, was called The Mount. I shall later describe my earliest experience of the school, and how it gave school a different set of associations. One of the rare friendships that my parents formed locally, which was completely unaccountable, was with a master who had taught at Ropers, named Stock. He was a tall, square-shouldered man with a thin bony face, a strong nose with hairy nostrils, and thinning fair hair brushed close to the skull. He had a wife, a big, raw-faced woman, who had been the matron at Ropers. He liked sport, and he wanted to have a school of his own, and, in addition, they both wanted to have love affairs. When I first knew the Stocks, they had a large, gloomy flat in what was one of the very few handsome buildings that survived in Walton-on-Thames: a sprawling Italianate pile, with a broad loggia on top, built by Sir Charles Barry, which commanded the Thames and a small backwater where there was a boathouse, and boats for hire, and families of swans. I went to the Stocks for boxing lessons, which were supposed to take up where Allen's had left off. By this time I was more wary, and I hated the way Stock would suddenly give me an upper-cut just when I thought we had broken off: but I confined the expression of my feelings to the angry way I struggled in and out of my gym-shoes at the beginning and the end of the lesson. A few years later, at Stock's school, I made a boy's nose bleed, and I could not be induced to box again.

Stock realized one of his ambitions. He bought a large

house, some twenty years old, with a stable with a cobbled yard, four or five acres of garden, a stream with stepping-stones, a field or two, and a high brick wall surrounding the whole property. I believe that my father helped Stock with the money, and I went to the school at the beginning of its second year. I had a very simple demand on school, which was uncommon: I wanted to learn. The favourite pastime of the other boys, when they had a few spare moments, was to open one of their textbooks at the end pages, and to do competitively elaborate drawings of stick-figures sitting on lavatories, and serving as crucial links in a complex excremental chain. Out of each figure a pile of faeces fell into the lavatory bowl below, and from there it travelled along a detailed plumbing system, like a switchback, at first losing height, until, at a certain moment, jets of water mysteriously propelled it upwards and sideways, so that it eventually reached a point immediately above the lavatory seat. Now it started on a downward track, pushing its way through S-bends and traps, until it was in free fall into the ever-open mouth of the figure who had, only a few minutes earlier, relieved himself of it. Then the journey re-commenced. I used to wonder whether it was a boy in our midst who had been the first to think up this kind of drawing, and his companions had latched on to his invention, or whether, on any given day of the week, all over England, Wales, Scotland, and Northern Ireland, in all the places whose names moved me, and that I longed to visit, schoolboys were crouched over their desks, one arm crooked around the book in which they were drawing to keep off idle observers, and they were all engaged in illustrating the same motif, but each one of them devising new twists and turns, desperately pushing forward and outwards the limits of the art form. Some of the bolder spirits made their stick-figures identifiably female. Most boys, I noticed through the haze of nausea that I felt, got angry as they did these drawings.

At The Mount, I had to play various games, most of which I initially liked, usually because they admitted of division and subdivision of parts, with many new names, whether these were for parts of the action involved, or parts of the equipment used, or parts of the field on which the action occurred. Once these names had lost their freshness, so that, for instance, it was no longer fun, in the half-hour or so when I was trying to go to sleep, to fabricate running commentaries on fabricated games between fabricated teams with fabricated colours, I lost all interest, and curiosity gave way to terror.

⌒

At a sale of the Empress Eugenie's possessions, which took place, I believe, in the late 1920s, though she had died in 1920, my father bought me two things: an album of pressed flowers from the Holy Land, which had heavy, hinged covers in *bois clair*, and a big wooden box, which, when it was opened out and laid flat, had a chessboard on the outside, and a backgammon board on the inside, and there was a set of stout wooden pieces massively turned. My father and I occasionally played chess on a Sunday morning, but he was generally too preoccupied to play well. Sometimes I was allowed to ask the guests who came down to the house if they would like to play. I played often with Noel H, and sometimes with Lucienne B, of whom more

later, and once with Kurt Weill, but he too was not able to concentrate because it was the day Hitler announced his intention of rearming. In the car, as we drove through the lanes of Surrey, he talked to me about Julius Caesar, the general and the writer.

My father took an interest in only one aspect of my education. He thought it essential that I learn foreign languages. What defeated my father's ambitions was his further insistence that, in speaking French and German, I should speak them impeccably, as he did, *sans accent*. In consequence, he could not bear me to speak a word of French in front of him, nor would he give any assistance in teaching me German, so that, though, in the course of my life, I have tried to teach myself German about thirty times, and I am enamoured of the sound of the language spoken slowly, with heavy cadences, I have forgotten it as often as I have learnt it: I find myself looking up the same word twice in the same paragraph.

When I was fourteen or fifteen, my father's interest in my learning French, which had half-conceded defeat, seemed to be re-ignited, and, to further this aim, he lent me a book, and implied that, if I read it carefully, my French would improve. The book was by Léon Blum, by this time the Socialist premier of France, and rapidly becoming one of my heroes, but it dated from a much earlier period, from his days as a young man, when he was something of a social figure, and a friend of Proust. The book was called *Du Mariage*, and it was a polemical work, intended to upset the conventionally minded of its age. It laboured the deficiencies of marriage, and argued for what was called "trial marriage". It mentioned approvingly the practice whereby fathers supervised the entry of their sons into sexuality by providing them with an older woman who was kind and experienced. I wondered if my father intended to do the same for me, and hoped so. I read the book dutifully. When I had finished it, I returned it to my father's bedside table, for it had not yet found its way on to his bookshelves. He was abroad at the time, but, when he returned, he never referred either to its content or to its power to improve my French, nor can I remember any perceptible difference it made. The loan of this book was what I have referred to as the second thing my father did for my moral education, the first being those sparkling mornings when he permitted me to watch him dress.

My father's work, as I can now see in retrospect, changed to a considerable degree over the years of my childhood, and this certainly influenced the background against which I grew up. When I was very young, or up to the age of six, my father was largely occupied with the Diaghilev ballet. I believe that he met Diaghilev before the war, for he is said to have taken him to see Adeline Genée dance in 1912. Whether the original meeting took place in Paris or Saint Petersburg or perhaps even in London I do not know, but from 1918 my father acted as the ballet's London manager, and also contributed to its survival in other places. He drew up the contracts, he made advance bookings with the theatres, opera houses, and music halls in which the ballet danced, and he endeavoured to raise money, to which end he acted as a go-between between Diaghilev and Lord Rothermere or the King of Spain. There was an almost daily exchange of lengthy telegrams. My father deeply admired Diaghilev, and he was, I feel, much drawn into his way of thinking and feeling. He was very sympathetic to the perfectionism, and I believe that he found the fury and the scenes of rage and jealousy very vital. In at any rate the moods that my father allowed himself to reveal, he was very different, and he tended to fluctuate between amused calm and a very self-assured irritability, but this does not mean that he wanted the world to be so circumscribed: indeed he could himself on occasion give way to towering rage.

My father was intrigued by Diaghilev's superstition and by his fear of water, and no small part of the special prerogatives with which he was credited came from the fact, magical in my father's eyes, that he was Russian. A

journalist once asked my father in what way Diaghilev was so Russian, and my father, who had no great belief in national characteristics, said that to see this you had to watch the great man in a hurry, because, the more worried he was about time, the shorter and shorter steps he took, so that, in the end, he was at a standstill.

And yet I do not think that all this would have added up to so much if Diaghilev had not in the last resort conformed to my father's fundamental demands on life, which brought him so much in conflict with me. Certainly the Russian ballet represented for my father a lost Arcadia, a worldly Eden of which the capital was pre-Great War Monte Carlo, but Diaghilev's ultimate achievement was that he took hold of all this, and he wrenched it out of the realm of mere regret or nostalgia, with which my father had no sympathy, and he connected it with what people, some people, enough people, wanted to see. He turned it into

what my father would have called, despite the debts with which it was encumbered, "a paying proposition".

My father set store by a few mementoes of Diaghilev: two photographs, one head-and-shoulders with the chinchilla streak carefully turned to the camera, and the other standing with Cocteau, both signed in French, which was the language Diaghilev and my father spoke together; a Malacca cane, which a burglar stole; and a watercolour by Picasso, which Diaghilev bought from a scene-painter for the ballet in order to give to my father, and which I still possess. Years later, when the picture came into my possession, I learnt that it was the handiwork of the scene-painter himself, called, I believe, Laforge

Years later I got to know Lady JD, one of the most loyal and tireless patrons of Diaghilev and his ballet, and her sweetness of manner dissolved me. Apparently she told my great friend MR that she knew my father well, a fact of which I was aware, but I never asked J what my father was like in those days, something that I devoutly wanted to know. I was too frightened. It is hard to reconstruct the precise nature of the fear, but I can say this much: I thought that I would be risking too much on a single throw. Later yet, in the early 1970s, I was invited to address the Harlech branch of the Fabian Society, and my host, with whom I was staying in North Wales, introduced me, and he said, with an inspired irrelevance, that my father had been "romantically associated" with Diaghilev. I bathed in this thought, but, looking round at the Welsh shopkeepers, and the respectable men who worked on the railways, and the workers from the iron furnaces, I felt secure in the thought that there could have been no audience on which such a remark, and its nuances, would have been more lost.

After the death of Diaghilev, my father refused to have anything to do with the ballet in any form. The new Russian dancers did not know how to use their arms: they thought that their legs were the only thing that mattered. There was no one left to rehearse them: that is to say, there was no one left to rehearse each single scene over and over and over again, until everything was perfect, and, as my father recalled, the blood seeped out of the dancers' toes. As to English dancers, my Anglophile father never believed that anything really good could come out of England. In consequence, throughout the Thirties, he concentrated on cabaret, and what had been his first attachment, music hall. He booked the cabaret for the Savoy and the Berkeley, and he became immersed in the daily life of the large hotel. He figured, he once told me, as a minor character in Arnold Bennett's *Imperial Palace*. He still found singers for Covent Garden, and he brought over whatever he could extract from the dying life of central Europe: the musical extravagances of Eric Charrell, *White Horse Inn*, *Waltzes from Vienna*, *Casanova*, Kurt Weill's *My Kingdom for a Cow*, the Ballets Joss.

One thing that my father refused to have anything to do with was acts involving animals. He did not believe that it was possible to train animals without great cruelty, and he instanced the way in which, when dogs were made to high-step, this was done through slicing open the pads of their paws, and pouring in iodine.

Gradually Europe became a smaller and smaller pond in which my father could fish, and his whole way of life, of business, was imperilled. In early 1933 he was staying in one or other of the Berlin hotels where he usually stayed, the Kaiserhof or the Adlon, and, as he got into the old-fashioned lift, he found himself alone with Hitler, and very slowly they travelled up several floors together. From that moment onwards he was a terrified man. I recall him on a Saturday night, crouched over the large walnut cabinet in which the radio was housed, smoking cigarette after cigarette, as he listened to the marathon speeches of Hitler, the fanfare, the angry rhetoric, the long ovations, the endless *Sieg Heils*, and, when all seemed over, the return of the Führer to the podium. At the same time, my father was aware that the part of the theatre he was interested in was being taken over by people with whom he found he had nothing in common: they were English-born, they did not

204

conduct business over long and large lunches, they smoked cigars to prove they were rich, they had bad haircuts. One of the new lot had once been an office boy in my father's office. Sometimes my father could relent: he formed a more favourable opinion of George Black, who was already a tycoon, when he learnt that he had read James Joyce.

In the 1930s my father increased his visits to the United States. He nearly always travelled by a French liner for the food, and I remember going down to Southampton and seeing him off on the *Ile de France* or the *Normandie*. He sent me postcards from the Waldorf Astoria, and brought me back elaborate toys, of which I remember with greatest excitement something called *The Knapp Electric Questioner*. It came in the shape of a box, which opened up like a backgammon board. The board had several rows of pins sticking up, on which one placed sheets with a line down the middle, and printed with questions on the left and answers on the right. Two plugs were attached to the board by a short flex, and the player, generally myself, put the left hand plug on top of a pin that corresponded to a question, and then, with the other plug, sought out the pin that corresponded to the right answer. When the answer was found, there was a sudden buzz, and a little tingling in the hand. The box came with, I believe, thirty-six cards, and one could write off for more. I formed a library of cards, dealing with flags, and capital cities, and books and authors, and butterflies, and quotations, which I loved most, and rivers and their lengths.

My father liked certain things about America, but he thought that nothing compensated for the food. On arrival in his hotel bedroom, he would find a large bowl of oversized fruit, and it tasted of nothing. Americans, he informed me, eat baked bananas with chicken, and chocolate ice cream with roast beef.

In 1935 or 1936, in desperation, my father, who thought that he owed it either to himself or to his family, decided to attempt to make his peace with the new regime in his native country, and he invited to England, and down to the house, the manager of a theatre in Munich. I remember the occasion vividly. I had just come in from a walk on which I had mistimed my visit to the lavatory, and had had what was called an "accident". I went upstairs, and changed hurriedly, determined not to miss the visitor. Herr Muller was a small, sandy-complexioned man, with wavy fair hair, which was thinning and brushed back without a parting, and a slightly effeminate manner. He wore a single-breasted brown suit, a cream-coloured silk shirt, a dark red tie with a large knot, and, in the lapel of his jacket, there was a diamond-shaped button with a black swastika on a white ground. As I shook hands, I stared, rudely perhaps, at the small button. My father did not pursue the arrangements with Herr Muller, who had already explained that he could not, for reasons of state outside his control, employ Jewish actors or artistes. He was one of the politest men I ever met.

The further decline in my father's fortunes lies outside the scope of my childhood.

I never knew whether my father had chosen his friends or whether they had merely come his way.

The first thing to be said about them was that they were

not the model of probity that he was. If he had promised to do something, he would do it, no matter how inconvenient it was. "I promised," he would say, or "I have given my word," thereby concluding a discussion. His probity existed not just in his own eyes, it was his reputation in the world of the theatre, and it was this reputation, along with his unlimited powers of discrimination and his legal mind, that accounted for a great deal of his success. My father was instinctively law-abiding, something that I have never understood.

His friends were often in marked contrast to all this: a number spent brief periods in prison, for, I believe, comparatively minor financial irregularities. I enumerate them, out of all context. There was Max L, the husband of Peggy, whose brushes with the law derived from what was then called "share-pushing"; Oliver W, who was "flashy" in his pale suits and his loud striped ties, which he bought from Sulka, and who, as I recall things, gave a dinner party to celebrate his release, to which I went; Lord C, who married the Australian Cora, who was at the Gaiety with my mother, and he was also "foolishly" involved in share-pushing; and Eduard S, a bare acquaintance, who went to jail almost immediately after he bought Claremont, the vast Palladian house that the nation gave to Clive of India, where I remember going to a birthday party for one of his daughters, and, halfway up the stairs, there was a large candle, divided into a hundred segments, one to be burnt at each birthday. There was also Mr Cox, the ex-husband both of Sigrid and of Muriel, of whom more later, himself a shadowy figure, and there was the stepfather of Muriel's lieder singer, the very old Lord W, who vouched for a

fraudulent prospectus, and who escaped prison only by fleeing abroad, which in turn required a change in the historic
order of the Coronation service, and I shall stop at Henry
F, a heavy man, about whom rumours were rife, who
hanged himself in a doorway in his London flat, and was
cut down by his wife in the early hours of the morning.

My father's closest friend was a man called David A, who
was a rich man, thin, with a pencil moustache, whom I
associated with the term "lounge lizard". He glided when he
walked, and he generally wore black and white shoes, but
sometimes shoes made of lizard skin, and he had a hooked
nose, and a tongue of which one was made much aware.
His father, whom I knew, had emigrated from Eastern
Europe, and, brought up in total poverty in the East End,
had, as still a schoolboy, come up with the idea of pushing
a wheelbarrow around the neighbouring streets, with a
placard announcing goods that the local shopkeepers had
for sale. Thus he invented the billboard, and, from these
beginnings, he built up the first advertising agency, and he
gradually bought up a number of the most valuable theatres
in London. I knew him during the war when he evacuated
his girlfriend, called, I believe, Lois, who was in her early
twenties, and himself, now nearly ninety, and they came to
live in Teignmouth, where they rented a large Regency villa,
with shutters against the sunlight, and pretty ironwork, and
a terraced garden, paced out with giant pots of hydrangeas,
from which steps curved down to the English Channel. I
recall him sitting, all day long, in a deckchair, either outside or just inside the conservatory, wearing a velvet
smoking jacket and a battered panama hat, a scarf across his
knees, smoking a meerschaum pipe, and he passed the

hours, paper-knife in hand, slowly opening his mail, which daily brought news of new property on the wartime market. He would hand the details over to my father or to my mother, saying, "A nice bit of property", as though it was something within their means. When the girlfriend could get herself out of earshot, she would discuss with my mother whether she owed it to herself to leave "the old boy", as he was called, or whether she owed it to her mother to stay with him. "I've always been a good daughter," she would say, and my mother would say, "So have I."

The son was very different from the father: avid, mysterious, indecisive, generally with a new girlfriend, whom he all but invariably failed to introduce. Except for his permanent friend Zoë, and Lady J, one of many Lady Js, of whom he was inordinately proud, he never mentioned their names, saying "the blonde girl", "the little girl who is actually very interesting", "the tall redhead whom I think you've met". For several summers in the 1930s, he and my father went on holiday together in Europe, sometimes taking one car, sometimes taking two cars, sometimes taking a chauffeur. I do not know why they went together, or what they did, or what they talked about. My father seemed able to relax in the company of the younger man, carefully overlooking his vulgarity. Once in the later years of the war, I arranged to meet my father in the bar of the Carlton Hotel, long pulled down, and I arrived, in uniform, with some of my fly-buttons undone: David noticed my mistake, and said, "At the ready, I see." My father never heard the remark, and slowly brought his martini to his lips.

A distinct group of my father's friends, which barely changed over the years except for new recruits, was made up of various women artists whom he regularly booked. One I have already referred to, Lea, Lehár's favourite, and another I shall introduce later, Lucienne B, who loved jigsaw puzzles, and sang of love, and both of them enjoyed a special place in my affections. As the Thirties wore on, there were younger women: a dancer, La Jana, Czech or Hungarian, with large dark eyes and plucked eyebrows, whom Hitler was said to have admired, and a young singer called Suzy Solidor, who was the first woman I set eyes on who was sexually provocative. On her first day in London, she had wandered into an ordinary shoe shop, and had "discovered" black Wellington boots, which entranced her: she bought them in schoolgirl size, and wore them with great pride when she came down to lunch, and, after lunch, she pulled a cushion into the dining room, threw it down in front of the fire, sat on it, stroked her boots, and, as she did so, sang, looking into my eyes until she dissolved in laughter. In wartime Paris, she graduated, I learnt years later, to studded belts and leather and whips, and, with a few lesbian friends, became the darling of the SS.

In the year or so just before the war the most common visitors to the house were two *apache* dancers, Rudy and Marietta. She was small and doll-like, the face the product of much surgery, and he too was short, and had very thick crinkly hair, and skin like a nut. Both had Hungarian accents. They and my mother and I would play tennis at a neighbouring hotel, and my father watched, and chain-smoked, as was his habit. Just after the war, I was going to Paris, and my mother took me aside, and asked me if I would try to see Rudy, and get back some money she had lent him. She slipped in the fact that she had had an affair with him, as she assumed I guessed. I met Rudy at a big café in the Champs Elysées. He had grown uglier and coarser. He said that he was sorry to hear that my father had died, and, when I brought the conversation round to the matter of the debt, which I did probably faster than I should have, but I could think of nothing else to say to him, he denied everything, and asked me why I did not just go and enjoy myself in Paris, instead of getting involved in matters that I did not understand. He walked off, and left me to pay the bill. It was Christmas Eve, though the weather was warm, and that night, after dining by myself in a small restaurant in the place Saint-Sulpice, mentally adding up the bill as I ordered, I took a train to Zurich, where I arrived as the snow was falling through the lamplight, to stay with Hans Feist: it was a flight from one family to the other.

The business friends of my father's to whom I felt closest were two brothers, who ended their lives being called the Charrell brothers, though they started life as the Loewenberg brothers. First Eric, who was originally a dancer, changed his name, and then Ludwig, who was originally a banker, changed his name. I loved the name "Charrell": it was one of those Central European names, like Putschi, or Czarkas, or Knize, which seemed, as is said of some wine, magically to fill the mouth. The two brothers were close to one another, very close, but they differed greatly in temperament. Ludwig was calm and worldly, Eric passionate, histrionic, and deeply superstitious. He had dark wavy hair, large black eyes, and he professed to think that every woman who caught sight of him was in love with him. On one occasion when the two brothers had come down to the house for lunch, we went afterwards to the swimming pool at the ornate hotel, and, at the end of the afternoon, we were walking back to the car park, and suddenly Eric had to stop: he stretched out a hand, and reached for the bonnet of the car, so as not to faint. Before leaving the swimming pool, he had, he confessed, exchanged meaningful glances with a young girl, and now he was overcome with her fate: he must walk back to the swimming pool to see if she was all right. Eric would suddenly delay, or advance, the staging of one of his productions to accord with the movements of the planets. In consequence he lost, for himself but also for my father, considerable sums of money. Ludwig continued to dress as a banker in dark, single-breasted suits with a waistcoat, and a very thin watch-chain, and he wore particularly beautiful ties. The brothers collected rugs, which they bought in Paris in the Marché aux Puces, and then later they formed the major collection of Lautrec prints.

One Sunday morning, when I was ten, my father summoned me to drive with him to London, so as to see Eric and Ludwig, who were staying at the Savoy. We arrived about 11 o'clock, and we went up to the suite they had taken, which smelled heavily of eau-de-cologne. The bedroom overlooked the river, and there was a slight air of disarray, with a vast double bed, and the bed-clothing piled up in confusion, and I was offered a bowl of stewed fruit from the breakfast trolley, which had not been cleared away. Typed papers, contracts, silk shirts were strewn round the room. Ludwig sat down at the dressing table, and started to tie his tie. It was made of very heavy faille, unbelievably soft to the touch, and with broad stripes of crimson and black of equal width. I could not conceal my admiration, and

Ludwig, halfway through tying it, stopped, took off the tie, and gave it to me. "It is my favourite tie," he said, "which I give to one of my favourite friends," and I was made to feel that we were living in the eighteenth century. I loved shows of manners, and, around the same time, I was, one day, lunching with my father, and suddenly someone whom I thought of as the most beautiful person whom I had ever seen, and also old, came up to him, and said to him that she had been sitting over there, pointing to a table behind him, and she had been saying to herself, "Could that be Eric?" My father touched the back of his collar, and said, with a suavity that took my breath away, that his neck was glowing, and now he knew why, but he put it better, and I felt proud of him. When she left, my father told me that it was Karsavina.

A year later, the Charrell brothers came down to the house again, and this time Ludwig presented me with a small, thick book, called *Routledge's Universal Encyclopaedia*, and he had inscribed it "To my young friend Richard Wollheim, hoping that this book will one day help him to a Professorship." The inscription was dated 1934, and the encyclopedia was a work of magic, for, in the years to come, there was scarcely ever a factual question that worried me to which I did not find an answer within its covers. It gave dates, and titles of books, and geographical information, and there were tiny portraits, and maps, and illustrations of animals, and flags, and the elements of heraldry.

Many years later, when I managed to resume my friendship with Lea S, I found in her someone who could keep her distance from the exaggerated world of the theatre, which had so frightened me. She told me of the delusions of Lehár, who, because of Hitler's friendship, believed that he was a composer of genius, and of his collapse, when, arriving at a first night in the Vienna opera house immediately after the war, he was booed by a group of young people. For a moment he turned in disbelief to his wife, who was Jewish, as though she could procure him immunity, but there was no one present who was unaware of the fact that Hitler had made her an honorary Gentile. On the same occasion, I asked Lea, who knew the Charrells well because she had sung in *White Horse Inn*, why she thought that they and my father, who was by now long dead, got on so well. "It's not hard," she said, "Jews from Breslau, they stick together."

It was not true. Just after the war, my father had sent the alleged Picasso watercolour that Diaghilev had given him and a chalk drawing by Utrillo to a London dealer to sell on his behalf in the hope of improving his position. The pictures were still unsold when he died, which was shortly afterwards. Immediately Eric and Ludwig got wind of the story, they arrived from Switzerland – I once asked my friend JR where he thought the Charrells lived, and he said that he always thought of them as "hotel people", which I am sure they were – they had a meeting with the dealer in the course of which they instructed him not to sell either work, saying that they would return in a day or so with an order to hand over the pictures to them in partial payment of an unredeemed debt of my father's. They were thwarted, and were apparently very angry. By this time, Ludwig was living with a great school friend of mine, Tony W-G, who loved all things Central European.

In their later years, the brothers, whom I had so admired

as a child, became, I am told, very exaggerated.

For one reason or another, none of my parents' friends, except for the jailed peer and his Australian wife, had children. There were no children at Sunday lunch.

⌒

I started to collect notes for this chapter over twenty years ago, when we were driving through the west of Spain. Before I left London, I had bought a large notebook with blue canvas covers, and, every evening, sitting at a café table, I wrote in it. I did this in Carceres, in Plasencia, in Guadalupe, in Trujillo, in Ciudad Rodriguez, in Albuquerque, and I then started to put my notes together in the town of Jerez de los Caballeros, where we found our-selves staying in a large rambling hotel with virtually no furniture, which had been built into the old city walls. Parts of the hotel seemed like a conservatory, other parts like an old-fashioned hospital ward, and the rest was a succession of big square rooms with the plaster flaking off, leading out of one another. A group of women in black, who sat side by side on bentwood chairs knitting, told us that the hotel was for sale, and for very little money, and, having arrived at midday, we had already, by the time darkness fell, formed the idea of buying the hotel, throwing out the iron bedsteads, reducing it to the seventeenth-century palace that formed its core, and living in it. In the evening we went out to look for a restaurant, and we walked in vain through the ill-lit streets, with mosquitoes clinging to the yellow light bulbs high above our heads, but we were either too late or too early, and only the chemist shops seemed to be open. In desperation we stopped a man, and asked him where we could eat. He said that he would accompany us to a place where, despite its looks, we would eat well, and, as he walked along by our side, he offered to collect us the next morning at our hotel, and to drive us through the countryside to visit some friends who had a big farm, and made their own sausages.

At the appointed time, our new friend arrived, and we set off through the narrow, winding roads of southern Estremadura. We drove through groves of cork and olive, from which, from time to time, a giant pig, red or black, would erupt from the shade, and crash against the wall or hedgerow that protected us from him: we drove past fields of the palest Brueghel yellow, where mules winnowed the corn: we drove across stark hillsides and through dry valleys, and we watched herds of bulls, bred for the bullring, wandering with their females, and, all the while, our driver, who turned out to be the kindest of men, humoured the fantasy that we would buy the hotel, and live in his town, and he kept on saying, "*Vous seriez les bienvenus ici*. You would soon meet two or three couples of your age, and you would find yourself part of the family."

It was the last word that came at me out of the blue, and, though I recognized the sound, nevertheless, for a second, for two seconds, I had not the slightest idea of what he was trying to tell me, or of what unexpected threat lay concealed in his sugary words. He was saying it again, "You would find yourself part of the family." – The sentence was still dying on the air when I pulled myself together, and, at the age of fifty-six, felt ashamed, ashamed for the momentary incomprehension for which so much had prepared me.

CHAPTER THREE

Love and Fear

Again I start with a memory. It turns up like the card in a card trick, so that, cut the pack, and it magically rises to the top, crisp and fresh as if it had been newly printed. The memory takes me back to a seaside holiday, and it must date from my sixth or possibly my seventh year.

For as long as my parents still went on holiday together, which ended around this period, there was nothing unusual in the fact that I should have been sent off with my nanny to stay in what was called a Board Residence in a seaside town on the south coast. The first two or three weeks of the holiday were divided between long periods of routine and brief moments of terror, with, I am sure, some pleasure in the middle. I call the parts "pleasure", "terror", and "routine" to mark the fact that for me in those years routine too was a kind of emotion.

Routine was established by the strict alternation of meals and walks throughout the hours of daylight. The table at which we ate breakfast was piled up with boxes of Shredded Wheat, and Force, and Corn Flakes: high tea was eaten while the sun was still elevated, and there was shepherd's pie, or rissoles, or fried plaice, followed by stewed fruit with custard or junket sprinkled with powdered nutmeg, and, on the sideboard, there were large Victoria plums with their skins marked by tiny mounds of yellow, deposited, or so I took them to be, by wasps. We had to eat our lunch out. If it was fine, the day between breakfast and high tea was measured out in walks: there was the walk to the beach, or the walk along the front, or the walk to the bandstand, where we sat on penny chairs and listened to the band of the Royal Marines, or, when luck was in, there was the walk on to the pier, and, on Sundays, there was the walk to church when I was required to regulate my pace to the intonation of an unfamiliar bell. I was frightened of a church that I did not know, for I feared that, at some point in the sermon, the clergyman might shake his arms free of his surplice, and, leaning over the side of the pulpit, in strange nasal accents harangue the congregation on the perils of hellfire. I would overhear what I did not want to hear. Then I visualised him, exhausted from the excitement, walking back to a bleak lunch, so different from my father's life.

Walks were sometimes enlivened by a form of manhunt, which was organized by one or other of the popular newspapers. Holidaymakers at specific seaside resorts, which rotated, were informed at the beginning of the week that, over the next few days, a man wearing such and such a sports jacket, and such and such a cloth cap, and answering to a certain broad physical description, could be seen loitering along the front, or on the pier, and anyone who had bought a copy of that day's paper, and thought he had spotted the mystery man, could go up to him, and, displaying the paper, challenge him, and, if right, would collect a reward. I never did this, nor wanted to do it, partly because I was frightened of a rebuff, and partly because I hated the way the crisp smell of the newspaper, even more of two newspapers, his and mine, would drift into my nose. Nevertheless knowledge of the chase lent excitement to daily life, and I wondered what kind of man it would be who would undertake to do this. Did a mystery man become something of a mystery to himself? I remember hearing the dismal phrase, "It's only a job," and I wondered what that explained.

Meanwhile the summer might be disrupted by another, graver, kind of manhunt, which swept holiday towns at the height of the season. A decapitated body, generally of a young girl with painted fingernails, would be found in a suitcase, abandoned in the Left Luggage office of a seaside railway station. A new series of "trunk murders" had begun. In no time a famous pathologist, the son of another famous pathologist, like Pierrepont the hangman, who was the son of another Pierrepont the hangman, had cut short his holiday, and visited the scene of the crime.

When the weather turned bad, and scudding squalls swept through the town, and mystery men stayed indoors, our walk turned into a race from one ornate shelter to another. For brief spells I was made to sit on the wet, slatted benches, restlessly knocking the heel of one gumboot against the toe of the other, waiting for the wind to drop, or staring far out to sea at the smudged horizon for signs that the rain was slackening. As I screwed up my eyes, putting on what were called my "weather eyes", people told me that I looked like an old sailor, which I took to show how readily a new life, someone else's life, could be assumed. If the bad

weather persisted, we were allowed to go back to the boarding house at three o'clock rather than the usual four, though
not a minute earlier. The elderly owner of the house, who
wore her hair in a grey, unwashed bun, needed the time to
herself in order to clean the rooms, to make the beds, to do
the cooking, and, above all, to rest, or, as she put it, to "rest
her limbs". She withdrew to her room, and lay down under
the religious prints in her grubby black clothes. She made it
clear to us that, if we did not like the terms, and she had
noted down, as she always did, on the pad by the telephone,
that my mother, in making the booking, had agreed to
them, we should not have come, she could always fill her
house with people who would accept them, and they were
clear enough: no one in the house between half past nine in
the morning and four o'clock in the afternoon. When we
did return early on wet days, the pervasive smell of rubber,
which I had lived with all day, abated, and was replaced by
the smell of old paper and, here and there, where the floorboards creaked, of sodden carpet.

Pleasure erupted into my life when fine weather allowed
me to arrive on the pier, and I was allowed to walk up and
down the row of black and silver boxes, which were
arranged along the boardwalk, until I chose the peepshow I
wanted to see, and for this I was allowed to divert a penny
from the buying of a comic. There, I believe,
peepshows for all tastes, and there might have been some
that were unsuitable for children, but I did not spare a
thought for them because I was interested solely in the
historical dramas, and supreme amongst them was the trial
and execution of Mary, Queen of Scots, in the great hall of
Fotheringay Castle. The momentous event, the inevitability

of which was conveyed in a way that no history book could rival, unfolded in distinct tableaux, in the third and last of which Mary, who had already faced her accusers, and had said farewell to her ladies-in-waiting, was found kneeling with her neck on the block. At a signal from the man with the long auburn beard, who was the sovereign's emissary, the masked executioner stepped forward, the axe rose and fell, and the head rolled. The great portcullis descended, and then there was a click, and the scene went dark. By the time the next person stepped up to the box, and another penny dropped, and the portcullis rose on the first tableau, the head was back on the young queen's shoulders, and she was ready to meet her stern tormentors once again, to pit in vain her beauty and her freshness against their heavy, grown-up authority. Sometimes, amidst the protests of my nanny – "Isn't it a waste of money?" "Isn't there something you'd rather spend your money on?" "You won't be able to sleep to night" – I would insist on watching the drama a second time through, for I needed to know that Mary could have life restored to her, even if only to lose it again, and as pathetically. I deeply resented the presence of the holiday-makers standing behind me, looking over my shoulder, waiting for their turn, but I told myself that they could not take anything from me, because, while they were con-demned to stay put amongst the crowd on the pier, eating ice cream or candyfloss, breathing in the salt air, listening to the waves lapping at the metal struts below, wrapped in noisy laughter, I could, through the power of con-centration, slip out of the present and escape back down the centuries to the scene of death and a woman's courage. Such experiences were what I meant by a holiday.

I try now, through the mists of time, to make out the precise tugs of sympathy that the death-scene of Mary, Queen of Scots, animated within me. As far as the central drama was concerned, I was wholly on the side of Mary, and wholly against Elizabeth. Elizabeth was, over the years of childhood, a recurrent figure of loathing, occupying a place in my historical animosities on a par with that later to be filled by Churchill. I had my reasons. First, she was a patriot. Secondly, as I was to learn from various novels, she was an enemy of love, and she oppressed it and its faithful devotees whenever she could: one victim of her destructive rage was the impetuous Essex, another Amy Robsart, who was later to become a favourite of mine. But, worst of all, there was the permanent imputation, never properly laid to rest, that the Virgin Queen was a man. But, if between Mary and Elizabeth my loyalties were clear enough, and, if, as far as Mary herself was concerned, it was my deepest loyalties that were engaged, what to think about the executioner caused me great turmoil. It was easy to think of him as the agent of badness, and there was some strand in my religious thinking that led me to entertain such thoughts only too readily. But I did not like this harsh way of thinking, and, in this particular case, I saw the man who wielded the axe as himself a victim, a victim indeed of that fate which claimed the young queen as another victim. And that he should live to see another day, whereas she could not, was not so obvious an advantage since, as every new penny proved, the day that he lived to see was only another day on which he was obliged to take a life: and whether it was another life, or the same life another time, was immaterial.

Terror, the third emotion of the holiday, for the most

part held at bay during the hours of daylight by sheer forgetfulness, set in as the daily routine wound down, and I had said my prayers, and been settled into bed, for, physically alone at last, I would be caught unawares by the sudden sight, through the net curtains, and over the slate roofs, of the stubby, grey gasometer, which, as summer progressed, grew larger and larger inside its metal frame. If it reached the top ring of the frame, it would, I had been assured in the car on the way down, explode, and, if it did, it would carry everything away with it: the little houses, and the corner shops with their supplies of comics and boiled sweets and cheap fishing-lines, and the giant cats who slept on the garden walls, and the men in overalls who walked the gangways of the frame, checking pressure gauges and tightening screws with gigantic spanners.

In the third week or so of the holiday, my father and mother came down for a few days, bringing with them, I think, my brother, and they stayed in the big hotel on the esplanade. It is to this moment that the memory I have in mind belongs. Every morning I would be brought round to the hotel by my nanny to have breakfast with my father in the large dining room, with its smell of toast melba, and its ample view through the curved plate-glass window over the English Channel, while my mother remained upstairs in her room. My father, who was waiting for me downstairs, dressed and scented, kissed me as I arrived, and, no sooner had we sat down to table than he invariably found something to complain about. He complained that the coffee

cold, or that the plates had not been warmed, or that
hotel did not know how to cook stewed apple as he
d it: the apples unpeeled and with the cores left in, no
r added, then sieved, and chilled. The manager would
e out and apologise, and my father would explain that
idn't want apologies. To me he wondered out aloud
re the manager had received his training: I fell upon the
sion to hear more place names.

fter breakfast I would spend some time with my mother
the beach. On this particular holiday my mother had
ught with her a friend, Peggy L, a young, dark-haired
man, with pretty eyes, and a small beauty spot on her
er lip, and whose husband was briefly in prison. She was
ass widow.

n the morning of the memory, the three of us, or, if in
my brother was with us, the four of us, had been in the
zing sea, and we came out, and clambered up the beach
vering. The sharp pebbles cut into the soles of my feet
ough the rubber bathing-slippers that I wore. In the pre-
ing weeks, when I had been alone on the beach with my
nanny, I had been expected to change with a towel held in
front of me, sheltering against one of the breakwaters, those
glorious wooden constructions, with their oversized nuts
and bolts covered with rust and seaweed, which for me had
all the grandeur of medieval fortifications. However, for the
few days that my parents were staying, we had rented a
small bathing-hut, which the light entered through a row of
holes drilled at regular intervals into the wood near the
ceiling. It was furnished with a narrow bench, and some
coat-hooks, and only a series of narrow slats raised the floor
above the level of the beach. With some assistance I

struggled out of my wet bathing-suit, and, as it was peeled down over my bottom, the sand, reinforced with fine shingle, was rubbed into my skin. Since my mother was unavailable, which does much to suggest that my brother was indeed there and with first call on her attention, Peggy was asked to dry me. I stood facing her, and raised my arms, as I knew to do when I got out of the bath at home and my nanny dried me. Peggy exchanged a look with my mother, looks changed to a quick smile, and, in my childhood, smiles – quick, amused smiles – did much work in telling me when, when and how, I had done wrong. I looked from one grown-up to the other, and it was Peggy, not my mother, who twisted her hand in the air to let me know that I should turn round. I did, and now smiles turned to laughter, and words, a few broken phrases, filled out the lesson that I was in the course of receiving, "A young gentleman", "At your age", "And a lady". She added with a special laugh, "You'll need to know such things." I kept my arms up as I turned round, and I took the feel of the rough, striped towel on my skin to be a mild, unspoken punishment for being a boy. It was about this time that my brother and I pretended that arms raised as we were dried was the same gesture as arms raised in total surrender. I was ready to learn that, just as pleasure is to be paid for in boredom, so the price of love is fear.

⁓

I have already written that it was many years after those visits backstage with my father that I first brushed against a woman's body.

It was in the late autumn of 1941, at 6 Oriel Street, Oxford, about six o'clock on a Sunday evening, in the rooms of an elegant young man with a pleasant drawling voice and pebble spectacles, worldly, famously avid for any piece of gossip about his friends and acquaintances, which he invariably greeted by throwing back his head and letting out a long, silent laugh, a series of sudden intakes of breath. Nephew of the Chief of the Imperial General Staff, who was a severe Ulsterman, VB was a pacifist, a convert to Rome, and soon to become a monk in a secluded order. In his first-floor set of rooms, the heavy brocade curtains were drawn against the encroaching mists, which, as we could see through the cracks, clung to the lamp posts and the medieval gargoyles across the street. Four candles were burning in the room where we sat, and on the gramophone a light tenor voice sang Italian songs, with their delicate defiance of the war. Two of the other young men, wearing, as many of us did in those days, large velvet ties, made by a local shirt-maker, began to take a furtive interest in each other. I was sitting on the arm of a chair, and in the chair was a girl to whom I had been talking over tea. I had never seen her until an hour or so before. She had strong features, which I could now scarcely make out in the growing darkness, an assured laugh, and a firmly made-up mouth. Our voices, hers and mine, started to trail off, mine through fear, which I thought augured well, and she was staring into the fire, in front of which, a short time before, we had craned forward to toast crumpets. Our heads came closer, and she leant back, I thought compliantly, and I ran my nose through her hair. She did not respond, but neither did she move her head away. At first I had no intention of repeating the gesture, yet I did not want the moment to end. This was, I found myself thinking, my last chance in life. I ran my nose through her hair again, and half-held my breath. Eventually someone must have suggested that it was time for dinner, and, since I had no money, I left the others, and went off to dine in College.

I saw Elizabeth a few times after that, and I have no recollection whether I ever repeated my advances, or whether she ever showed that she had noticed them, or whether this is how she would have described my behaviour. I suspect that the answer to all three questions is No. Once, when I was in the army, I took her to lunch at the Causerie at Claridges, where for 5 shillings it was possible to eat as much as one wanted. Later, by which time the war was over, I rang her up, and got the mad Lady L, who was either Elizabeth's mother or her stepmother, a situation which was left unclarified by Lord L. Lady L said that Elizabeth was serving in Germany, and that, in due course, she, Lady L, would write to me, and ask me to dinner, which she did. We dined at a Polish officers' club in Princes Gate. We got on well, though I do not know how, and, at the end of dinner, she pushed her face into mine, and I heard her say, "I do not mind what you say to people about our friendship, you are a young man, you are bound to talk, you will talk, but there is one thing you must promise me you will never say, and that is that Violet L is the sanest person you know." She also made me promise that in future, if I wrote to her, I would always date my letters. It was a sign of having been well brought up. She said that, whenever I liked, I could stay in her flat, which was in a large mansion block off Bryanston Square, and was occupied only by a maid. I did stay there once, possibly twice, but, though I was touched by the generosity of the gesture, I found the experience unnerving. Lady L was a well-known shoplifter, but was virtually immune from prosecution because she was a close friend of the then Queen Mother. Every unoccupied inch of floor, behind the doors, in between the large oatmeal-coloured sofas, under the round library table, in the folds of the enormous coromandel screens, was piled high with books commandeered from Bumpus, or Hatchards, or Heywood Hill. I never saw Elizabeth again.

In 1943, when I was in the army, at an Officer Cadet Training Unit at Heysham, every Wednesday or Thursday night we would walk the two or three miles into Morecambe, and go to the dance in the Floral Hall. From about eight to midnight, several hundred men and women, nearly all in uniform, were packed in under a pink and gold

dome, and wandered round in a haze, searching for a partner. I danced badly, and I was convinced that I alone of everyone under the great dome could think of nothing to say when the music stopped. In my nervousness to find a partner, I often asked first and looked later, and thus came to regret my choice. Then one night I found myself dancing with a tall uniformed girl, pretty in a heavyset way, with big lips. As we sat in the smoke-filled bar, drinking gin and lime, I discovered that she also came from suburban Surrey. She talked to me of her father and her mother and her brother, and revealed a simpler, fuller, life than anything I had ever known, replete with friends, and dogs, and parties, and the tennis club, and her own pony, and skiing holidays before the war. I had some knowledge, mostly from out of the backseat of the car, but also from the one time that I had taken my dog there for a walk, not daring to let him off the lead, of the expanse of heather and gorse and blackberry bush that she could have seen from her bedroom window every morning, and which was where she used to ride her pony, and I found myself, in distant wartime Lancashire, trying to pretend that my life had been much more like hers than it was. She believed me, clearly finding it difficult to think that anyone had not led a life exactly like hers. After the band played "God Save the King", and the whole hall had stood to attention, the two of us went out into the blackout, and walked along the front, where in the darkness I could hear the sea like a great monster gathering force to wash over the road. For a moment I paused, and she turned through a right angle, and was leaning back against the wall of a building, and pulling me towards her. I was facing her. "I do want to," she said, as though I had asked her something, "But I can't." She pulled me tighter against her. "Can't you feel the swelling? Down there." I was uncertain whether I really understood her. Her breath was hot, the breath of a grown woman, which I had not expected. I could hear in her voice an aching desperation I had never heard before, and I never thought that, the first time I heard it, it would be so close to my own ear. Inside her tight Air Force uniform, her breasts rose and fell. "Next time it'll be all right," she said. I said that I would be there next week, and, having said goodbye, I walked home through the pitch dark, listening to the waves beyond the bungalows as they crashed on the beach, and I felt that some miracle had happened to me. Life had moved very fast, and then the week to come moved very slowly. However, on the night of the next dance, I was C.B., "confined to barracks", for sloppiness on parade. We had had to parade in full battle order, and, before falling in, I had, at the last minute, loosened my belt, and the half inch of webbing that was thus exposed had not been blancoed. The following week, I went looking for her, but she was not to be seen, nor, as I went from one WAAF to another, could anyone give me news of her. I came, somewhat prematurely perhaps, to the conclusion that she had found it difficult to form friendships in the ranks, and that, if only we could have met again, I would have rectified this for her, but the truth is that, though I could readily enough identify her self-confident, easy-going manner for what it was, and could place it, it was, as far as my actual acquaintance of life was concerned, as unfamiliar to me as it must have been to her fellow-conscripts.

Around this time I gave up going to the Floral Hall.

Training got increasingly arduous, the arches of my feet once again began to hurt, and I did not really like the routine of the dance floor. I was apprehensive of the greedy looks, given and taken, which served as introductions. It, the whole thing, was something for which I was too little prepared, and the trains of thought that ran through my mind in rapid succession amazed me with their absurdity. I never believed that any girl wanted me, but I was terrified of being entrapped. Desperate for the mere recognition of my existence, I felt that anyone I danced with completely owned me, both in her eyes and, for the duration of the dance, in my eyes too. My feet were not free to dance as I would have liked them to, my mouth was not free to form the words I wanted to utter, my eyes were not my own to turn in whatever direction they were drawn. My only desire was to please the girl I was with, but, inside the body which my arm lightly, gently, encircled, I could feel waves of scorn rising and crashing against the ribcage.

Looking back on those evenings, I find one thing that delighted me, and that was the sudden, poignant moments when a group of girls, fifteen or twenty of them, irritated either with the attention they had received or with the lack of it, fed up with the flirtatiousness that was first expected of them and then resented, banded together in a great anarchic ring. Girls of a seventeenth-century prettiness, and girls with dark, angry blotches spreading across their faces, and little nondescript girls levered out of their fathers' corner shops and now with corporals' stripes on their sleeves, put their arms around each others' waists, and swept round the floor in a large, defiant circle, kicking up their legs, their high, sing-song voices breaking out into a chorus of "Run, rabbit, run", or "We're going to hang out the washing on the Siegfried Line", or "Pack up your troubles in your old kitbag", the cracked vowels rising up into the ceiling, and then, when they could bear it all no longer, the conspicuousness, the isolation, the dependence on each other, they dissolved in laughter, and slowly merged back into the vast supply of complacent partners. And all the while I lived with this terrible premonition: that, were a girl in uniform, through what I recognized would have been an act of random kindness on her part, actually to have taken upon herself to initiate me into the pleasures of upright sexuality, fully dressed, one eye kept open for the military police, the cries of soldiers revelling in the distance, the rough salt air blowing off the Irish sea, I would have responded by falling so desperately in love with her that, as likely as not, my feeble sense of what being a soldier required of me would have crumbled, and the next night, and the next night, and the night after that, would have seen me standing under her window, a common deserter, shouting out her name through my tears.

It was some time in the autumn of 1943, or in the spring of 1944, that I lost my virginity. It is a not unusual story, but I have told it only once, one warm night in the early 1990s, when I was staying alone with IB in Oxford, and we were sitting up after dinner in a room scented with the smell of hyacinths. Every half-hour or so, we took it in turns to say that it was time to go to bed, as we had for more than forty-five years, but we did not move. He was dressed in a thick tweed suit with a waistcoat, and a fawn-coloured cardigan over the waistcoat, and, as the hour hand came close to two, we quite unexpectedly broached the subject of our first sexual encounters. "When did you lose your virginity?" I heard him ask me. I told him in outline the following story, but, when it came to his turn, he stared up at one of the corners where two walls met the ceiling, as he used to do when he stood on the rostrum and the words poured out towards his audience in a magical flow, he pursed his lips, and he said only how old he was at the time. "Very late," he added, "very late indeed. But there it is." And in that "There it is," he put all that deep acceptance of life, which started from the acceptance of himself, and which made his friendship so sublime. As to the conversation between us, I suspect that we both put into it, and, for that matter, got out of it, precisely what we wanted, what we needed, that spring night.

It had all happened, I told him, a mere two or three years before he and I first met, and I was by this time an officer, stationed at Hythe, and I managed to get to London fairly regularly, and I would stay with my close friend JR. A certain kind of evening, which J half-organized, half-improvised, from out of his already vast circle of friends, invariably ensued: amusing, filled with young effete officers from the Brigade of Guards, and middle-aged aesthetes, and druggy women in dark glasses, people coming and going as we moved through the blackout from one night club to another, The Nut House, The Caribbean, The Four Hundred, The White Room, The Romilly Club. But such evenings, for all their radiance, were for me ultimately frustrating. I had put one foot into the stream of life, but how about the other foot? Everyone around me owed their glamour to the fact that they kept theirs permanently submerged in the water. Accordingly, on this occasion I was determined to tell no one of my visit, and to see no one I knew. I packed a small bag, put into it a volume of Proust, which I had just started, walked down to the station, caught a stopping train, and found myself in Piccadilly in the blackout close to midnight. The streets were crowded with fast-moving anonymous bodies. I walked round and round, along Piccadilly, through the backstreets, past the Regent Palace Hotel, across Regent Street, down Swallow Street, back to Piccadilly, then round and round again. I passed the same unlit shop-fronts five, ten, fifteen times. At least two hours had passed, and I could tell that a kind of dreaded squeamishness was entering into me, which foretold a lonely end to the night. It was just as I was thinking this thought that I paused, exhausted, outside the great ornamental portico of the Piccadilly Hotel, and I found myself approached by a young girl in a brief belted coat. I could see, by the light of the match that I covertly struck for her, that she was pretty, short with curly fair hair, and a somewhat blurred poetry around the eyes. She was dressed in blue. I could also see that she was nervous. She suggested that I follow her back to her flat, which was off Orchard Street. I asked her if she would go ahead, and, as I followed her, the street stretching out before us, here and there broken up by low walls of sandbags, I felt inordinately proud and free, and it was only after she had fumbled for her keys, and opened the front door, and gone up the steep flight of stairs, and told me not to make any noise and to avoid the creaking stair, and had got me into the warmed flat with the gas fire that had been left burning, and had shut the flimsy door behind me, that I felt myself her prisoner. She had gone out into the wild streets of wartime

London to capture me. My freedom had suddenly evaporated, and I felt a little sick. For the first time, I noticed quite how pretty, and quite how nervous, she was. She was French, she was nineteen, and she had, she told me, a brother in the Free French navy. As I was slowly undressing, struggling with my Sam Browne, she picked up a silver-framed photograph from the dressing table, and, giving it a quick kiss, put one knee on the bed, and passed it to me. It showed a very good-looking young man who was wearing a sailor's uniform, and so, in her own way, I now saw, was she. She started to cry, and I told her that, if she liked, she could forget what I had come for, and I would pay her all the same. She dismissed the idea: it would bring bad luck, she said, and I believe that now I cried. What happened on that bed I cannot remember, but a frontier, an undefended frontier, was rapidly crossed. When I was once again outside in the blackout, I was overcome by her sweetness, and I might have gone back, had the thought not suddenly struck me that perhaps her brother lived in the flat, and that she was already in his arms. Then the sense of reality broke in. I hailed a taxi and got it to take me to the Russell Square Hotel, and I went to the Turkish baths, which were about four floors down. On every floor there was a strange damp echo thudding through the tiled halls, and now and again there was the silent apparition of a bald-headed man in a white towelling dressing gown. I rented a cubicle, about which I remember only the enormous size of the key, and I lay down to sleep, but I couldn't. I passed the night with a high fever, travelling through strange, lurid nightmares. In my lucid moments, I thought of the young French girl's total charm of appearance, her modesty, and the dreams that must by now have passed behind her eye-lids. I wondered how many clients she had already told to avoid the creaking stair, and whether she still remembered me. In that moment I knew that what I wanted, and wanted inordinately, was, not so much to have her, though I also wanted that, as to be her.

Each time I recall the event, what is brought back to me with painful vividness is an alternation of mood from which I have never learnt to escape altogether, and to which I readily fall victim on autumnal nights and spring evenings: fierce, overbearing loneliness giving way to a suffocating togetherness, the two separated by no more than the shutting or the opening of a front door, or the climbing of a staircase, or just the turning of a key in an innocent enough lock.

Readers who recognize the contrast on which the penultimate paragraph ended, "to be" against "to have", something which, along with other things, I left out of the story as I told it to IB, are likely to think that it is only with hindsight, and more, that I am able to formulate the distinction, let alone apply it to my twenty-year-old self and its urgent, tangled desires. That may well be true, but it does not mean that there was not, at the time, some form that my desires had taken on, some shape that their many baffled attempts upon reality had conferred upon them, some kind of incipient articulation, that justifies the solecism. Of course, in reconstructing my first conception of love and its kinds, I cannot hope to sort out the contributions of infancy, childhood, and early adolescence. I can only say that, when the many different things that I learnt from my frightened experience of the body, from long hours of reading the great poets and novelists, and from much solitary day-dreaming, were ready to come together, they did so with a sense of fatality. They came together with a crash. Fifty, sixty, seventy, years later, I take them apart only with diffidence.

I start with what was for many early years the most recalcitrant of problems, even though, before my eyes, grown-ups with no particular skills dealt on a daily basis with its practical implications as though they presented no difficulties. This was the distinction between the sexes, and the difference in which it was grounded, and, in saying that grown-ups appeared to find no difficulties with it, I have in mind the obvious fact that men and women of the most ordinary sort can, seemingly without any special powers, tell each other apart, and respond accordingly. They pair off, linking themselves by special bonds of affection: sometimes, if the story tellers and poets are to be believed, they fall in love at first sight. No account of the difference between the sexes could be right if it made something, which in fact is easy, seem difficult, indeed difficult beyond belief, but what account made things come out as they actually are?

From an early age, or at least early enough for me to have understood Peggy L's gesture as she twisted her finger in the air, I was aware that, between my legs, I had an appendage, which was, or would eventually be, of interest and concern. It was also an object of considerable fragility, for, when its lower protuberance was touched by chance, or flicked by a finger, or I merely thought of such things, it set up shudders throughout my whole frame that could not be stilled for some minutes. Years later I recall the tremor that could not be disguised when, in class, we read the great *Adonais* poem of Catullus with its gory epic of self-mutilation: I shivered, and could not stop. I never ceased to wonder how anyone could be a surgeon, or even a doctor.

I had learnt of this object largely in the bath, and in two distinct ways: from the outside, and also from the inside. I had observed the object with my eyes, through the slats of the soap tray, which, once I had got into the bath, my nanny would move from behind my head and place modestly over the middle part of my body, and I had also experienced it directly when, for instance, the bath water was allowed to grow cold, and my thoughts turned in an historical direction, and strange tingling sensations made it their home, rather like bees swarming in a beehive. However if, about the same time, I came to accept the fact that girls, that women, that the opposite sex, did not have this object, I still rejected the view that this anatomical difference was the difference I was after. It could not be, because it could not explain what happens in those moments before love arrives, before even attraction sets in, but upon which both love and attraction depend, such as when, in a crowded, smoke-filled hall, or across a grill-room, or at a bus queue, a woman notices a man, she notices that he is a man, or when, as I was made aware, not only through the print over my bed, but also through a large book I had been given, with pieces of tissue paper over the illustrations, a man, once upon a time, upon a bridge in Florence, saw a woman, and knew it. Unless I was

singularly unobservant, and, as a child, I was more usually
accused of the opposite, or unless, which was as unlikely, it
was a skill that the eyes acquired only with maturity, the
presence of the penis was not something perceptible, at least
in the middle distance, or through adequately cut clothes.
Was not this some large part of the lesson that I learnt from
my father on those bright, scented mornings when he
turned away from me to pull his shirt tail between his legs,
and carefully splay it out, and then turned back to face me,
by which time the thick fold had been secured by his but-
toning his silk underpants tight across his stomach, and I
could admire the thoroughness of his workmanship? In the
case of the young girls standing around in milk bars in their
semi-transparent skirts, or of the old, broken-down man
slouched outside the pub with his distinctive smell, it was
perhaps different, these things were perceptible, but, in
what I was somewhat encouraged to think of as ordinary
social life, where staring was said to be unacceptable –
though there was little in the way the people whom I saw
behaved to confirm this – the appendage could not conceivably ground the big distinction, on which unimportant,
as well as important, things seemed to turn, such as who
paid the bills, or the length of one's hair, or whether it was
necessary to take a job. The matters that the appendage
could account for were minor, such as that women urinated
differently from men, or perhaps did not urinate at all, but
this pointed, not to the real difference between men and
women, but to the superiority of women over men, which
I took for granted.

If the penis did not differentiate the sexes, I could think
of other views of the matter, of other anatomical views of

the matter, and also of one that made no reference to anatomy.

One view was that the difference was facial. Men had one set of features, women another, and that by which they were commonly told apart was what in effect made them different. It was a view with the merit of obviousness, but very early on I had learnt a lesson, which cautioned me against obviousness. It was the Christmas Eve of my fourth year, and the bed next to me was occupied, not, as normally, by my nanny, but by my brother. Around midnight, unable to go back to sleep, I saw a small hooded figure, with a long beard that had the consistency of the cotton wool with which my ears and nose were regularly cleaned, approach the foot of my bed carrying a stocking, but, noticing some movement on my part, it commanded me to go to sleep, which I was expected to obey without paying attention to the words used. I said sleepily, but so that my brother over-heard it, "Sounds like Nanny's voice." It was the obvious thing to say. Next day, though it was Christmas Day, I was made to notice the chill in the air: I was held to have corrupted my less free-thinking brother, who was not ready for such ideas. The following Christmas, on the suggestion of my father, who seldom intervened in such matters, I was given a large beaker of warmed Beaujolais, so that I would sleep the deep sleep of oblivion in which the obvious would be swallowed up, and so for every later Christmas.

In point of fact, I came, in due course, to see that the view that sexual difference lay in the face was not as obvious as I first thought. Often on long spring or summer evenings, having stayed up later than usual with my parents' friends waiting for dusk to fall, and then gone to bed, I would try to amuse myself, as their voices continued to drift up to me from the garden, by conjuring up their faces in detail. As I did so, I would concentrate on, say, a man's face, and then ask myself whether, holding it clear in the mind's eye, I could, in a series of steps, each involving no more than a visible change in the facial features, pass from it to a woman's face, that is, to any woman's face, and then I would try it on the other way round. But, lying awake long after the voices under my window had vanished, and I was left only with images in the head, I had to conclude that, either way round, the answer was a clear No. How to start – that was easy enough. If the move was from a man's face to a woman's, what was demanded was an initial lightening of the features, if the move was from a woman's face to a man's, there had to be a corresponding coarsening of the features. But how to go on was the problem. For it was possible for a man's face to achieve real lightness, a woman's face to be thoroughly coarsened, and yet for both to remain within its original sex. There was some aura that this view overlooked. Not even God could, with just the face and a surgeon's knife at his disposal, change a man into a woman, or a woman into a man.

Of the other views about what distinguished men and women, two, both anatomical, went too deep into the formation of the body for the comfort of a little boy, even in the darkness of his narrow bed.

One view was that women were made women by the swelling of the breasts, and men were men by default. I was loath to give the breasts such importance. My knowledge of the female breasts derived from the few occasions when my grandmother came to stay, and I was made to share my bedroom with her. For, as she dressed in the morning, despite the protection given her by a screen covered with pictures from nursery rhymes, I saw her wiggle her breasts into her stays, and, later in the day, I recruited my brother into a rare act of masculine conspiracy, when I got him to agree with me in comparing her breasts to torpedoes that might, when ammunition ran short, get shovelled into the breach of an enormous cannon, or (a word I liked) a howitzer, and then sent screaming through the sky into the enemy lines. The unattractiveness of the breasts was not conclusive against their determining sexuality, but it surely was against their demarcating the beautiful sex.

The other view stressed the bottom, and not so much the shape of the bottom as its responsiveness to pain, and also to pleasure. This view fitted in with observations, made or imagined, that a woman would never naturally put this part of her body, except out of bravado, to some of the uses that were normal amongst men, such as riding a bicycle, or wearing clothes tight around the lower body. And further there was what I took to be the timeless fact that girls, even in the strictest households, were by and large exempt from a form of chastisement regularly and immemorially – though never in my case – applied to boys. At Burwood Park School, I was severely shaken one morning when Diana, a twin, arrived in a state of extreme distress, and, not able to keep back her tears, described to a mystified audience, which quickly gathered in a circle around her, how, immediately after breakfast, which was only three-quarters of an hour ago, her father, whom we all knew as a good-looking, dapper man, had used a fine cane on her bottom for the telling of a lie, and then, breaking off to catch a train, had promised her a continuation that evening. What baffled me most was how, once the punishment was thought appropriate, no time was lost administering it. How, in a house where there were only daughters, was there a cane to hand? Had it been borrowed from the house next door as a special favour, or had it been bought before the sex of the children was known? Or did it go further back still, say to the months before the young couple got married, when, for once putting aside the light-hearted tone that came to them naturally, they settled down in front of the fire to a larger conversation about their deepest needs and wishes: they talked about where they would live, and the kind of house they would have, and how they would bring up their children, and suddenly, from one moment to the next, they were discussing the one great temptation to which, as God-fearing parents, they would never give way, which was that of spoiling the offspring of their loins, and it was to make certain that this would never happen, even inadvertently, that, with a quick exchange of glances, one or other picked up a fountain pen, and added a cane to the Wedding Present List?

The view of sexual difference with which this story engaged in such a disturbing fashion was to some degree confirmed for me by a passage in a book, which had already seduced me with its crisp, sparkling prose, and I was not ready to believe that something so dedicated to beauty would want to lead me astray on a matter no less important than beauty. The book was *The Black Arrow*, and I loved it for the way there seemed to blow through its pages the light winds of the English counties, which I could imagine rippling the surface of some osier-fringed stream as it meandered through water meadows and between low pollarded willows. The passage in question comes fairly soon after a description of how the clouds are reflected in water as "crumbs of smiling blue", and it tells how the honest yeoman, who has just escaped from the castle of his Yorkist enemy through the courage and assistance of a young companion, starts to query the sex of his rescuer. The boy's clothes that the rescuer wears do not altogether convince him, and now he thinks of a trial that will, and, in a flash, he has undone his leather belt, pulled it out of the loops, ordered his companion to bend over a nearby tree trunk, and, without troubling to improvise an excuse, he sets about whipping the exposed bottom. Momentarily the victim is taken aback by this turn of events, but no more than I was by reading of it, and what impressed me was that, apart from a leap into the air at the first lash of the belt, and then a question asked about what kind of gratitude this is, nothing was given away. I do not remember how the young yeoman dealt with his suspicions.

The substitution of either of these more private parts of the body for the face as the mark that distinguished men and women gave to sexuality a curious vagabond quality, wandering fitfully through the body, and I noticed that, as I started to insert this sentiment into the labyrinthine stories that I told my governess on our walks along the leafy streets and avenues of the neighbourhood, the disturbing effect that these stories had, if not upon her, which I could not determine, then upon myself, increased. A familiar figure in many of these anecdotes was the wily courtier who, foregoing, at least initially, any direct advantage, undertook to find companions whose liveliness in the royal four-poster, the *lit carré*, would bring pleasure to his royal master, and ultimately credit, and thus, in the fullness of time, reward, to his faithful servant. I now know that, in the telling of these stories, I was explicit beyond my years about the significance that the artful pander attached to the different parts of the female body as he pinched and pro-voked them. I vividly recall, from my twelfth year, an occasion when I was about to go to London to see a play, and, already dressed in my best clothes, I was, to my com-plete surprise, allowed out for ten minutes or so on my bicycle, and I must have been so exhilarated that I decided to spend these minutes telling myself a story about the selection of women for the bed of the young Edward VI, whom I had decided to think of as outwardly prim, but in fact totally lascivious, provided only that he didn't have to notice what his body was engaged in: so rich in anatomical detail was the story I told myself that, when I eventually fell off my bicycle in the heat of the excitement, and was sent sprawling across the road not more than twenty yards from our house, I chose to find the iodine that was poured directly out of the bottle on to the open wound on my right knee suitable retribution. As for the old courtier himself, I tried to soften his predatory nature by modelling his manner and his appearance on my father as I imagined him in some foreign opera house, craning forward over the edge of the box, and taking his gold pencil from out of the inside pocket of his dinner jacket to note down on the back of his programme the finer points of the singers whom he admired. To all the disclaimers that my father usually made to the effect that he derived no particular pleasure from music, to all the modesty that went into his insisting that he was in effect tone-deaf, but had a very good ear for certain features of the human voice, I gave a different meaning, and I never ceased to place total confidence in the skilled eye and ear with which he discerned qualities that, brought to Covent Garden and displayed for all to hear, would surely be greeted with rapturous applause, perhaps given a standing ovation, and all of this would contribute to the repute in which he was held.

A final view about the difference between the sexes, which abandoned anatomy altogether, held that we all carry around within us an inner voice, and this inner voice, which speaks as if from the outside, and always in the clearest accents, announces to each of us the sex to which we belong. In speaking to men, it adopts a tone of resignation as though our fate is a second-best fate which we had better get used to. It says something like, "Well, my boy, you're a man." But, when it talks to women, it addresses them with the soft lisp of flattery. The voice announces, "You are, my dear, my loved one," then a pause, then a crescendo, "a woman," in the tones appropriate to declaring the winner of the lottery.

What I liked about this view was that I seemed to have some direct evidence for it. I had myself heard such voices, at once comforting and belittling. Let me make clear that, as a child, I was totally averse to views that were not confirmed in experience. However, as a result of the kind of life that I lived as a child, and its solitariness, I found myself satisfied with what others would have barely regarded as confirmation. Being without companions, I was never reasoned out of any view before I adopted it, nor was I ever, once I had accepted a view, laughed out of it. Beauty, such

as the beauty of Stevenson's prose, encaged me in beliefs
that a child endowed with my degree of curiosity might
have been expected to reject, and it led me to read portents
in nature, of which I should have been sceptical. An
important belief in my childhood was the belief in
immortality, and evidence for it was precisely what I
thought I had when, on a summer morning, looking up
into the sky, I there saw a vast pyramidal mass of cloud, the
palest pink, the palest blue, the darkest cream, resting for its
base upon a row of diminutive fir trees, or upon the cut-out
edge of a corrugated iron fence, which then, turning round
and round upon itself, here and there overlaid with a veil-
like formation, which had the texture and the colour of
dark smoke, ascended into the heavens. For, in this strange
formation I saw with the greatest clarity a broad spiral staircase, its shallow steps edging their way upward, one by one,
towards the great portal, which itself remained far out of
sight, while, in the reverse direction, there was a downward
movement of long shafts of coloured light, pale lucid blue
and yellow, with here and there intrusions of rose and a
darkish orange. Scrambling up these stairs was a group of
figures, irregularly spread out, but never more than six or
seven visible at a time, their clothes billowing out around
them, and seen so much from below that it was impossible
to make out their faces or to tell whether they were on all-
fours, like penitents, or whether they were on their feet,
walking. The topmost figure, of whom little more was
visible than the dirty sole of a foot and a turning ankle, was,
even as I caught sight of him, about to disappear into the
heavenly tunnel, which constituted the last stage of his
journey to the giant terrace of Heaven, where he, luckier

than most of his contemporaries, would live for ever. To the
suggestion that I would never have seen any of this in the
sky if it had not been for my intense desire to do so, I could
reply that, in seeing what I wanted to see, I also had to
accept certain things that no one could want to concede.
For one thing that the great opera in the sky made clear was
that, of the many thousands who died every day, no more
than the handful whom I saw up there in the clouds ever
made their way to the life hereafter, and this was something
that no one could have wanted to accept for it must mean
that the God I believed in was a God far more vengeful than
anything I could have thought up in my darkest moments.

But I realized that the view of the inner voice as
annunciate of our sex could be no more than an account of
half the matter, for if it answered the question how we
know the sex to which we personally belong, it left un-
answerable the real question, of how we can tell the sex of
others. For who is to say that we hear their inner voices?

As a child, I certainly had my share of magical beliefs
about the transmission of thoughts, but each belief I had
concerned the commerce between myself and just one
other, and then only in favourable circumstances. So I
believed of Dr Barclay that, when he put on his ice-cold
stethoscope, and pressed the pad against my chest to hear
the many internal rumblings that wandered around inside
me, he could, if he chose to block out these noises, listen
instead to my innermost thoughts. Naturally there would
be a moment of recoil on his part as they reached him, and
his eyes would furtively seek out mine, but then he would
overcome his personal feelings, as a doctor must, and he
would in time become an archive of myself, each revelation

having its own special conditions of privacy affixed to it. Similarly, there was the possibility of a magical form of communication with my father, which, though dependent on very complex conditions, was likelier to bring some understanding between us than the means we usually relied upon. What was required was that I should go to the lavatory, urinate, and forget to pull the chain, that my father should follow me, not notice my oversight, and then inadvertently urinate on top of my urine, for then the fusion would, in an unobserved way, drag the whole of the contents of the lavatory bowl up into himself, finding a way up the very stream that flowed out of him, and it would get first into his body, then, through various dark channels, into his mind, and there, riding alongside my fluids, like the cavalry protecting a caravan of gold from the New World, would be all the wishes, all the fears, all the hopes, that I had unthinkingly expelled from myself when, leaning forward over the white pan, I had emptied my bladder. And finally there was the form of thought-transmission, which I dutifully took to be not only infallible, but inevitable, so that it barely called for a belief on my part, and that was when, kneeling by the side of my bed, bathed and powdered in talc, with my dressing gown tied neatly around me, I clasped my hands, and all the contents of my mind willy-nilly flew up to heaven, and lodged themselves for ever in the divine ear.

But these, as I say, were special cases, and otherwise I had to recognize that our thoughts, our inner voices, and none more so than those which were declaratory of our own sex, seemed condemned to be earthbound within ourselves.

So what, in the face of all this, was a small boy to do or think?

I say "to do" as well as "to think" because, around this time an incident led me to worry that the difficulty of telling the sexes apart might have practical consequences to which mere growing-up might not provide the solution.

It was about eight o'clock in the evening, which was after my normal bedtime, and I was standing with my father in the foyer of the restaurant of the Savoy Hotel, breathing in the delicate, warmed smell of the chafing dishes. Looking through the large sheets of plate glass at the far end of the restaurant, I observed lights going on along the line of the Embankment, promising those who were able to stay up hours of pleasure ahead. It was like a scene from a Hollywood musical, a class of film I detested for their lack of rectitude, or their dissolution of the unities of time and place to which I was so attached. Nevertheless, I had drifted far enough out on thoughts of dancing the night away, and of hearing the milkman on his round, and of watching my companion let her black satin dress fall to the ground that it required my father to tap me gently on the shoulder to gain my attention. I followed his gaze down the passage that led past the private rooms named after the different Gilbert and Sullivan operas, and there, coming towards us, swaying irregularly along the thick Turkey runner, was the debonair figure of the Prince of Wales, wearing a light grey double-breasted suit, and holding in one hand a black cigarette holder. As the passage opened out into the space where the two of us were standing, he straightened himself up, he stuck his cigarette holder between his teeth, and both hands flew up to adjust the large knot of his silver tie, which protruded from the famous cut-away collar of his shirt. Momentarily assured of his appearance, he paused. Then, the next moment, under our very eyes, he dived into what was the ladies' lavatory. My father, noticing the error, tried, as a loyal subject, to move me on, but not before I had observed the heir to the throne re-emerging backwards through the heavy mahogany swing door, trying, as he regained his balance, to take fresh stock of the world, which had so suddenly deceived him. Which, I wondered, which of the many blurred clues to life, which I had been struggling with for so long, and to such little effect, had the young prince scrambled in his head?

I do not know what precise degrees of ignorance or knowledge my parents attributed to me, and what dangers they inferred I ran, or whether they acted out of something they had read in a manual, but when, at the age of thirteen years and four months, I was about to go to boarding school, they told me, in the middle of one week, that, the next Sunday morning, instead of going to church, I would get on my bicycle, and go and see Dr Barclay, who, they did not need to remind me, had first introduced me to the novels of Scott, and he would instruct me in "the facts of life". Having said this, they made it clear that they did not want any further discussion of the matter, nor of what the matter was. Sunday came round, and I felt somewhat unshriven for not going to church, but I got on my bicycle before the congregation would have come out of church and had time to spill out over the neighbouring roads. I rode very carefully, and, having concealed the bicycle in the clump of rhododendrons that encircled the drive outside the doctor's neat, half-timbered house, which was called Woodlawn, I rang the bell, and was placed in what alternated as waiting room in the day and family dining room in the evening and on weekends. I was alone with the mahogany sideboard, and the Georgian candlesticks, and the pattern-books that were being considered for the daughter's coming-out dress. I felt cold, cold with a coldness that reached me only when the bath-water went cold. I went to the lavatory twice, each time, as I returned, pretending to the empty room and to the large watercolours of the Highlands that I had had no reason to leave it. At last the maid in her starched apron and cap came in and summoned me. Dr Barclay was sitting at his desk, wearing one of the dark blue bird's-eye suits that he ordered from my father's tailor, and he threw one arm over the back of his chair, as he turned to talk to me. "Now, let us see," he began, "when does term begin?", then correcting himself against an error, he asked me, "You do call it 'term', don't you?" Staring beyond him into the garden, I answered him. He then asked me if I was excited. I said Yes, though reluctantly. I knew of about ten kinds of excitement, and, as a child, though I was generally prey to one or another, it was seldom the kind I was being asked about. By now Dr Barclay had released his arm, and he was opening and shutting his gold fountain pen, which made a faint sucking noise. There were certain things, he told me, that I needed to know if I was to be happy at school, and to be able to concentrate on my work as he knew I would want to, and it was better that I shouldn't first learn them from other boys. Boys sometimes got things wrong, or they put them in ways that made natural things ugly. Did I, as a point of curiosity, know what kind of thing he was talking about? I thought it wiser to say No. He asked me if I had ever kept rabbits, and I said Yes. Had I ever noticed that overnight there might be, not just two rabbits, but some little rabbits? I said Yes. He said, Had I any idea how that came about? I said No. He said, Had I ever asked myself how it came about? I said No. He said, If I hadn't thought about it until now, could I suggest something here and now? I said, after further hesitation, No. Did I think that there was anything like this amongst human beings? I said No. For a moment, he tried to think of another question to ask me, his small dark eyes darting at random, and, with a deep breath, he

255

gave up. He rose from his chair, adjusting himself in his suit as he did so. He wished me good luck, and suggested that, at a later time, I might want to come back, and talk more. He slapped me on the upper arm.

I was sorry that I had said No quite so often, but it was a matter of survival. What I could not tolerate was the sense that, under guise of being told something, I was in effect being told what I could know and what I couldn't know. I

could not bear the drawing of a line. By the time I had bicycled home, Dr Barclay had telephoned, or so I inferred. Later that evening, coming down the stairs, and having reached the very point where, a few years earlier, I had overheard the conversation about my ears, and how they might get trimmed, I once again paused just in time. My parents were talking: Bunty and Noel H were there. Dr Barclay, it seems, had been amazed. My mother repeated the phrase that had been used to her, "His ignorance is complete." Apparently my ignorance was so complete that it had made it impossible for Dr Barclay to know how to proceed. She said, "He had to give up." My father said to my mother, as he periodically did, "You always think that he knows so much." If my father had known, which he did not, about my fearless expeditions up the cliff-face of his books, and the samples of rare learning that I had brought back with me, would he still have inclined to the view, as he clearly did, that my ignorance was complete? Noel, who had had tyrannical parents, ventured, "At that age, there are a lot of explanations." Once again in retreat up the stairs, I suddenly felt sorry for Dr Barclay, who had, I reflected, not particularly that day, but on other days, or in general, done more for my education than anyone except myself.

⌒

I too find it incongruous exactly how the belief in the inherent superiority of women survived effortlessly all the difficulties that I found in distinguishing between the sexes. But, despite the secrecy that surrounded their nature, I knew three things of women, and all pointed to their superiority.

The first was that women were beautiful. Women were beautiful in paintings and in photographs, and so, with only two horrific exceptions, were the women I encountered in life. It is true that, if I stood back far enough from them, my nanny and my governess were not beautiful, but then I loved their faces with such passion that for them to be judged from any distance greater than that at which I could trace with my finger or with the tip of my nose the nooks and crannies of their features would have seemed irrelevant. The true exceptions were two sisters, called Winifred and Eileen W, who lived together in a small flat in Wargrave-on-Thames, and I never received any explanation how, or why, they were a part of our lives. There was nothing that, as far as I could tell, they shared with either of my parents. Eileen was, I believe, retarded, and spoke little, but Winifred, who was the uglier, was voluble, and her interests precisely coincided with what could be found within the covers, or read between the lines, of *Burke's Peerage*. She was interested in heraldry, in titles and courtesy titles, in genealogy, in the seats and the London clubs of the aristocracy, in cavalry regiments, in high-born scandal, and in nothing else. Though I was sometimes rebuked for the dread I had of seeing the W sisters, particularly since there were some historical interests that I shared with Winifred, no one in my childhood ever suggested to me that there was anything untoward about my physical recoil, or that it was uncharitable to judge people by their looks.

The second way in which women showed their superiority was in the more interesting and enjoyable lives that they lived. Men had to make money, which women, on the whole, did not, and this had the striking consequence that, whereas men were never permitted to talk about how they passed their days, it was something that women discussed continuously. Women could, I knew, be painters, sculptors, poets, dancers, actresses. There was no limit to the paradise that opened up at their feet and stretched forwards indefinitely, whereas for men such possibilities existed only rarely, and then mostly in the past, in history.

Thirdly, women could love, they could fall in love, they could be in love, they could be lovesick. They could feel. Sometimes, after a man and a woman who had come down to the house for lunch had driven off, one of my parents would say, not exactly to the other, for that was not how they talked, but more into the surrounding air, "Why does she go on doing it?", "What does she get out of it?", "When will she settle down?", "Why is she throwing away the best years of her life?" If only, I would feel, these questions had been asked of me, I, though not able to put it into words, would have had much to say. I would have begun by saying that these were women, something that my father had never been, and perhaps something that my mother had forgotten how to be, and I would then have gone on to say that, for women, for some women at least, love, love in itself, love unrequited, love that did not even seek for anything in return, in other words the pure culture of love, could be a way of life. If asked for examples, I had them. There was Peggy L, the grass widow, who pined for her husband, though she wished that she wasn't married to him; there was Suzy the dressmaker, the chain-smoker, with her assortment of dashing men-friends, who wore their hair enviably long; there was Daisy B, a friend of my mother's from the stage, who ran a boarding house in Highgate in a house where Coleridge had once lived, and who went everywhere with her younger sister, Pauline, arm in arm, both women always in dark red velvet, and it was only years later that my mother told me that Pauline was really Daisy's daughter by some ne'er-do-well, one-night lover. And there was Muriel, my mother's oldest friend, also from the Gaiety, who might easily, but wrongly, have been excluded from this list because of the slight laugh that was always present in her voice and in her eyes, which my mother called charm, and which prevented her from showing any excess of feeling or conviction. Rumour had it that Muriel had once sung in cowboy bars in the Wild West. Married, as long as I knew her, to a rich wine merchant called Wilfred, in love, vainly, with a rich lieder singer called Eric, whose concert programmes she organised, she had the will to make the three of them more or less inseparable. They would go to the opera together, and Wilfred slept, which he was allowed to do until he snored, and Muriel and Eric talked, and talked, and talked. When Eric died, his place was taken, and the flame of impossible love kept burning, by Gerry, who had been British Minister in a small country, and who was invariably accompanied by a good-looking young man from the Post Office. Then there was Sigrid, the Swedish wife of Muriel's first husband, Mr Cox, whose voice and furs and pale hair I recall, but nothing else to any degree of precision, except that one year my parents, when they still went on holidays together, took her with them to Marienbad, to help her get over some unfortunate affair of the heart. Then there was Molly Marshall, a tall thin dyspeptic woman, with features like my mother's, whose black crêpe dresses smelt of stale cigarettes, who had to work for her living, and who talked endlessly about "the girls in the office", and who redeemed herself in my eyes in two ways. One was by giving me for my eleventh birthday Gibbon's *Decline and Fall of the Roman Empire* in eight small volumes: the other was by being unshamefacedly in love with Barry, the understudy for Ivor Novello, and there was a recognition, not concealed from me, that he never would, that he never could, reciprocate her love. All he could ever give her was front-row tickets for the play when the principal was sick and he took over, and she went unfailingly. And there was Zoë, Zoë of the many scarves, scarves from Lanvin, scarves from Schiaparelli, scarves from Patou, the girlfriend of my father's closest friend, David A, but who came to the house with him only two times out of three. With the exception of Molly and Muriel, all these were women with long earrings and with what I learned to think of as tinkling voices, and I would have added to this list Lucienne B, a singer, who, whenever she arrived for lunch, brought with her to my utter delight a jigsaw puzzle of great difficulty, with vast monochrome expanses of sky, or smoke, or ocean, which she and I would work on together at a special card table set up in the garden until the sun started to go down. She was invariably accompanied by a suave Frenchman called Carson, with prim lips, which he barely opened when he spoke, and the only reason I have for associating her to this group of women in love is that she made famous all across the world a song called "*Parlez-moi d'amour*", which I knew by heart, and, at that age, I could not visualize what an art would be like that was not in some large part autobiographical.

In thinking of women as the natural habitat of love, I did not envisage this condition as one of pain. Rather I conceived of the pangs of love as a sort of internal flame, which warmed the soul rather than burnt or singed it, and it gave a sumptuousness to women in glorious contrast to the partially frozen condition in which men, grown-up men, passed their lives. What made their condition fortunate, if not exactly happy, was that it transported them to a land, not otherwise visited by adults, where passion and excitement, the raw stuff of poetry, flourished, and where languor and even boredom, though not of the cruel kind visited upon idle boys, sometimes took over.

This state of love, which was open only to women, though not all women availed themselves of it, was, I concluded, an internal state, but what made it tolerable was that it was not innermost, as was the life of children. A gulf separated it from the shrill, high-pitched despair, from the never distant scalding tears, which I saw as belonging exclusively to a child's existence, and which I believed were comprehensible to God alone. Grown-up love did not bring with it that constant need to talk to oneself, which in my experience led so readily to prayer. When women fell in love, every step in their condition was carefully tied to some outward action, which expressed and relieved it. They picked up the telephone, they lit a cigarette, they bought more than ordinarily expensive shoes, they got someone to draw their portrait. The rearrangements that all this might, might not, necessitate were more like changes of train or destination, caused by the need for a foreign holiday, or by the sight of a young face, or made in response to a sudden judicious absence abroad. Every Sunday this fact was pressed home to me, when, immediately on my return from church, my father would suggest that I go with him to meet the guests who were about to arrive for lunch, either on foot to the station or by car to The Bear at Esher, which was about as far from London as anyone could be expected to drive who had not done the journey before. Men came to lunch with much younger women than I had seen them with before, women with fair hair just touched with grey produced ever older, ever more silent, men who wore shirts of expensive cotton threaded with fine satin stripes and smoked heavy cigars, all of which I appraised at leisure. Even when women cried, they cried to an end: they did not cry the futile, solitary, acid tears of children, nor, as their crying stopped, did they finish on a snivel. There was a word, a very special word for women in love, a word which I spent years brooding over, and which I did not fully understand, but which had the effect of diminishing somewhat their ultimate vulnerability, and of returning them, by however roundabout a route, to somewhere not so far outside the ranks of ordinary grown-ups, who, on Sunday mornings, walked to church, and dropped to their knees, and had nothing to say to a God who failed to understand them: they were – this was the word – "sophisticated".

In my view of the lovesick condition as something peculiarly within reach of women, there was a lacuna, a hole, which, until it was filled in, deprived the picture of all sense. When women are in love, who are they in love with? And I knew deep down one thing for certain, and that was that the right answer was not: Men. There was nothing about men, not their manner, not their faces, not their bodies, not the way they talked, not their minds, not their feelings, if they had them, not even their elegant shirts and ties, that could make it plausible that they were the real objects of women's love: it was a thought that could not ultimately be taken seriously. And, if this was so clear to me, after all a boy myself, was it conceivable that women, the monopolists of beauty, who knew what beauty was from the inside, would betray their inheritance, their birthright, so lightly? I understood that women had to behave as though they loved men, otherwise they would starve, and such behaviour on their part was totally honourable, just as it could be totally honourable for men to die in battle for their country. Love of money, love of country, were not, in my eyes, good things in themselves, but it might be inevitable that, in certain circumstances, one should sacrifice oneself for them. There was, I knew from books and from my father's conversation, another mysterious word for women, which was really supreme praise, though stupid people could not see this. Some women were "adventuresses", tawny-haired women who hacked their way through the jungle of men with a deep inner pride.

The true answer to the big question, or what, for many years to come, I took to be the true answer, did not dawn on me until, somewhere around my sixteenth year, about half past eight one foggy evening, having finished my prep early, and having got permission to do private study, I read for the first time the five *pièces condamnées of Les Fleurs du mal*. So much of life, so many things that had been kept from me, suddenly became clear, and Baudelaire became one of my great prophets.

From this time onwards, an image of great vividness, of great poignancy, of some delicious sadness, haunted me in a number of variations. Often, when I went to foreign films, I hoped to see the very scenario enacted on the screen. I state it in a particular version, but there were many, many completely interchangeable, completely equivalent, versions. A young man with dark eyes, wearing a foulard tie of some rich colour with large polka dots, and carelessly knotted, stares, as dusk settles in, at a young woman with fair hair, a pianist perhaps, perhaps a sculptor, and she absent-mindedly but insistently runs her fingers over his hand, while in turn she looks across at another, slightly older woman, around thirty, with black hair, silhouetted against the window, and this other woman looks down, through the ironwork of the balcony, on to the streets of a great European capital. People are leaving work and walking home, or they sit in cafés, and the smells of the kitchen and the sounds of modern life rise from the streets, and penetrate the room, and, as the lights start to go on outside, reflexions are thrown up on the low ceiling, where they flicker and fade. All three are enthralled, and only one of them has the power to break the spell, and to move, or even to wish to move, without the others. It is she, the dark woman, who alone has the power to get up, and, with heavy, sleepy movements, shake out her hair, and go. She exerts it. She gets up, and, as she does so, she touches the other girl's hand, and, without looking at her, she goes. They will meet later. The man goes on looking at the fair-haired girl, the fair-haired girl goes on looking at the spot where her friend was sitting, and they can hear the sharp click of heels on the cobbles as the woman, who is such a tempestuous figure in their lives, walks into the evening: she leaves only to return. She is tempestuous despite the softness of her gaze and the full, slightly trembling, rather Egyptian, lips. The man sighs, he is close to fainting, and the girl who remains weighs up the careful balance of pleasure and pain that this elegance of despair gives her.

Tucked into this vignette was also the conclusion I had come to about the only way, though not an easy way, in which, in a world in which women love women, a man might come to win a woman's love. He could try, in thought, in speech, in gesture, to become as like women as nature would permit, in much the same way as, within religion, which was only just beginning to lose its command over me, or perhaps to exchange one form of command for another, the believer tries to come closer to Christ through the imitation of Christ. The way to a woman's heart, I had come to believe, was along the hard, stony, arduous track of effeminacy.

There were two girls who irrupted into my life before the incident in Oriel Street.

The first girl was at the school I went to after my convalescence from pleurisy came to an end. She was called Mary, and she lived in the great port of Bristol.

I have the feeling that Mary was one of two or three girls who boarded at the school, and I also have the feeling that she was poorer than the other girls in the school, and that made her attractive to me. But the truth is that we had not paid much attention to one another, apart from one long walk, which took up the whole of the twelve o'clock lesson, when we went with butterfly nets to gather tadpoles. The path we followed, which skirted a lake, was half-buried in a wood that came right down to the water's edge, and, from time to time, I held the branches back so that she could pass without being forced into the reeds. But now the end of term was approaching, and we were both leaving school. The pangs of separation, stretching ahead across the endless years, came to seem unbearable – would we ever, ever, see one another again? – and, at her instigation, we decided, standing up in one of the big, whitewashed corridors that had formed part of the original kitchen of the house, to link ourselves with a vow that could never be broken. I owned a penknife with a view of Cannes, and I used either it or a needle to draw a drop of blood from each of us, and we then mixed the blood, and rubbed it over our wrists, looking into each other's eyes as we did so. I thought of Mary as "the nut-brown maiden", but I do not remember what aspect of her looks this singled out. Sometimes I think that her features were small and carved, sometimes I think that her complexion was dark, and I believe it is likely that she was partly Indian.

We said that we would remember each other for ever, and I seem in a way to have done so. I can just recall her standing barefoot on the large flagstones, in a pale blue linen dress with smocking, which was the school uniform for the girls, and her dry, black hair was about to fall down, and she was shivering. The word "love" did not pass our lips, but the concept of friendship, which would, over the years, come to ride roughshod over such brutal ideas as duty, and blame, and responsibility, had, I believe, begun to lodge itself in our childish hearts. I think back on her sometimes as the original pagan in my life. Had we met later in life, I would not have been surprised if, without giving the matter a second thought, she had dropped her blue dress to the floor, and slipped into bed with me. I know that I have traduced Mary because of the many later experiences through which I have filtered her, but in my reverie I think of her as too profound to think it worthwhile denying anything seriously asked of her.

Next there was Jill, Jill with the double-barrelled name.

It was September, 1939, and war had just been declared, and my father had decided that we must evacuate ourselves immediately, even though there was no sign of war nearer than the Polish frontier, which the German Army, under the leadership of the mythical Guderian, had just crossed in force. We packed our bags, closed up the house, and drove down to Devonshire, where my father installed us in a large early nineteenth-century hotel on the front at Teignmouth. The façade of the hotel was decorated with a pediment, and the pediment contained the arms of George IV. It was less expensive than the small, luxurious hotel, to which I shall return later, a ferry's ride away across the estuary of the Teign, where we had stayed briefly a few years earlier, and where my father felt at home, with walls painted burnt orange, and large vases of orchids at each turn of the stairs. It was also much more expensive than the "private hotel" to which my mother and father moved after a few weeks, and where they stayed for another year or so. For the whole of the war, my father refused to be within fifty miles of London.

A regime was established, part of which was that I could have breakfast in bed, which for me had the charms of convalescence, and a newspaper was brought up with breakfast, which I could endure because I had ordered it. The paper I had ordered was the *News Chronicle*, a paper of strong liberal sympathies. Every morning the newspapers carried on their main page large maps with arrows showing the different offensives that opened up daily, carrying the *Blitzkrieg* deeper and deeper into the heartland of Poland. Optimistic correspondents from the front would occasionally tell of counter-offensives by the Polish cavalry, their sabres being, we were told, more than a match for the cannons of the advancing tanks, which could, through some design fault, fire only on fixed lines. These engagements, in which it was admitted there were losses on both sides, invariably cost the enemy this or that amount of armour, such and such reserves of motorised infantry, which it could ill afford. It was hard to take these stories seriously, hard not to.

After breakfast I dressed, and came downstairs, and made a careful decision about where to sit for the morning and read the English poets, or the harsh denunciations of war and capitalism that I had brought with me. On the second or third day, I noticed a girl of my age leap up from her chair, cross the road in front of the hotel, and walk rapidly towards the sea. She moved with great speed, her fair hair was cut in a bell, she wore a tartan skirt and very shiny black rubber boots, and she always carried a book. Sometimes she read walking, but it did not slow her down. She was staying in the hotel with her mother, to whom she seemed to have a great deal to say. Would I ever talk to her, this creature from Mars, this character from an Aldous Huxley novel? I assumed not, but to my amazement I found a way of doing so, I do not know how, and straightaway we were walking together, slightly faster than I would have chosen, round and round the municipal flower-beds that stretched from the hotel to the seafront, pausing to watch the old men playing bowls, or, standing on the front, looking at the up-ended fishing-boats with their fresh coats of tar. We barely had to remind one another that these were the sights on which the young Keats had fed. She told me that she lived in the Lake District with her mother, who ran an hotel, but she boarded at a convent school in Berkshire. She knew a boy I knew at school who, by this time, had graduated from being my worst persecutor to being my accomplice in all kinds of literary and political subversion. She had read Marx, and Auden, and French poetry, though surreptitiously, because the nuns didn't like it. However what brought us together was Russia, which was for me so much the past, and the present, and the future. Our conversation suddenly lit up, like a great firework display, when we started to talk about Dostoevsky, and our versions of the Russian soul and the Russian Revolution.

As to the war, neither of us cared a great deal about the future of Poland, or, at any rate, about the future of Colonel Beck's Poland, and we were in agreement that it was the

worst issue over which to have started a war. Did I really think, Jill asked me, stopping abruptly, and staring at the splash of colour in the flower-bed, that intervention in the Spanish War would have made all that difference? Did I admire Orwell, did I read Lorca, was I sympathetic to Kropotkin? Did I think this, did I think that? I was amazed at these questions, since it was I who wanted to know everything that she thought. She was serious and intense, something that boys could be only under the lash of being bullied or in the throes of adolescent desire. It was only when I saw her coming from a distance that I dared look at her, and then I scrutinized her body from the top of her head and her straight pale hair to the toe of her boot. As she came closer to me, I took my eyes off her and stared straight ahead, so that, by the time she reached my side, I professed to be taken by surprise. It has been pointed out to me that this is something that to this day I do with certain people, with people I love, and I do it, I suppose, to avoid some unfathomable disappointment.

Term started soon afterwards despite the war, Jill and I separated, though I do not recall the details of the parting, and my school was evacuated to the Sussex coast, where it shared buildings with another school. I was anxious to see my school friend, my one-time persecutor, now unique to me as the friend of Jill, and to tell him about the conversations on the seafront, and I believe that he encouraged me to write to Jill. I did, more than once: long, flowery, scented, perhaps even literally scented, letters, with quotations, I am sure, from the French and Latin poets, but I never had a reply. I believe that I was upset, but I was inclined to think of the whole incident, and the fast walks, and the conversations, and the questions, as a dream. I was certain that none of it could have left a residue in Jill's clear, forceful mind, which strove so hard, as I saw it, to be un-encumbered, and ready for ever new truths about ever new things.

That was how things were, more than sixty years ago, and that was how they remained until about ten years ago, when the philosopher who gave me my first job died, and the event achieved wide recognition, and I came to write an obituary in a leading newspaper, in which I tried to defend him against the petty moralism that I foresaw. Some weeks later, a letter arrived for me in California. I could not tell from the envelope who had written it, and I opened it with eagerness: it was from Jill. She had read the obituary, and she explained to me, but as though it was something I knew already, that my letters to her had been stopped by the nuns, and so, she eventually discovered, had her letter to me. When she did find out what had happened, she had told our common friend, and had asked him to tell me.

Whether I already knew all this or not was hard for me to tell, but it was Jill's continuing awareness of me that took me by surprise. Her letter evoked with great force the memory of those walks against the background of distant battles. She wrote with great charm and with great precision of phrase, and said that the first awakening of intellectual curiosity, or excitement – I cannot remember the word she used – could, though often unattended to, be as important an experience as the first awakening of physical love. She had read some philosophy, she told me, but nowadays she mostly tended her garden. From the postmark I gathered that she lived in a large midland city, but she omitted her address, and gave only her maiden name, the double-barrelled name that I have now forgotten. I say her maiden name, though she did not indicate whether she had married. She asked me to think of her as she then was. I did not need the injunction. The image of the girl with the fair hair, and the tartan skirt, and the shiny boots, cutting through the damp, balmy air of the Devon coast, was impervious to decay, and I hope that it has escaped any clumsy retouching. I found a safe place in which to keep her letter close to my bedside, but it was so safe, so unlikely, a place, that now I cannot find the letter, which saddens me. The letter made me think, amongst other things, this: that, if my letters had got through to Jill, if I had heard back from her, if somehow what I call my life had started from such an early point, when I was under the same roof as my parents, and still found it conceivable that I should talk to my mother, and lived on pocket money kept in a leather purse with a flap, then not only would my life have been different, it would have been the life of a very different me. It would have been the life of someone who remained the permanent spoiled convalescent that I wanted to be for ever.

⌒

I shared a pram with my brother, and I endured his kicking me without interruption. Though I was three years younger, he was born in June, and I in May, and he was convinced that it could not really be true that the birthday of a younger brother came before the birthday of the elder brother. Every year there were outbursts of rage as my birthday approached, as a result of which it was barely celebrated. By contrast, when his came round, it was a rather elaborate event, and I recall one year, or perhaps two years running, its taking the form of a re-enactment of the Mad Hatter's Tea Party, with all the children in fancy dress, and my brother in a large top hat. It was modelled, not on the Tenniel illustrations, which I never saw as a child, but on a big horizontal drawing, in part collage, which was hanging on the walls of the nursery, and which my father had commissioned from Ernst Stern, who had been Reinhardt's favourite stage designer, and from whom he also commissioned a bookplate, showing a mask. I have never minded suffering injustice, and I certainly prefer it to any show of anger. It was consoling to feel that my brother most disliked me for something that was, without a doubt, beyond my power to change.

If there was early fear in my life, long before the word "love" was breathed, it was school that introduced me, not to fear, but to the idea of a world of fear. By that I mean a world that fear stalked like a wild animal bent on indiscriminate revenge. When, years later, I began hesitantly, and never with complete success, to read Dante's *Inferno*, the wolf was like the fear felt at school.

It was within my first week at The Mount that I witnessed a ceremony which abruptly enlarged my experience of life, and, across the years, it still has the power to transfix me.

Morning assembly took place in a big, sunny room with French windows, which gave on to a slatted wooden balcony, below which the garden sloped down to a narrow stream with stepping stones. On the far side of the stream the garden rose sharply, first to some grass tennis courts, and then to a dense shrubbery overlooking them called the bowery, and farther on was the gym, a big Scandinavian structure, and, beyond that, a large walled field, where we had to run and play cricket in the summer, and football or hockey was played in the winter. Opening out of the room where assembly was held, on the opposite side to the French windows, was a small room, terminating in a semi-circular apse, where we changed for sports, and, in the basement, was another room where, on arrival in the morning, we hung our bags, and put on the elastic-sided slippers, which turned out to be a momentous part of our uniform.

For assembly we sat at small wooden desks, putting our pencil-boxes in front of us, and I used to stare at mine with childish piety as though it were a small travelling altar. Facing our little desks was a big knee-hole mahogany desk, the desk of a company director, and on the wall behind it was an oilskin map of England, divided into the old counties, with the county towns in bold print. At nine o'clock a bell was rung, and Mr Stock walked in, and sat down behind the big desk, and then, leaning forward, and putting his weight on his elbows, said a couple of prayers. Today his face was set in an unsmiling, skull-like mould. After prayers, he stood up, and, in accordance with what must have been a prearranged plan, he called out a boy's name. I have tried to remember the name, an ugly name, beginning with an S, but I cannot, and the boy, who was a weak-looking boy, with a short neck, and afflicted with large orange freckles which looked like dark confetti thrown all over him, stumbled out of his chair. He was Stock's nephew, but, on this occasion, this would not protect him:

nothing would. Without a word Stock held out his hand, and the boy pulled off one of his slippers, and placed it in Stock's open hand. "Bend over," we heard. Boy and man now formed a frieze in front of the assembly, and, with a sudden access of energy, which we all felt, Stock beat the boy four times, using an upward cut of the slipper. On the fourth stroke, it seemed all to be over, but the boy fell over, and Stock's interest was reignited. The boy got up, Stock weighed the slipper in his hand, and, taking a short run at the boy's bottom, gave him another two noisy blows with the leather sole. For a moment he had his arm raised high above his shoulder for another stroke, then he dropped it, and instead he flung the slipper to the far end of the room, and roared at the boy to go and get it. The boy hobbled over, and, slowly rubbing his bottom, resumed his seat, and Stock waited for him to wince.

As things turned out, this was not a unique event, but no later repetitions had the same startling effect. On one occasion, a group of boys were called up to be "slippered", and they stood in a queue for their punishment, and I think of them when I read how, in abattoirs, calves are protected from seeing the fate of other calves who go ahead of them. A year or so later, when Stock was trying, with some difficulty I remember, to explain to us older boys how to solve a new kind of equation, there was a gentle knock at the door, and a very young boy of great sweetness of expression was waiting outside. He said that Matron, who taught the youngest boys, had sent him to ask for the cane. Stock opened the drawer of the desk at which he sat, and brought out the cane, and handed it to the boy. As an after-thought, he asked "Is it for you?" The boy nodded, and, for a moment, I thought that he was going to appeal against his fate to whatever forces in the world looked after justice. But he didn't. "Bring it back," Stock went on, "as soon as you've had it." He paused. "Do you understand?" The boy came back five minutes later, and Stock, who examined the cane to see if it needed replacement, was evidently satisfied with its condition, and he paid no further attention to the boy. The boy's face was stained with tears, which attested to the suppleness of Matron's wrist.

Matron was young, had a strawberry and cream complexion, and curly fair hair, and I remember begging my mother to allow her to come riding with us on a Saturday afternoon. She was invited, and I prayed that her horse would bolt, and that I, who was a much better rider, would rescue her. I would gallop alongside her, and, leaning forward, would grab her reins close to the bit. In fact, I believe that something like that happened, but I lack certainty. She stayed to supper, again at my insistence, and my father could find nothing to say to her. I do not think that he was even struck by her looks, to which I thought no one could be impervious. All the while she was engaged to a master, called Mr Rossiter, who read *The Yorkshire Post* and taught us hockey, which also frightened me.

If by this time I had acquired, as I was expected to, the concept of punishment, it was not the concept that my teachers thought they were teaching me. I came to think of punishment as essentially a transaction in which two people, patron and client, executioner and victim, colluded with one another in order to bring about pain for one of them. The coming years at school enlarged my awareness of what might count as collusion, but without tampering with my sense of the character of punishment itself. Certainly the most vaunted aspect of punishment, which I had read a great deal about in the Bible in connexion with Jehovah's punishment – that is to say, the link between punishment and some prior offence – seemed to me appearance, which I could credit with little reality. It struck me as at best an excuse, invented by the two parties in some further form of collusion so as to keep those who would ask curious, spoilsport questions at bay. I do not, for instance, remember that any of us had ever asked, or that we were ever told, what the offence committed by Stock's nephew had been. None of the standard answers – that he had lied, or that he had cheated, or that he had made a noise in the corridor – would have seemed to us boys as true to the facts as the brute, sweaty game between man and boy, boy and man, played out to the fear and excitement of an audience. But what precisely had to go on between the two agents to make the result collusion, hence punishment, how the actions of one had to be entwined with the thoughts of the other, went, I knew, well beyond the simple cases where the victim handed over a slipper to the executioner, or the client asked the patron for the cane, or the two prayed before and shook hands afterwards. Might it not be enough for one party to fall in love with the other, and then the axe could fall with all the authority of a court come to judgment?

Beside the fear of punishment, there was the fear of disappointment. In punishment the victim hands himself over to the executioner, and then waits, expectantly, to see what the executioner has chosen to do to him. In disappointment, it is the victim who chooses what the executioner will do to him, for he attributes to the executioner all kinds of promises, which the executioner, ignorant of what they are, is unable to keep. "But you promised, you must remember, you promised, you said that you would" is the cry that goes up, the great anguished cry, the cry of righteous indignation, as if the whole city of the disappointed burst into one great Biblical wail. In the last muffled moments of a telephone conversation, or at the end of dinner in a restaurant as the candle burns fitfully, some words are said to have been said, or, if they were not actually said, they were not denied, which, in the circumstances, they should have been if they were not to be honoured. "But I took it as a promise, you know I did, don't say you don't because you do, you do." And then comes the great untruth, "I shall never believe you, ever again." For how, if the victim stopped believing, would the disappointment so dearly loved ever be possible again?

For my ninth birthday I was promised a pony. I had long said that I wanted one, and, the year before, during a holiday in Devon, I had won an event in historic Widdecombe Fair, and I clearly deserved something to record my victory. A very large brown paper parcel arrived for me about ten days before my birthday, and it waited for me in the ominous cloakroom. From time to time I went in and pinched it, and, though it did not seem to be alive, nor to have the shape of a pony, I continued to believe that it was a likelier eventuality than not that, when my birthday came round, and the parcel was opened, I would have been given a pony. If I did not know exactly how this would happen, there were two broad possibilities. One was that the parcel in the cloakroom, which I had examined so carefully, was a proxy for the real present, keeping a place warm for it, and then, on the day, there would be a substitution of one for the other, making me then look rather foolish for having paid so much attention to, or having fretted over, a mere place-holder. The other possibility, which I favoured, was that the parcel in the cloakroom was, and would on the day turn out to have been, the real thing all along. Under the folds of brown paper and the Harrods label was a live pony, expertly anaesthetized, then dehydrated, which allowed it to be folded flat, and stacked up, first in the delivery van, then in the only storage place that our house had to offer.

When the day came round, what emerged was this: because of a diet I had been put on, which included a large cup of hot chocolate for breakfast, I had gained weight, and this had apparently become a matter of concern to my parents. In consequence, when, on the morning of my birthday, the brown paper package was brought into the night nursery, and I, in trying to open it, took the greatest care not to do any damage either to the paper itself, which could be used again, or to its inhabitant, I discovered that what my parents had given me was a rowing machine. Miss King, who had been recruited, I chose to think reluctantly, into the deception, saw my disappointment, and told me that it would be good for me, and then added that I could learn to like it. I swore not to, feeling that I owed this to the pony that never was. How I kept my oath, and the revenge I took upon the hated machine, which I modelled on the work I had put into destroying the Kum-bak, is a long story. Every time I got on the rowing machine, and dragged the handle up to my chest, in simulation of pulling in on a pair of oars, I gave the wood a sharp sideways twist so that the long rubber bands joining the handle to the frame were scraped against the metal bracket through which they were threaded. Evening after evening I watched them fray, until I saw that it now needed only one exceptionally sharp tug, which I gave it, and the bands would break, and I would fall backwards and hit my head on the floor, for which I got a little of the sympathy that I had been denied on the morning I opened the parcel. In time the post brought with it a new package of bright blue bands, fresh from the manufacturers, and disappointment was renewed.

From then onwards, the only present I trusted was money, with which I could buy books and ancient coins, or which I could save up until I had enough to write off to Bruton Street and order a large painting by Picasso, which no one had promised me.

It was in my tenth year that paintings came to join books in my own palace of love, by which I mean that, not only were both objects of love, I loved them, but they became shrines in which lovers, people in love, could enjoy shelter from the cold blasts of grown-up disapproval. I can date the moment at which paintings came to share this position, for I preserve the catalogue, now a pale faded violet, of the exhibition at which the sombre austerity of Poussin, and the delicate blues of Claude, and his shepherds like garden statues, first burst upon me. It was the exhibition of French paintings held at Burlington House in the winter of 1932 to 1933. In the car on the way back, I developed a temperature. A little later I found in the book section of a department store four slim volumes on individual painters: they were Correggio, van Dyck, Tintoretto, and, I believe, Rubens. The painting that intrigued me most was Tintoretto's *The Origin of the Milky Way*. I had no idea what the subject was, except that it recounted some deep change in the elements around us, which allowed me to assimilate it to one of *The Just-So Stories*. It was not for another two or three years that I started going to museums, for the majesty of which I felt that I had in some measure been prepared by large, expensive hotels.

Ordinarily, when I read a book, I forget it in a very short period of time. Paintings are less fugitive. Sometimes, it is true, when I am travelling through Germany, where I am totally at the mercy of my sentiments, I sometimes cannot recall a painting that I saw only a few hours before. However, if I see a reproduction of it years later, it will strike me as familiar, and I shall perhaps go on to recall aspects or details of it that the reproduction does not even register.

Nevertheless there are a few passages from books – and I shall consider three – that have survived from childhood with the unfading colours, the vivacity that will not go away, of early mornings when the dew has not dried out, and voices, a garden away, speak as if direct into my ear. In strength these passages rival the most stubborn memories of actual events in my life, such as my five days as a prisoner in enemy hands, or, more diffusely, the dawning of new love, or, without rhyme or reason, my second arrival in Piacenza when, to please my travelling companion, I took a snapshot of the equestrian statue in the ruined piazza, showing in soft focus the underside of the horse and its enormous testicles.

The first passage comes from Charles Reade's *The Cloister and the Hearth*, read most probably when I was between nine and ten. The hero is travelling to meet Erasmus, a figure who, with his judiciousness, his irony, and his remoteness from the sort of fevered issues with which I was plagued, depressed me, first as a child when he appeared in historical novels, then later in adolescence, when we read his *Fpistolae* in school. He was the complete grown-up. But this is irrelevant to the passage that stays in my mind, in which the hero, who is still some way away from his destination, stops at an inn where there is much smoking of long clay pipes, and drinking of beer, and loud peasant talk. Above the din and the smoke he notices the girl who serves. He notices her beautiful hands, and the long fingers, and the whiteness of the skin, and then he notices that he is not more observant of them than she is. Every movement she makes is designed to show them to best advantage, but she takes no pleasure in doing so: she acts out of a coldly conceived duty. She is the servant, servant and guardian, of her hands, and something tells him that the fact they will soon fade, or coarsen, is familiar to her, she has reflected on it, and this has even been something of a relief to her. But, when he tries to convey to her in a single look everything that he has noticed, she resents his gaze.

The second passage comes from the opening chapter or so of *Quentin Durward*, which was the first novel of Scott that was read to me. When, one morning, on putting down his stethoscope, Dr Barclay had pronounced me ready to start on Scott, he had also suggested that I might be eased into it by leaving out, not only the endnotes and appendices, but also the long descriptions of nature and the customs of the times to be found in the main body of the text, for these were likely to be "heavy" for a child. At first I tried not to hear of the plan, and I abandoned my ordinary passivity as a convalescent to the point of threatening that, if I suspected that something was missing from what had been read to me, I would scream. The threat was unwise, since it only reinforced the view that reading that was too advanced for my years would be bad for my nerves. I was too "highly strung" for such risks to be taken lightly. The matter was still unsettled when, one late afternoon, my pillows arranged behind my head, and a dab of eau de cologne put on the sheets, I settled down to listen to the description of the young man with a springing gait, who is engaged in deep conversation with an older companion. The two of them make their way across a meadow, sown with wild flowers, towards a walled town, which stands on the far bank of the Loire. Heraldic pennants are flying from the white turrets. The liquid colours of the morning, with their clean outlines, delight our hero, who, in pursuit of his livelihood, has been newly recruited into a company of Scottish archers in the service of the King of France. He wears a multicoloured doublet, and, as fashion dictates, his penis is neatly enclosed in a swelling codpiece, on which subject our author had, or so I remember things, appended a learned endnote, with antiquarian references.

At this point in the reading a double disappointment was in store for me, and, if Miss King could do something to mitigate the first, the second was completely out of her control. With a speed that completely surprised me, she found a solution to the issue of the footnote, which an asterisk in the text and a reference at the bottom of the page told us was suddenly upon us, by agreeing to the ruse that, provided that I didn't draw her attention to the fact, I could read the footnote to myself while she was out of the room either making me a drink of lemon barley water or, itself a touch of the middle ages, emptying the "po". However, the effect of this solution was to pitch me, even more precipitately, into the further content of the conversation between the two men. As they walk through the morning air, the older man begins to feel that he cannot keep to himself any longer his gloomy reflexions about the changes that are all but certain to engulf the fair land of France. With the ascension to the throne of the new king, who was cold and avaricious, the age of chivalry was about to pass: the pennants that now fluttered in the air would soon be taken down as an unnecessary expense, and, if – and, at this point, the older man turned to face the younger man – if honour, and romance, and glory were what he had crossed the North Sea to see, he should feast his eyes on them now while he can. As I listened to Miss King's uninflected voice, I knew that my fate was destined to replicate that of the young archer. For I had come to Scott, just as he had come to France, for love of the middle ages, and yet here I was, at the beginning of the first book of his that I read, confronted with a lamentation upon their waning. By the time evening fell, by which time we were well into the book, I had come with some sadness to the opinion that, if I had to learn about the relentlessness of history, it was better that I should do so from someone who had such a deep sympathy for its victims, and who cast in such a favourable light the chances of standing out against it.

The third passage came either from *The Water Babies*, or,

somewhat more likely, from a story in a boys' annual that derived from Kingsley's novel. The king of the world that lies at the bottom of the ocean is entertaining his subjects to a lavish tea party. In front of him, there is a low curving table laid with a tablecloth and an enormous teapot and elegant cups, and, behind him, the space in which he has chosen to give his party vanishes into mysterious caverns and dark chambers. The king is wearing a crown, and, though still in his prime, has a long, flowing beard that bifurcates, and both strands curl down to his navel. Meanwhile a young girl, who belongs on dry land, but who has, I think, been freshly transformed into a mermaid, is also a guest. The girl knows that these unfamiliar circumstances require her to be on her best behaviour, but, unaware of exactly what this asks of her, she is under great stress. In her nervousness, she knocks over a jug of milk, and an illustration shows her hands flying up to her cheeks in horror. I knew that this was precisely what, in my clumsiness, I too would have done, had I been her, and I also sensed that the misadventure would turn out to be a larger matter than I could even dream of. The king, who had, up till that moment, been leaning back in his throne, the genial host, his fingers clawing the ends of his beard, while the waves swirl around him breeze-like in a gently refreshing manner, lets out a sudden roar. He has noticed the jug on its side, and the milk spreading across the low table. On dry land, this would be of no moment, but, at the bottom of the sea, where all is liquid, any additional liquid, which one might be forgiven for thinking, as the girl thought, completely harmless, is fatal, or near-fatal. Combining with the water of the sea, which ordinarily does not enter the orifices of those who live within it, the milk is completely invasive. There is no way of blocking the ears, or the nose, or even the eyes. Will no one, the king asks, save his kingdom? Meanwhile the girl cowers. She does not know what she has to fear for herself, nor from the strange scaly people who surround her.

One might have thought that the "rectitude", as I have called it, which made me on many occasions resistant to hybrids or artificial mixtures of things, such as films in which one place dissolves into another, or novels that put modern idiom into descriptions of historical time, or military regroupings in which units of different regiments are combined into special task forces, would have made me just as resistant to stories constituted of characters drawn from different novels. Yet I doubt that I gave the archer and the servant-girl and the mermaid sanctuary in my mind only to place them in solitary confinement. I have no direct recall of the telling of stories in which they meet one another, but certain synopses regrouping them into new narratives so speedily form themselves in my mind as to suggest that they possess some authenticity.

The archer will go to war, perhaps will be involved in the killing or the maiming of someone, but then will return and, with an operation as simple as that of washing his hands, will be able to present himself before the servant-girl, fresh and sweet and feminine. He will woo her, and will win her. His charm for her will be, not the exploits that he has lived through, but the laconic way in which he can recount them.

He has carried out his duties as she has always carried out hers. She listens to his words of love, turning over her hands as he speaks. They live for ever afterwards: without fear or intimacy.

Or he dies on some foreign battlefield, a round bullet-hole in his forehead, and there is no one to tell her. She allows someone else to marry her, but dreams that the archer will arrive and disrupt the wedding festivities. She stays married, but only so that he will know where she is when, returning in the middle of the night, he throws a stone up against her window, and carries her off pillion on his great white horse. Eventually she dies in holiness, surrounded by a large and happy family, but, as she breathes her last breath, she looks out of the corner of her eye in the hope that she has not lived in vain.

Or he returns from the wars, clean it is true, but uncertain of himself in a way she does not remember. She sees him across the smoke-filled room, she comes over to his side, and asks him what he desires. He asks for a tankard of beer. "Is that all?" she asks, looking him in the eye. "I may want something else: in which case I'll tell you," he says. "That will be the day," she says, a phrase that will stick in his mind for ever, even as her beautiful hands, reaching down, find their way through the codpiece, and close in upon him, and she drags him upstairs into her unmade bed. For the first time, the ghosts of warfare are laid to rest, and he does not wake up to the clash of armour on armour. The next day he rises early, he observes the storks on the high rooftops, and, like them, he is ready to move on. She has purged him, and now he is too afraid to look her in the eyes. He says that he must be in search of his fortune. He never forgets her.

Or he returns from whatever adventures he can find, and she is sitting there, waiting for him, and a pale flicker of a greeting passes between them. Not tonight, she intimates: nor the next night, he proposes. They do not want to do anything precipitate without first gaining their parents' approval, or seeking the priest's blessing on their union. But, in times of civil war or sectarian conflict, families are broken up beyond recall, and new religious loyalties form. Our young people believe that true love can put up with procrastination, which, if it must, it will. In due course the two grey-haired lovers, assuming their nightly place in the deep shadows of the tavern, are pointed out to newcomers, to guests from other countries, and various calculations are made, and bets are taken out, about how many years they have waited for each other, how many candles they have seen gutter to extinction, how many times they have renewed their vows. Now, without recalling why, he washes up the glasses to spare her hands, which are red and chapped, and she shows no evident gratitude. Sitting side by side without a word to say to each other, they think exactly the same thought: Which of us designed this hell for the other?

Or he goes to the wars, but he misses the great battle. It is still daylight as he returns to the smoke-filled room. She sees him, but cannot display any pleasure she feels. He persists, she becomes visibly irritated. Anger flares up, he can go and stand on his head, she tells him. Wondering whether it makes any sense for him to have come so far just to be brushed aside, he falls prey to another fear. Is not the large man at the far end of the table the recruiting sergeant who, two months earlier, had given him a bag of coins on the understanding that he would take part in the coming battle, which in fact he missed? When battle was finally joined, it was fought out, as the light was fading, in the narrow, congested lanes of a small village. Mercenary grappled with mercenary without any enduring interest in the outcome, but with none the less murderous intent. The archer has no hope of explaining that it was through no fault of his own, that it was solely because of the height of the hedges, that he never found the battle. He is, in very different ways, frightened of the girl and of the man. To justify himself to the man, he would need a measure of pride that would be fatal in the eyes of the girl. He pulls his purse out of his jerkin, and, though he has now more need of it than ever, empties its contents on to the table, and leaves.

I leave these narratives with the reader, aware that, apart from any claim to veracity they might have as a child's own thoughts, they fit in with a predilection on my part, in the matter both of literature and of life, for half-stories, for beginnings without endings, for passion that succumbs too readily to confusion, for feelings that choke on themselves, for beginnings that are in themselves endings.

But what of the third passage, with its single act of carelessness, which threatened to turn a whole kingdom into a vast watery mausoleum? And how about the third character, and the singular mindlessness with which she surveys the doom that she has brought down on herself and others? As I retell the story to myself, as I see in the mind's eye the line-drawing that emphasizes the royal beard and the pot-belly and the overturned milk jug, and the whiplash line that encircles the milkstain, and the fish, "the dim moon-eyed fish" as the poet calls them, fluttering their eyelids at the disaster that is about to break out down there, and which, when it does, will surely engulf them too, I feel that the mermaid, unlike the archer and the servant-girl, persists in my mind, not so much because of any narrative that she brings with her, as for certain deep-seated characteristics of mind, which belong to me, and which dogged me as a child, particularly as the day sunk into evening, and some of which are themes already woven through this memoir, and some are thus far left out like a bunch of unused threads by the side of a tapestry.

The most arresting theme in the mermaid's story is fear, but it is no ordinary fear, though it is also a fear not unknown to children. It is the fear that arises in a world of which you suspect that you have only to add to something that is good, or to something that you love, a little more of itself, and the whole becomes the opposite of what it was until now: something alluring becomes something drab, something exciting turns disgusting, what was originally fresh and sweet-smelling is now found cloying. And, matching this fear, there is the hope that you have only to add to something bad, or to something that you don't like, more of itself, and the bad thing becomes something good.

More than once, crouching down by the edge of a flower-bed, cut by the gardener's hoe with a precision that I worshipped, I would hold the small folded bud of a rose up to my nose, and it was sweet and delicate, until the warm breeze would bring the smell of other neighbouring roses towards me, and the two smells, one from close to, one from far away, each in fact the same smell but with different intensities, would blend, and the smell that came from farther away, though the weaker smell, would, by being added to the nearer, stronger smell, turn it into the dry, musty stench of stale powder, which is how nowadays roses invariably smell to me.

Visualise a woman's bottom, or a woman's nipple, and imagine the skin of the bottom taking on an edge of grey, or the volcanic form of the nipple growing a darker, an angrier red, and though, for the first degree or two of change, the body part will retain, or just conceivably increase, the pull it exercises, it is at risk, and suddenly, from one second to the next, disgust strangles desire, shame smokes out lust. Even in the mind's eye, there is a harsh, suffocating smell.

And there is the transformation the other way round. Sometimes, on late summer mornings, when I was playing in the garden with racquet and ball, and the time was getting close for my drink of warmed orange juice, which ordinarily was brought to me outside, a darkening cloud suggested a change of routine, and I would be called inside, and seated at the kitchen table. But what I had to be prepared for was a sudden consternation when it was decided that, though the kitchen floor had been swept once, it was not clean. Abruptly I would be asked to sit sideways, and to put my feet up on the crossbar of the neighbouring wooden chair. Meanwhile, with the magnificent, old-fashioned, sweeping gesture of a sower casting the seed, sowing the germs, familiar to me from the illustrated Bible, a handful of dust, or of old tea leaves kept specially for this purpose in a cheap enamel bowl, would be scattered across the cleaned floor. Then, with the handle of the broom held almost parallel to the floor, everything would be swept up, old dirt, and new dust, and tea leaves, and, to a child's unbelieving eyes, the linoleum floor, with its alternating squares of dark blue and light blue, would sparkle in a way it never could have if it had not first been dirtied in this methodical way.

The mermaid had one great fear, whereas my fears were many, but her great fear was, like many of my many fears, the fear of inundation, where that in turn was twinned with what I took to be its opposite: that is, a sense of inner dryness, leading to a sudden depletion of the body so that it would be wrong, wrong for me or anyone else, to ask of the body that it should stand up to a new physical challenge. Fears arising from the depleted body include the fear of heights, the fear of boredom, and a fear, which was commonly experienced in childhood, that, while I was sitting in the dentist's chair, the drill would fall from its cradle, and, describing a parabola that I could see drawn in the air, would land, the point or bit uppermost, on my genitals.

As to the fear of inundation itself, inundation in liquid, inundation in sound, inundation in smell, were all to be feared.

In the summer of either 1932 or 1933, my father arranged that we would all spend a holiday together in England. It was the only time that we did such a thing, and it was because my father knew of an hotel that was sufficiently comfortable and where the food was good enough. This was the hotel I have already referred to, which was across the estuary of the Teign from Teignmouth, and thus only a ferry-ride from the hotel where I was destined, some six years later, to meet Jill with the double-barrelled name. In the car on the way down, I formed two ambitions. One was to start a novel, modelled on Walter Scott, and for this purpose on arrival I bought myself a pencil, about two inches thick and a foot long and decorated with tartan, and the other was to learn to swim. For two or three summers now, I had had swimming lessons, but to no avail. A variety of aids had been used: water-wings, rubber tyres, an inflated mattress called a Li-lo from which I would imperceptibly slide into the water, a long pole attached to which was a harness made of canvas in which I was supposed to rest my body while I concentrated on my strokes, and, worst of all from my point of view, the support of two human arms, one placed under the chest, the other holding up my ankles. My terror of water, and my terror of dependence on another, were proof against all these methods. "I can, I can, just let me alone," I would say as each new teacher seemed prepared to take me on, as each new contraption was got ready, but I would make two or three strokes, and then my feet would drift downwards. If they could not touch bottom, I knew that I had been betrayed.

My bedroom in the hotel was on the top floor, and I soon noticed that it had two aspects that made it highly suitable for the attainment of my two aims. In the first place, it had sloping ceilings, which, my father explained, when I initially complained of them, was how writers lived in Paris: it was the setting for the *vie de bohème*. Secondly, the bed was extremely soft, thus favouring my new plan for learning to swim, and which I believed to be foolproof. On rising, and before going down to breakfast, I would stand, facing the bed, about two or three feet from it, with my hands brought up to my chest and parallel to the floor, in the first position of the breaststroke. Then, shutting my eyes, I would thrust my hands forward into the second position and, at the same time, fling myself on to the bed, my legs pushed out behind me. I did this a dozen or so times every morning, telling no one, and then I went down to breakfast where I ordered myself a meal as close as possible to what I saw my father eating. My resolve was that, in the solitude of my bedroom, I would so perfect this leap that, when the time came and I was in the sea, it would be a kind of second nature, and the presence of water would be a matter of indifference to me: the sea would feel like eiderdown, sheet, mattress, satin. Meanwhile, until the leap was perfected, I kept away from the water.

At last the time was ripe, I asked to be taken to the beach. I waded out into the water, brought my hands up to my chest, and then, thrusting them forwards, flung myself into the oncoming ripple of waves. I was afloat. However, after only a few confident strokes, the double pretence that I was really swimming and that the sea was not liquid was severely tested. Facing waves that rose above my head, I used my feet to feel for the sand below, and, when they found nothing, I had only one idea: I was drowning, and, if I was drowning, would it please God to let me get it over as fast as possible, and, with that idea in my head, I opened my mouth to take in as much of the water that washed over me as I could. I did not believe that anyone could help me, nor did I want to be helped. Distrust had entered so deeply into me that, as I was forced to recognize on numerous occasions, there was no real difference between the silent wishes of the cause of death and what the cause of life clamoured for. In the course of a holiday a year or so later, when my mother, my brother, and myself, were staying on a farm with long views over the England that I would never know, I climbed up on to a haystack no more than seven or eight feet high, but, once there, could not, would not, move or be moved. I vented my hostility alike upon those who tried to help me by pointing out that, to get down, I had only to do the reverse of what I had done in getting up, upon those who tried to make light of my situation by offering to bring up lunch, my meals, my bed, and upon the burly farmhand, who, observing that nothing remained of my will but the resolution to fend off all help, climbed up, put me over his shoulder, and, despite my kicks and tears and piercing screams, carried me down to safety. I treated them alike because they were all telling me what was unbearable for me to hear: that there was something to trust in the world. The only thing I thought worth doing was to scream, and it is easy to believe that an elderly lady, shopping in Chipping Camden for wool for her knitting, or a shepherd with his flock high above Ebrington, one a mile or so to the south, the other the same distance to the north, chancing to hear my screams, might have wondered what ancient rite was being revived at the midday hour.

I have never rejected the idea that, behind each fear I have, there is a specific defect of the body. If, to this day, when I take a shower, and the water runs over my face, I cannot open my eyes until I have found a towel with which to wipe them dry, I nevertheless hear of people who, getting out of the shower, or the swimming pool, or the ocean, can, as they surface, shake the water out of their eyes like dogs. Who are these people? I ask myself, and when I go on to ask, Why am I, who am really so similar, so different? I wonder whether I have, say, a layer less of skin over my eyelids, or a gap between them that I am unable to close. I have never found the courage, and never shall, to ask a doctor whether this is so, knowing that, if he said Yes, I would then have to think that I had, by acknowledging his answer, brought my deficiency upon myself.

Yet this I know well: that however cleverly a doctor might be able to explain my fear of drowning in water by invoking a bodily weakness, what he could not explain is something present in all my fears, but at its most florid in the fear of drowning, which is the discrepancy between what I fear and how I behave under fear. Why is it that, as the waves break over my nose, I seek to drown? Fear, so far from making a coward of me, calls upon me to flee safety, as though it is only so long as there is safety that danger exists.

Next to drowning in liquid, drowning in sound.

The hardest battle I have fought in my life, the fortunes of war going, now one way, now another, and I too sometimes on one side, sometimes on the other, has been my struggle with music. For many years, I used to declare that I hated music, and the cruellest blow was to be believed. What I needed was a saviour, but I have had to wait until now even to formulate the need.

I remember, when I was about the age of seven, and my love of uniforms and of battles in which no one would ever suffer was at its height, coming back, very late one summer night, from a military tattoo staged with intense, floodlit drama on Salisbury Plain, past the barrows and the single trees like dark, fleeing figures, and, stretched out on the back seat of the car, where I was expected to go to sleep, I recited over and over to myself the following two lines:

> Orpheus with his lute made trees
> And the mountain-tops that freeze

thinking that they made a couplet, and that the sense stopped where I made it do so. In thus innocently over-ruling the great poet's intention, I assumed that what his poem was telling us was that the notes, as they fell from the lyre, brought trees and mountains into existence. Music, in other words, was a kind of witchcraft, and this I came to accept, and, along with it, the necessity that, if I was ever to get equal with music, I must find my own magic, which I would pit against its magic. Once I thought that I had found my magic: it was at the time when I was learning to play the piano, and, getting hold of some sheets of stave paper, I covered them at random with crotchets, and quavers, and semiquavers, with chords and rests, adhering only to the basic rules of measure. I had not the slightest knowledge of how what I wrote would sound, nor did I greatly care, for had I not opened myself to the pure flow of creativity? On two occasions I asked Miss King if she would play my compositions for me, and her shake of the head led me to feel that she had denied herself a remarkable opportunity. As I grew up, I came to accept that my cause required me to abandon magic, and that, if only I would pause and get myself to listen to this great monster, this sad minotaur, I might eventually find myself able to lie down within his embrace. – It is far outside the temporal confines of this memoir that the fiercest battles of this campaign have been fought.

In recounting my piano lessons with Miss King, I have described how, in the earlier days of the week, striking the keys hurt the pad of flesh exposed by the freshly cut finger-nails, and this may have suggested that the original site of the pain that music caused me was the fingers. This would be wrong. The original site was the ear. I can recall earlier experiences in the dining room, where the gramophone in its dark-stained, fretworked cabinet was kept, when my father, on a weekend, would put on records which bore a special white label, indicating that they were not for public sale, but were samples specially made to convey the merits of some singer or some composer. Sometimes the music did not hurt me, but when a symphony was played, or a deep Russian bass sang a slow song from the furry depths of his entrails, I heard the swell of the sea above my drowning head, or I was caught below a great, thundering waterfall, which swept into my ears, and through my ears into my nose, my eyes, my throat, and I ran upstairs to cry in the lavatory. Even as I tried to cry the music out of my head, I could feel unlocated waves swirling round inside me, and attempting further attacks upon me, now from within.

With this form of inundation too, I harboured the belief that perhaps there was a physiological explanation. What was for me pure surge, which knocked me over, and pinned my body down while the shingle was dragged across it as it was sucked out to sea, was something that others could "follow": they could hear in it a narrative, a pattern, which I couldn't, and so I wondered whether, in my case, the fault lay in the ear. In my first week at boarding school, I was given a test by the Head of Music, a boy who later became a great friend. He struck two notes, and asked me which was the higher. I had no way of answering the question, and then he struck another two notes, and this time I could think of a hundred reasons on both sides. I saw a look come over my interrogator's face, which once again meant, "His ignorance is complete."

If the fault lay in the ear, could a doctor help, or must I look exclusively to the power of love, working like one of those powerful pumps which pushes a large body of water through the head, and, after a great rumble of liquid close to the brain, a block of wax, which has caused the trouble, is now ready to float out through the ear and into a special steel container, which has been positioned against the neck, just below the ear lobe? Sometimes I was certain that, so long as I was unable to follow music, I would never be able to understand any way in which the future emerged from the present, and that my knowledge of the world would be confined to the lugubrious succession of facts without rhyme or reason. I have felt that I would never complete this memoir.

Finally, there is inundation in smell.

Smells of all kinds, some good, some bad, have played a big part in my childhood: the smell of lilac, most beautiful of all, the smell of orange, the smell of coal, the smell of furniture polish and the acrid smell of metal polish, the smell of fried bread, the warm smell of the airing-cupboard with its promise of new clothes, a new day, and many camphor-filled hours of convalescence, and the beloved smell of eau de cologne. However, one smell played, and continues to play, such a spectacular role in my life that no book would be about me if it did not refer to it, and that is the smell of newspaper. It is the most persistent thread in my life, stronger, more unchanging, than any taste or interest, more demanding than any intellectual challenge, and I have never seen any way in which the power of love could transform it. It was like a ghost in a house that could be expelled only by demolishing the house.

I have an early memory, which I have recently, after much effort, called out of decades of dormancy, and which internal evidence dates to November 1925, when I was two and a half. It is teatime, the light of early winter is fading, and my nanny is sitting next to me in a big wicker chair, with a newspaper held wide open in front of her. She has fallen into a pose of great stillness, which, in a few years' time, or when I could, I would associate with the great lyricist's phrase "*vieille à la chandelle*". Her lips move, and she is reading with great sorrow of the death of Queen Alexandra, the Queen Mother, to which a full spread of two pages has been devoted. At this point my brother got annoyed: he could not bear my physical proximity to our nanny, and I believe he anticipated her intention, once she had finished reading the sheet of paper that absorbed her, to pin it up on the nursery wall as a memorial that we would wish to have to the passing of royalty, and this too he could not bear. To stop both he hit on a plan. Surreptitiously he slipped a page out of the newspaper, and, making certain that Nanny didn't notice, he began to tear it up into small

pieces, and then to roll the pieces between his fingers into tiny pellets. These pellets he then stuck in his mouth and moistened them, and then, placing them one at a time on his thumb, he flicked them with unfailing aim so that they landed in the middle of the page that Nanny was reading. As the pellets hit the paper with a slight thud, they clung to the page like the scabs in some children's disease. For a while Nanny preserved the fiction that she saw nothing, knew nothing, and she may indeed have been so absorbed in the great news that this was no pretence, but I knew very well that this was something that only my brother, never I, could have got away with. After a while, she lowered the paper as if to reason with my brother, who was now signalling to me that he wanted me to say that it was I who had been doing it. In fact, I might easily have done so, for, by this time, the juices that had risen up into my mouth in sheer horror at the scene seemed to duplicate the taste of the little pellets in my brother's mouth as he rather awkwardly dipped them in his saliva, so that it might have as easily been I as him who had done it. It would have been a small departure from the truth for me to have confessed to what he wanted me to. But I didn't. The next thing, and it is the point at which the memory breaks off, is that the sheet of newspaper slips out of Nanny's hands, and, as if in slow motion, slides over her knees, where, for a moment, it forms a protective apron, and then falls on to the linoleum, and there it lies like a great injured bird. A last look on my part shows me that, as the paper billowed up in my direction, the embroidered bodice of the dead Queen, to which the court photographer had endeavoured to do justice in the flat, took on sculptural form, but with a terrible difference. The legendary face, to which, rumour had it, the queen's lady's maid daily applied the finest layer of porcelain, and the priceless emeralds, and the fichu, and the small satin buttons, were now desecrated by spit, and smell, and the signs of disease, and it was hard any longer to believe that, as the Nation had been told, death had come to the Queen peacefully.

The newspaper that my nanny had been reading was in the small scholarly type that, in those days, was invariably used by that section of the popular press which was represented by *The News of the World*, or *Reynolds*, or *The Sunday Dispatch*, and which specialized in reporting in dry detail gruesome murder trials, sexual scandals involving the aristocracy, and physical deformity uncovered in high places. I mention this fact because one of the remarkable things about aversions such as this one of mine is the acuity of perception with which it endows one. Some forty years after the incident I have described, I called on an old friend of mine in his rooms in the Oxford college where he taught. He was alone, it was just before lunch, he offered me some sherry, and, opening a corner cupboard, he took out a decanter and two glasses, poured out one glass for me, one for himself, and brought mine over to me. Barely had I lifted it to my lips than I was, without warning, overcome by nausea. I told him what I knew had happened. The college scout had washed the cupboard, and he had then lined the shelf, before it was fully dry, with a sheet of *The Daily Mail*, and on it had arranged the glasses rim down. I opened the cupboard, and it was so. My friend understandingly took my glass out of my hand, tipped the sherry down the pantry sink, washed the glass, poured out some more sherry, and brought it over to me. What it did not occur to him to do, so that I found drinking out of my clean glass only a small improvement, was to do the same for himself.

If my aversion to newspaper is primarily rooted in smell, then I ought to be able, in fact I would have to be able, to order it amongst the other smells I find bad, so that I rank it better than, worse than, the same as, say, the smell of excrement, which I also, in common with the rest of humanity, find unbearable. But I have no answer except perhaps this: that, for all their horror, excremental smells do not infiltrate the inner world, nor do they have the protean character of the smell of newspaper, changing from smell, into sight, into taste, into sound. If I catch sight of a newspaper across a café, or the length of the dining car of a train, my stomach closes up, and I know that I should give up all thought of eating. If I persist, every mouthful that I swallow, and I can swallow only a mouthful or two this way, and of fish or eggs not that much, offers to rise up out of my body as it goes into it. And all this happens before the smell has had time to reach me, or I have had time to imagine the smell, or, for that matter, I have formed the slightest desire to eat. If I now try to look away, and to take advantage of there being no smell to pretend that the newspaper isn't there, I now invoke all the terrors of safety, as when the young farmhand told me that there would be nothing to fear if I looked up into the sky as I walked backwards down the ladder. The obliging creak when someone quickly hides a newspaper under the cushion on the sofa, or slips it into a briefcase, tells me, as if I needed telling, that there is nothing, could be nothing, worse about newspaper than the fact that I need to be protected against it. – And why do I say "I", when I know full well that newspaper has as great terrors for others as for myself, though they fail to recognize it?

If I seem to have come a long way from the stories that I told Miss King based on my early reading, this is because in none of the stories that I have resurrected have I confronted the question: How prepared is the gentle archer for the simplest, the sweetest, of all prospects – that the servant-girl should abandon her devotion to her beautiful hands, and, drawing upon the reservoir of affection unexpectedly put at her disposal, should suddenly, of all things, reciprocate his feelings? Suppose that what she did precisely fitted a phrase that he had occasion to observe was dear to her lips: suppose that she "opened her heart" to him. Suppose that the passion that, until that moment, she had recycled within her own frame, along channels deceptively simple in

their layout, was allowed to break its banks, and to flood over him in an altogether abandoned way, the unmaking of the Zuider Zee, what would he, poor archer, make of it? Suppose that the little milk jug, which she kept inside herself, were to fall on its side, and its contents spill, but reaching out towards the man of her desire, would he take shelter, how would he shield himself, against the new simple inundating force of love? What would he, in this new life, come to think of as danger, and what as safety?

I have called this book a memoir of childhood, and so, if not at the outset, then as it draws to a close, I should have something to say about when childhood itself ends.

I remember when, and also where, this question first

arose for me. I was walking along a sandy path which I often took to go to the two nearest shops to our house: one was a bicycle shop, the other was a shop where they sold sweets and comics and toy soldiers, and I was perhaps eight. The path was dead straight, and at either end was a stile and a picket gate. Along one side of the path there were iron railings, each rod tipped by an arrow-head, and, beyond the railings, a grass embankment rose precipitously up to the railway line. On the other side was a scruffy hedge of hawthorn and Alexandra rose, though neither ever bloomed, and beyond the hedge was a ditch, where the water seldom ran, and beyond the stale ditch, there was, for half the length of the path, a secondary school with a concrete playing ground in front of it and a rugby pitch behind, and, for the rest of the way, a small field with black and white cows, who always followed me with their heavy eyes. The school was that from which the errand boys who terrorized my childhood came, either as apprentices or as truants.

I was walking back home along this path, and, out of the blue, the thought struck me that very soon I would be asked to put away my toys. Lessons at the nursery table and much reading of the Epistles caused the famous words of St Paul to ring in my ears, and, throwing myself to my knees on the sand, I swore in God's presence that I would not be like St Paul, and that I would never put away my toys, which would be an act of desertion, and I had particularly in mind a small white dog, the wires of whose legs were beginning to work their way out of his body through his paws. I called the dog Andrew, out of my love for Scotland. Instead of two glass eyes, he had only one, and he had survived many shipwrecks in the storms that so regularly convulsed my sleeping body. I doubt that my prayer did much to stave off the end of childhood, and I am more inclined to think that it precipitated it, for one way in which childhood can end is with the first recognition that childhood will end, no matter how fiercely the prospect is resisted. It was in this cause that Sir Walter Scott rode by my side.

Another way in which childhood can end is when the hour between nine and ten o'clock in the morning, which until then had stretched out indefinitely, often to the bright sound of the cuckoo, contracts. I recall childhood mornings when I had accomplished all the things that I had charged myself to do, and then, looking at the wristwatch, which I still wore, noticed that it was only eight minutes to ten. In eight glorious minutes, I could read another couple of pages about a plot on the life of Charles II, or I could complete another proverb in my copybook, or I could insert, from above, so as not to disturb the scene, another platoon of soldiers into the great, frieze-like battlefield I was composing, or I could put another touch to the ongoing saga of a daydream, in which the hero was part-soldier, part-poet, part-lover, part-traveller, mortal and immortal. The eight minutes finally up, by which time I had possibly done two of these things, and also had the leisure in which to admire the posture of the minute hand as it stalked the most imposing number on the dial, I looked forward to the way that all the gilded mornings that were to make up my life would have the same compendiousness. How completely alien to childhood would have been the feeling, by now so familiar, when, waking up at a decent hour, not late, I decide to lie in bed for a little longer, luxuriating in the warmth of the bed and in what I take to be my control over life, and so the time passes, and first I allow it to be eight, and then I allow it to be nine, and suddenly ten minutes later the conviction has formed that the day is already ruined, and that, as far as hope is concerned, I must wait for tomorrow: for Wednesday if it is Tuesday, for Thursday if it is Wednesday, with the great Nordic beauty of these mythic names already a bit tarnished.

And a third way in which childhood can end, and which worldly readers can discern has been much of a spur to the writing of this memoir, is when, no longer reconciled to the cold fact that there are things about ourselves we cannot say but can at best express in tears, we try obliquely to conquer the inability to say one thing through the hard-won ability to say another thing that neighbours on it. I have known occasions – as who hasn't? – when I was ready to whisper into the delicate shell of a woman's ear, needs that I never had, desires that I knew only from my father's books, in the desperate hope that one thing I could say, but only just, would, once said, lead to the saying of another thing, once impossible but now just conceivable. However little there was in the way of truth to the first thing said, there might be more to the second thing said, and eventually, or such was the hope, I would, in saying one thing after another after another after another, each with a grain more of truth to it than its predecessor, come to spill the beans: I might, if only the ear stayed steady, and that was another hope, find myself, with one broad archaic gesture, scattering the germs.

Richard at His Desk
(1993)
by
Mary Day Wollheim

LIST OF ILLUSTRATIONS

308 *Richard at His Desk*, 1993, by Mary Day Wollheim, reproduced by kind permission of the artist.

A NOTE ON THE TEXT

Richard Wollheim died before *Germs* had been submitted to Waywiser for consideration. In preparing the book for publication, Waywiser had the guidance of Jane Miller, who was once Richard Wollheim's editor at Cape and is now a trustee of his estate. His idiosyncratic spellings and punctuation are as far as possible preserved. Some obvious slips have been corrected. Elsewhere, uncertainties have been left to stand, as in the case of "Jacobite" on p. 111, where "Jacobean" might appear a possibility. "Jacobite", after all, accords with the importance for Wollheim's development of Scott's Waverley novels. A misremembered episode from Stevenson's *The Black Arrow* is another case in point. The "mistake" has been respected, in the belief that this is a book in which memory is, among other things, the power to imagine and create, a work of self-expression.

ACKNOWLEDGEMENTS

For supplying photographs, as well as information about their subjects and dating, we should like to thank Hermann da Fonseca-Wollheim, Polly Toynbee, Jean Tsushima, Anne Wollheim, Bruno Wollheim, Emilia Wollheim, Mary Day Wollheim, Nikki Wollheim, Pat Wollheim and Rupert Wollheim.

For agreeing to let us reproduce his drawing, *Wollheim and Angela*, we are indebted to R.B. Kitaj.

We are likewise indebted to Mary Day Wollheim for allowing us to reproduce her drawing, *Richard at His Desk*.

For having read the memoir in typescript and made a number of helpful comments and suggestions, we are grateful to Malcolm Budd, Peter Dale, Karl Miller and Rupert Wollheim.

Our greatest debt is to Jane Miller, on whose judgement, tact and good humour the editors have been able to rely throughout.

A SELECTED LIST OF FINE WRITING
AVAILABLE FROM BLACK SWAN

77207 0	THE AARDVARK IS READY FOR WAR	James Blinn	£6.99
99914 8	GALLOWAY STREET	John Boyle	£6.99
99704 8	A SHORT HISTORY OF NEARLY EVERYTHING	Bill Bryson	£8.99
77161 9	HOLD THE ENLIGHTENMENT	Tim Cahill	£7.99
99926 1	DEAR TOM	Tom Courtenay	£7.99
77119 8	EDUCATING PETER	Tom Cox	£6.99
99923 7	THE MYSTERY OF CAPITAL	Hernando de Soto	£8.99
99981 4	A PROFOUND SECRET	Josceline Dimbleby	£7.99
99858 3	PERFUME FROM PROVENCE	Lady Fortescue	£7.99
99850 8	THE RIGHTEOUS	Martin Gilbert	£8.99
99983 0	OVER THE HILLS AND FAR AWAY	Candida Lycett Green	£7.99
77098 1	GETTING TO MAÑANA	Miranda Innes	£6.99
99958 X	ALMOST LIKE A WHALE	Steve Jones	£9.99
14595 5	BETWEEN EXTREMES	Brian Keenan and John McCarthy	£7.99
77133 3	MY WAR GONE BY, I MISS IT SO	Anthony Loyd	£7.99
77108 2	NOTES FROM A ROMAN TERRACE	Joan Marble	£7.99
99967 9	A GHOST UPON YOUR PATH	John McCarthy	£7.99
99964 4	GLOBAL VILLAGE IDIOT	John O'Farrell	£6.99
99982 2	THE ISLAND AT THE CENTRE OF THE WORLD	Russell Shorto	£7.99
99988 1	BEFORE THE KNIFE: MEMORIES OF AN AFRICAN CHILDHOOD	Carolyn Slaughter	£6.99
99750 1	SPEAKING FOR THEMSELVES:THE PERSONAL LETTERS OF WINSTON AND CLEMENTINE CHURCHILL	Mary Soames ed.	£15.00
99929 6	DOWN THE HIGHWAY: THE LIFE OF BOB DYLAN	Howard Sounes	£8.99
99928 8	INSTRUCTIONS FOR VISITORS	Helen Stevenson	£6.99
77124 4	ANDALUS: UNLOCKING THE SECRETS OF MOORISH SPAIN	Jason Webster	£7.99
99891 5	IN THE SHADOW OF A SAINT	Ken Wiwa	£7.99
99366 2	THE ELECTRIC KOOL AID ACID TEST	Tom Wolfe	£8.99